The Uses of Greek Mythology

The Uses of Greek Mythology offers an overview of Greek mythology – what it is like, where it comes from, and where it fits in Greek history and landscape. Ken Dowden outlines the uses Greeks made of myth and the uses to which myth can be put in recovering the richness of their culture.

This book begins by considering the nature of Greek myth and goes on to show the diversity of the ways the Greeks used myth. 'Greek mythology' forms a virtually closed system, and Dowden considers how it was formed and who its creators were. Special emphasis is given to the way the Greeks themselves viewed their mythology and the way they did not quite distinguish it from history. The investigation sheds light on many aspects of Greek history and culture: prehistory, including the supposed Trojan War; ethnic identity and the rival claims of cities; the importance of cult-sites; the language and practices of initiation; the meaning of gods, heroes, monsters and legendary kings; the rejection of matriarchy and the establishment of the boundaries of sexual behaviour.

Ken Dowden is Lecturer in the Department of Classics, University of Birmingham.

Approaching the Ancient World
Series editor: Richard Stoneman

The sources for the study of the Greek and Roman world are diffuse, diverse and often complex, and special training is needed in order to use them to the best advantage in constructing a historical picture.

The books in this series provide an introduction to the problems and methods involved in the study of ancient history. The topics covered will range from the use of literary sources for Greek history and for Roman history, through numismatics, epigraphy and dirt archaeology, to the use of the legal evidence and of art and artefacts in chronology. There will also be books on statistical and comparative method, and on feminist approaches.

The Uses of Greek Mythology
Ken Dowden

Art, Artefacts, and Chronology in Classical Archaeology
William R. Biers

Ancient History from Coins
Christopher Howgego

Reading Papyri, Writing Ancient History
Roger S. Bagnall

The Uses of Greek Mythology

Ken Dowden

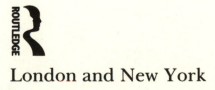

London and New York

First published 1992
by Routledge
11 New Fetter Lane, London EC4P 4EE

Simultaneously published in the USA and Canada
by Routledge
29 West 35th Street, New York, NY 10001

Reprinted 1994, 1996,1997

Typeset in Baskerville by Computerset, Harmondsworth, Middlesex
Printed and bound in Great Britain by
T. J. Press (Padstow) Ltd, Padstow, Cornwall

British Library Cataloguing in Publication Data
A catalogue reference for this book is available from the British Library

Library of Congress Cataloguing in Publication Data
A catalogue record for this book is available from the Library of Congress

ISBN 0–415–06134–2 (hbk)   ISBN 0–415–06135–0 (pbk)

Contents

Part IV The world of myth

Preface

I make no apologies for this book: it has been enjoyable to write, I think it will be interesting to read, and it is rather different from previous books on the subject. There are plenty of books to retell Greek mythology: a Greek, Apollodoros, wrote a useful one himself and I have put references to his account into this book wherever possible. The business of this book is not the telling of myths, though naturally some, particularly the more obscure, are outlined: I have envisaged readers who can turn to their own handbooks (see the Topic bibliography) and who want to know more about Greek myth. Equally, though I consider methodology and theory more important than some previous English writers, I have tried not to act as a salesman for a particular brand of ideas. Or at least not too much.

I have tried to write a book which will give a sense of what Greek myth is like, where it comes from and where it fits in Greek history and landscape. But I have paid particular attention to the various uses which Greeks made of myth (and which moderns think they made, consciously and unconsciously), above all the use of myth in place of early history – where it performed much better at defining the basis of the present order than a real history would have done. The result, I hope, is that we gain a better idea of how we ourselves may use Greek myth to uncover areas of Greek history, culture and experience.

A glance at the contents page will show my attempt to redefine the subject so that we can say practical, interesting and admittedly 'speculative' things about it. But the book cannot possibly deliver a complete account: such a project would be beyond the scope of any single volume and maybe any single author (certainly the present one). Nevertheless, I have tried to make it more than just a random sample ('Aspects of . . .') and to stimulate a larger sense of what mythology does. I hope that even those with quite different priorities will not feel that what they consider important has been totally overlooked. At the same time, I have tried to keep close to the actual myths and the localities to which these traditions belonged, whilst retaining some sensitivity to issues of ambience and cultural significance.

Mythology is a complex and interwoven subject and, though I have imposed a degree of organisation on this book, it will become apparent to the reader that each topic in mythology presupposes a knowledge of every other topic and that organisation at times is little more than sleight of hand. Here I hope the indexes will be found more than usually useful – because more than usually necessary.

I had originally intended to include some illustrations of myth in Greek art but felt that after the appearance of Carpenter's (1991) beautifully illustrated and easily accessible volume, I had ample justification to devote more space to words instead.

Greek mythology is most naturally, though not exclusively, studied by classicists, whose sense of international community is strong. For those who will venture beyond the English language into continental Europe, there are some outstanding works of scholarship to explore. I have not hesitated to include these in the bibliography. The rest is up to the reader.

The University of Birmingham
Spring 1992

Abbreviations

Ancient authors

Ap   Apollodoros (*Ep.* = the *Epitome*, or abridgement); see pp. 8–9.

P   Pausanias; see p. 17.

Works of reference

CAH3   *Cambridge Ancient History*, 3rd edn, Cambridge, 1970–date.

FGH   F. Jacoby (ed.), *Die Fragmente der griechischen Historiker*; see p. 173.

KIP   *Der Kleine Pauly: Lexikon der Antike*, Munich, 1975.

OCD   *Oxford Classical Dictionary*, 2nd edn, Oxford, 1970.

Other abbreviations follow the usual classical practice, as found in tables of abbreviations in J. Marouzeau, *Année Philologique* (for periodical titles), the *Oxford Latin Dictionary* and H.G. Liddell and R. Scott, *Greek–English Lexicon*, 9th edn:

AC   *Antiquité classique*
CQ   *Classical Quarterly*
CW   *Classical World*
HR   *History of Religions*
JHS   *Journal of Hellenic Studies*
LCM   *Liverpool Classical Monthly*
PCPhS   *Proceedings of the Cambridge Philological Society*
REG   *Revue des études grecques*
SSR   *Studi storico-religiosi*
ZPE   *Zeitschrift für Papyrologie und Epigraphik*

Part I

Attitudes to myth

Chapter 1

Myth and mythology

1.1 WHAT IS MYTH?

It says here: 'Peppino is a myth in the world of Italian song'. He looks real enough to me. Perhaps they meant a 'legend'.

(Terry Wogan, commentator on the
1991 Eurovision Song Contest)

A lie?

If it's a myth, it's untrue. That is what we mean today – or part of what we mean. But a myth is also enticing: it lures not just a stray, mistaken individual, but whole groups and societies into believing it. Perhaps superior courage or skill was the key to the defeat of the Luftwaffe by the Royal Air Force in the Battle of Britain. Or is that just the myth of Britain's 'most glorious hour'? Was it in fact more about intelligence derived from the breaking of enemy codes (the 'Ultra' intelligence – Cave Brown 1976: 36–38). If so, the 'myth' brought great satisfaction to the (undeniably courageous) participants in the battle, to a nation on the brink of defeat, and to the post-war nation adjusting to a reduced position in the world. Few would welcome the rejection of this myth, if myth it is.

This is the paradox of myths. They are not factually exact: they are false, not wholly true, or not true in that form. But they have a power which transcends their inaccuracy, even depends on it. I do not think this is just a fact about modern use of the word 'myth'. It lies at the heart of all myths and in particular of ancient myths: myths are believed, but not in the same way that history is. Those who, let us say, 'subscribe to' a myth may well express their acceptance of it by asserting its 'truth'. Certainly they will not wish to call it 'false'. A Christian who denies that the virgin birth actually happened will not say that it is 'false', but rather that it has some valuable meaning, that it has its own 'truth'. As we follow myth in Greek history, we should be sensitive to the variable meaning of 'truth'. Language is an approximate tool.

A Greek word

'Myth' goes back to the Greek word *mythos*. Like any other word, its meaning has shifted over the centuries. Back in the days of Homer, at the beginning of Greek literature (*c.* 725 BC), a *mythos* was not necessarily false. Here is a servant replying to Hektor's question about the whereabouts of his wife Andromache: 'To him then the trusty stewardess spoke her *mythos* in return: "Hektor, since you really tell me to *mytheisthai* the truth" ' (Homer, *Iliad* 6.381–2). The woman proceeds to give an account, as asked – this is her *mythos*, a worked out string of ideas expressed in sentences. I suppose it amounts to a 'speech' here. So, in *Iliad* 9, when the delegation has tried to recall Achilles to the battle and he has given devastating expression to his rejection of the request, the three envoys sit silent, 'in wonderment at his *mythos*' (9.431). Only after some time does aged Phoinix reply, referring to Achilles' father's instructions that he, Phoinix, should teach Achilles to be effective in war and in assembly, 'to be a speaker of *mythoi* and a doer of deeds' (9.443). These are the twin competences of the Homeric hero: to kill efficiently and to persuade through impressive *mythoi*.

The earliest Greek literature had been in verse. Prose only arrived in the mid-6th century BC and was part of the deeper penetration of writing into what was still very much an oral culture. *Logos*, the noun corresponding to the verb *legein* ('I speak'), was the word chosen to describe prose. It covered both the verbal expression ('speech') and the enhanced possibilities inherent in committing prose to writing ('rational account', 'discourse'). Early writers frequently refer to their book as a *logos*, including our first historian: 'I must tell [*legein*] what people tell, but I am not at all obliged to believe it – and this principle can be taken as applying to my whole *logos*'. (Herodotos, 7.152.3). Indeed, Thucydides refers to all early historians as *logographoi* ('*logos*-writers', 1.21), a term which has passed into modern handbooks on these 'logographers'.

This development of the word *logos* to cover extended utterances, pushed back the frontiers of the *mythos*. Though fifth-century tragedians, in their archaic way, might preserve something of its original application, by now *mythos* was usually applied to fiction – the sort of material associated with the early verse writers. The predominant contrast is no longer between *mythoi* and battle-action, but between *mythoi* and *logoi*, a word now close to the heart of the new enlightenment. Thucydides, implicitly distinguishing himself from his predecessor Herodotos, asserts the scientific value of his work at the cost of lessening its entertainment value: it does not appeal to *to mythodes* ('the *mythos*-quality'). A *mythos* may have retained its sense of a developed utterance, a whole narrative, but it has become a mere 'story', a 'tale' (Burkert 1985: 312 with 466 n.4).

This was the crucial development in the history of the word. Since then, it has changed less: it has always been able to apply to the inherited stock of Greek traditional stories ('Greek myths'). This view of *mythos* is, for instance, passed on in the mid-80s BC by a Latin rhetorical author: '*fabula* ["story", Latin for *mythos*] is defined as including matters which are neither true nor probable, for instance those handed down in the tragedies' (Anon. ('Cicero'), *Rhetorica ad Herennium* 1.13). Changes in its meaning since antiquity have only reflected our changes in attitude to that stock of stories – and all stories which are told and enjoyed in spite of the fact that they are 'false'.

'Myth', 'history' and other terms

History is what myth isn't. What history tells is true or else it would not be history, only failed history. What myth tells is in some way false or else it would be history. Yet within mythology there are gradations of credibility. To take an example: there is a myth that Athene was born from Zeus' head. It is wholly false: Zeus never existed, neither did Athene, and no one has ever been born from anyone else's head. On the other hand, many believe that history underlies the myth of Agamemnon's expedition against Troy (though see chapter 4.3). On that view the 'Trojan War' is partly historical, if not in the form we have it (if Homer's *Iliad* were literally true, it would be an historical record and not a version of myth). To many writers it is important if there is an historical dimension, and they like to reflect this in their choice of terminology, distinguishing between various types of traditional story:

saga and legend, on the one hand, and myth and folk-tale on the other. Broadly, these terms have the following implications:

Saga, is applied to myths supposed to have a basis in history. So, for instance, Rose (1928: 13) thought that 'The Homeric account of the Trojan War is one of the best possible examples.' 'Saga' is an Icelandic term and was originally applied to supposedly true histories of families/clans or of kings. Perhaps it is best restricted to myths which tell the history of a family.

Legend: originally traditional stories about saints that were 'worth reading' (Latin: *legenda*). As stories about saints rarely have much historical value, the term is applied to any myth with only a kernel of truth or historicity.

Folk-tale: this term was invented during the early nineteenth century (like 'folklore' and 'folk-song'), to serve as a translation of the German word *Märchen*. This was when scholars such as Jacob and Wilhelm Grimm (1785–1863, 1786–1859) imagined, and persuaded their readers, that they were collecting traditional tales which ordinary folk used as a sort of moralising entertainment. Some think their motifs derive from long lost myths (as the Brothers Grimm did).[1] Others think that all nations have always had folk-tales for their entertainment. In any case, European literary sources have been found for some of these supposedly oral tales.

In content the tales of the Brothers Grimm are not always easy to distinguish from what people class in other societies as myths. Maybe they tend to contain types rather than individuals. Bettelheim (1976: 39–41) accounts for this psychoanalytically by distinguishing the roles of myth and folk-tale: folk-tales are about everyman, 'facilitating projections and identifications' and resolving anxieties, whereas myths 'offer excellent images for the development of the superego'. You may believe this if you like, but folk-tales can be just as vague about locations. Perhaps, too, there is some delight in the magical and rather an obsession with princely courts – as one might expect from that period in German history. But in any case the unthinking application of the term 'folk-tale' to the oral traditions of other nations has obscured the difference (if there is one) between myth and folk-tale and trivialised those traditions. Merely to register a tradition as folk-tale too easily evades their specific social and historical context and leaves only their motifs to be classified. We will be looking at analysis of hero-myths by motif in chapter 8.3.

Fairy story is often used as a variant for 'folk-tale', but is rather useless for Greek culture (low on fairies). Interestingly, however, when used in a derogatory sense, it captures something of the contempt which Greek thinkers could occasionally feel for 'myth'.

Myth is often reserved for tales which do not fall into the above categories, which perhaps have a clear involvement of gods or a clear religious or philosophical purpose.[2]

I have tried to be less discriminatory. It seems to me that attempts to distinguish between these terms have failed and that it is best simply to allow all Greek non-historical narratives to be 'myths'. Otherwise we will suffer from terminological difficulties of our own invention and prejudge the nature of each of these narratives, with its own identity and its own history. However, I should mention that there is a school of thought which recognises a regular pattern of 'degeneration' of myth:

stage 1: the myth is associated with religious ritual and that is its function;
stage 2: the myth has become 'history';
stage 3: the 'history' has turned into folklore;
stage 4: the folklore is turned to literary purposes.[3]

There are some problems of detail in the application of this scheme to Greek mythology: it is not clear (and most scholars will refuse to believe) that all myths began as partners for ritual. In classical Greece, as we shall see, the myth has indeed largely turned to history, but it also has something of the entertainment value of folklore about it and most certainly the literary artists are busy with it. Nevertheless, the reader may find this a useful pattern to hold against the shifting role of Greek mythology from prehistoric to Roman and modern times.

1.2 GREEK MYTHOLOGY

Greek Mythology, a total system

It is one thing to decide what will count as Greek myths, another to know what 'Greek Mythology' is. 'It is a matter above all of written material, of texts' (Brelich 1977: 6). There is no doubt that we access Greek Mythology above all through texts and that even in ancient times texts, read or performed, were instrumental in forming the Greeks' own sense of mythology. But texts were not the only medium for mythology (unless you have a very broad definition of 'text').[4] Myths may be told orally, without reproducing a particular author's account – it is simply 'how the story goes'. Art too displayed myths and in both senses offered a view of them. We think of the surviving remnants of sculpture and vase-painting, but of course there were wall-paintings too – now lost but for their reflection in the humbler art of vase-painting. All of these are media through which Greek Mythology was presented and, by being presented, reinterpreted.

In fact Greek Mythology is a shared fund of motifs and ideas ordered into a shared repertoire of stories. These stories link with, compare and contrast with, and are understood in the light of, other stories in the system. Greek Mythology is an 'intertext', because it is constituted by all the representations of myths ever experienced by its audience and because every new representation gains its sense from how it is positioned in relation to this totality of previous presentations. In this book I will use the term Greek Mythology, with capital letters, to denote this (evolving) total system.

Today handbooks play a special part in communicating Greek Mythology. It is their job, sometimes alphabetically, more often chronologically, to lay out before us a tapestry of Greek myths. At the beginning: the origin of the gods (and the world). At the end: the aftermath of the Trojan War. We need collections of stories to help us know them. The Greeks, however, were brought up on their mythology and it is only relatively late that we find a collected Greek Mythology. The first surviving collection, and the best, dates from the first century AD. It is by an '**Apollodoros**' (so the manuscripts claim, perhaps thinking wrongly of the scholar Apollodoros of Athens), and is headed *The Library*, to mark its comprehensiveness. The end is missing, but we also possess an abridgement, the *Epitome*, which is complete. Apollodoros is of great importance to us, and as he is the most useful single source for Greek Mythology I have included where possible in my text references to his tellings of stories I am discussing. He does not actually tell all Greek myths – there were so many in every Greek hamlet – or include all details, but he does give some account of most of the myths that had come to matter beyond local city-state boundaries. It is his interpretation of what counts that has above all shaped our present, relatively frozen, idea of Greek Mythology.

Presently I will sketch the contents of Greek Mythology as in Apollodoros. But first we should look at how this system of myths came to be formed.

Formation: archaic texts

As we shall see (chapter 4.1), the Greeks had always had myths. But in order to form a national Greek Mythology, local stories must cluster with the stories of other localities. This is what provides the characteristic geographical range in Greek Mythology. This clustering could only occur in a time of good communications and shared culture, when the entertainers of the age, epic poets, found an audience in any major Greek centre. This was possible during the Mycenaean Age and it clearly became possible once again as prosperity was restored during the Dark Age. So what we find when the darkness recedes is that the manufacture and maintenance of national mythology is in the hands of poets – and two types in particular, epic poets and genealogical poets.

In epic we think immediately of **Homer**'s *Iliad* and *Odyssey*, but the slow narrative pace, unusual originality and wilful silences of these texts make them less important from our point of view than other more routine and more action-packed epics, now lost – though a detailed summary of their plots survives. These works of Homer's successors (mainly seventh century) enshrined the stories of epics composed by his contemporaries and predecessors. Their authors are referred to as the **Cyclic poets**, because the epics in their final form, together with the *Iliad* and *Odyssey*, made up an omnibus edition or 'epic cycle', telling the complete story of the Trojan War with its preliminaries and aftermath. By contrast, the *Iliad* itself covers a mere fortnight. Other epic poets, however, were telling the tales of Thebes – particularly the tale of the 'Seven against Thebes' (chapter 4.3) – of the voyage of the first ship, Argo, with its complement of Argonauts and of many other parts of the mythology. So these epic poets can be viewed as transmitting various cycles of myth often associated with heroes, military campaigns and other adventures. We have no good information on how these individual cycles came to be put together, but they are clearly ready, in place, and in general circulation by the end of the Dark Age.

I should mention at this point a problem in approach to our limited evidence. One pattern of scholarly thought upholds what may be viewed as high standards in the acceptability of evidence: thus no myth can be proved to have existed until the date of our first evidence for it. In itself this sort of proposition seems obvious enough, but it perhaps makes too little allowance for the large gaps in our evidence for mythology. A story which first appears in Apollodoros (first century AD) or Pausanias (second century AD) or even Nonnos (fifth century AD) need not on that account be a late invention. We should not overlook the obvious corollary that no myth can be proved *not* to have existed before a certain date simply because that is when it is first attested. Associated with this difficulty is the difficulty in establishing the degree of inventiveness of authors at certain periods. It used regularly to be supposed that the Cyclic poets had improvised freely around Homer, but increasingly it is being recognised that the problem may often lie in the character of Homer, who is a deliberately omissive and selective author. Equally, it is hard to be confident about the extent to which tragedians modified individual myths.

The other strand which emerges from the Dark Age is genealogy. The most important work, of which many fragments survive and more have been recovered this century, was one ascribed to the Boiotian poet **Hesiod**, though it was probably set down in its final form in Athens in the sixth century BC (West 1985: 164–71). This was the *Catalogue of Women*, also known as the *Ehoiai* ('Or-likes') because the transitions to new subjects were made by that formula and stuck out like a sore thumb:

> Pindar got the story from an *Or-like* of Hesiod, which begins thus:
>
> 'Or like her who dwelt in Phthia, with the beauty of the
> [Graces,
> By the water of Peneios, fair Kyrene.'
> (Hesiod, fr. 215: Scholiast on Pindar, *Pyth*. 9.6)

This work was of major importance, as it used mythic women to draw together the genealogies and mythologies of most of Greece.

The dreariness for modern audiences of 'catalogue poetry', which lists names and of which we see a reflection in Homer's

Catalogue of Ships (*Iliad* 2.484–877), and genealogical poetry, which organises names and family trees, is exceeded only by its fascination in its living context. Genealogy must have mattered to the well-born in the Dark Age: it stated their place in the world and linked their famous ancestors to the famous ancestors of others. This has the effect of systematising not only family trees but also the internationally famous mythic adventures of the past. But it goes deeper than this too. The concern of myth-genealogists is to map a world and its people. To write a genealogy is to make a series of links between names enshrining peoples and places, assigning each their position. Using the model of family relationships, something immediate, accessible and powerful to close-knit pre-industrial society, statements are made about affiliation (closer or more distant) and seniority. Thus genealogy, though limited by facts of history of which its audience is securely aware and by traditions which the audience generally accepts, is by nature ideological.

This was not something whose interest and effect died out with the Dark Age or Archaic period. It continued to matter to Arcadians whether they could endorse a genealogy by the poet Asios (sixth century BC?) and whether a Pausanias could be persuaded to accept it (p. 72 below). And it mattered to a Pausanias what the answers were, for otherwise the map was deficient and *terra incognita* was left:

> I was especially keen to find out what children were born to Polykaon by Messene. So I read through the *Or-likes* and the *Naupaktia* epic and, in addition, all the genealogical works of Kinaithon and Asios. However, on this subject they had written nothing.
>
> (Pausanias 4.2.1)

The achievement of epic and genealogical poetry has been to create cycles of stories clustered around particular heroes or events, to establish the family relationships between the heroes of different stories well enough to arrange the stories in sequence, and as a result to develop a sense of mythical chronology. There is even a saga aspect: we can follow the fates of some families in successive generations. Thus Greek Mythology now unfolds like the history it can never be: it is a para-history, a proto-history, a phase in the development of the world and of man. And the 'Theogonies' ('births of gods') written by Hesiod and other authors plug the gap that could all so easily have existed at the beginning of the world.

Myth and art before 500 BC

We are not able to identify with any certainty scenes from myth on Mycenaean vases. And after the end of Mycenaean civilisation, pottery decoration became increasingly a matter of mere patterns – hence the description of this period as the 'Geometric' Age. It is only in the mid-seventh century that scenes from myths appear on vases – the 'Archaic' Age has begun. So, for instance, an Attic vase of around 660 BC shows Herakles' defeat of the centaur Nesos (Ap 2.7.6). This vase was intended to be used, as so many of these were, to mark a grave. Another of this painter's works showed Herakles releasing Prometheus. To about the same time belongs a vase from Eleusis depicting Odysseus blinding the Cyclops Polyphemos and Perseus dashing away from two Gorgons – in hot pursuit after his murder of their sister Medousa. Artists of the Archaic period thought Gorgons specially striking.

The last example shows something important about how artistic depictions work. Perseus is not only shown killing Medousa the Gorgon, but also with the Gorgon's head, being chased by other Gorgons – bringing home his slaughter rather better than the mere scene of beheading. Because art cannot narrate, but only offer still photographs, it must choose 'telling' moments. Wrestling with the Nemean Lion, though often uncomfortably like a tango, displays Herakles' imminent lion-skin on its original owner. Up on the east pediment of the temple of Zeus at Olympia (c. 460 BC), we are at the line up for the chariot race between Pelops and Oinomaos, a moment pregnant with all that will ensue, a frozen scene of deceptive stillness – as the Seer must know. Likewise, when Exekias paints Achilles and Ajax playing draughts, it is not just a jolly idea, but contrasts with the fury of the battlefield and, in particular, looks forward to those other scenes that relate the two heroes: Ajax's recovery of Achilles' dead body from the battlefield and his devastating loss of the contest with Odysseus for the arms of Achilles, leading to his suicide.

It is beyond the scope of this book to give a detailed history of myth in art, so let us make quick progress. By 600 BC Corinthian pottery was displaying an enthusiasm for decorative features imported from the Near East and is therefore described as

'Orientalising'. This increases the range of mythic creatures without necessarily increasing the range of myths: amongst exotic animals we find rather a lot of sphinxes and griffins. This decorative use of mythic creatures shows the greatest distance from our notion of myth as narrative – only the Oedipus story involves a sphinx and only the weird epic of Aristeas of Prokonnesos (chapter 8.2) involves griffins.

Also around 600 BC, the black-figure technique of vase-painting was being developed, a technique which was practised above all at Athens until around 500 BC. The distribution of mythical subjects in this period has been conveniently summarised by Boardman (1974: ch.13; ch. 11 for monsters). Overall, Herakles is consolidating his hold on the artistic imagination in this period. His feats are more popular than those of any other hero and even than scenes from the Trojan Cycle. These latter scenes are less often from the *Iliad* than we may expect: other parts of the Trojan story, told in the Epic Cycle, were more action-packed, telling for instance how Achilles ambushed the boy Troilos – a son of Priam who would have guaranteed Troy's survival had he himself lived to the age of 20 (i.e. to the age of the warrior, p. 111 below), but Achilles outran his horse (hence Achilles' epithet, 'swift-footed') and slew him.

The sculptures that decorated the pediments and metopes of archaic Greek temples share the early interest in Gorgons and constant interest in Herakles. In addition, the battle of the gods and Giants, the 'Gigantomachy', catches just the right monumental tone (as we shall see in chapter 9.2).

Formation: the Classical Age

500 BC is a watershed. In written texts, the change-over from verse to prose (beginning amongst thinkers in the sixth century) reaches accounts of myth, and we find ourselves in a new world of para-historians giving a *logos* of the mythic period. We call them 'mythographers', and the major names are **Akousilaos** in Argos (*c*. 500–490 BC) and **Pherekydes** in Athens (*c*. 460–450 BC). But their work continued with **Herodoros** of Herakleia (*c*. 400 BC). We will take a look at these writers in chapter 3.

Simultaneously the age of monsters and omnipresent Herakles is over in the decorative arts. In Athens, where so much of our

Table 1.1 Themes in architectural sculpture to 500 BC

Date	Location: building	Theme
Late 7th cent.	Olympia	Plaque: mother and baby griffin
	Syracuse	Plaque: Medousa and Chrysaor
600–580	Corcyra: Temple of Artemis	Pediment: Medousa, birth of Chrysaor, Gigantomachy, Neoptolemos kills Priam?
575–550	Paestum: Temple of Hera	Metope: Herakles steals Apollo's tripod, and other stories
560	Selinous: Temple Y	Metope: Europa and the Bull
560	Delphi: Treasury of Sikyonians	Metopes: scenes from voyage of Argo, hunt of the Calydonian Boar, Europa and the Bull
560–550	Athens: Temple	Pediment: Herakles, Iolaos and Hydra Pediment: Herakles fights Triton
550	Athens: Temple	Pediment: Herakles fights Triton (again), monster(s) with three human tops and snake bottoms
550–525	Athens: Temple of Athene Polias	Pediment: Gigantomachy
540	Selinous: Temple C	Metope: Herakles and Kerkopes
540–520	Assos, nr Troy: Temple of Athena	Metopes: centaur, sphinxes, Europa and the Bull, Herakles steals Apollo's tripod Frieze: Herakles and Tritons, Herakles and Centaurs
525	Delphi: Treasury of Siphnians	Frieze: Gigantomachy, including Herakles? E Pediment: Herakles steals Apollo's tripod and other stories
520–510	Delphi: Temple of Apollo	Pediment: Gigantomachy
510	Eretria: Temple of Apollo	Pediment: Theseus and Amazonomachy
510–500	Delphi: Treasury of Megarians	Pediment: Gigantomachy
500–490	Delphi: Treasury of Athenians	Metopes: deeds of Theseus, Amazonomachy, deeds of Herakles
500–480	Aigina: Temple of Aphaia	W Pediment: Trojan War E Pediment: Herakles' Trojan War

evidence comes from, there was a limited transfer of interest from Herakles (promoted, art historians claim, by the Peisistratids) to Theseus as a symbol of the new democracy of 509 BC. This may be especially true of public, monumental sculpture, where Herakles' appearances are no longer a matter of propagandist routine. Even at the Temple of Zeus at Olympia, the metopes of Herakles' labours furnish the subject for the metopes for reasons of local tradition – this son of Zeus founded the Olympic Games. The sequence of labours of Herakles on metopes of the Hephaistieion at Athens (maybe designed earlier than the Parthenon), seen by Boardman as old-fashioned (1989: 170), may be needed to add importance by association to the sequence of deeds of Athenian Theseus. But on the Parthenon there would be no interest in Herakles.[5] The reduced importance of Herakles in (Athenian) red-figure pottery may again be associated with the ending of the world in which his ideology had been important, but in a broader sense – Theseus is not overwhelmingly common either. There is a wider, almost more 'democratic', spread of interest across mythological and divine themes on vases – to the extent that it serves no purpose to put together the sort of list I present above for the Archaic period.

The fifth century was, however, a golden age of myth (Boardman 1975: 223). The work of the old poets found new expression in the mythographers. A broader band of myths was now depicted on vases and presumably on the mural paintings that they often imitated. The great temples – for instance, those of Aphaia on Aigina (completed after the Persian Wars), of Zeus at Olympia and the Parthenon – were lavishly decorated with scenes from myth. And mythology, as understood in the light of the mythographers, was almost the exclusive source of plots for the **tragedians** in Athens (the big three, Aeschylus, Sophocles, Euripides, successively dominating the stage from 484 to 406 BC). The practicalities of theatre and the increasing social awareness of tragedians naturally affected their selection and projection of mythology. They focus on the human crises that prevail in the Greek Mythology that has reached us. Of course there had been others who added to the intertext of Greek Mythology: one may think, for instance, of the lyric poet Stesichoros (c. 550 BC) or the post-archaic 14-book epic on Herakles by Herodotos' uncle, Panyassis or the suggestive hints of Pindar in his lyric poems (written 498–438 BC). But overwhelmingly the tragedians, the mythographers and the early poets of epic and genealogy were the suppliers of myth to later generations and art, ancient and modern, has accepted their definition of Greek Mythology.

Formation: Hellenistic and Roman Ages

We can briefly mention the tendencies of the Hellenistic Age (323 BC to Roman times). It was notably a learned age. Even in poetry, Callimachus (writing *c.* 275–240 BC) showed a path for new writing which depended heavily on reference books full of fresh, local mythical colour which had not previously found a place in Greek Mythology. And this was the material that the prose-writers of local histories, now sadly lost, uncovered and recorded. New methods of sorting the mythology too could produce interesting aesthetic results, whether in Boio's *Ornithogonia* (presumably a 'theogony' of birds), Nicander's *Metamorphoses* (changes in shape) or the *Catasterisms* (becoming stars and constellations) of Eratosthenes – all three lost. Perhaps, too, these principles of selection led to a proliferation of the material to suit them: so, if you are confronted by several variants of a given myth, you will suspect the one in which the hero(ine) turns into a star of being a Hellenistic development. It is not necessarily so: way back (600 BC?), 'Hesiod' had written an *Astronomia*.[6] Nevertheless, metamorphosis and catasterism are particularly prevalent in the Hellenistic version of Greek Mythology – together with pastoral themes and tales of unhappy or forbidden love. Some idea of the pathetic development of Hellenistic myths is given by the second century AD prose collection of stories from Hellenistic poets, the *Metamorphoses* of **Antoninus Liberalis**.

This more sentimental mythology had little influence on Apollodoros, and would probably have had little influence on us were it not for the alluring epic of **Ovid**, the *Metamorphoses*. This 15-book 'epic' presents a mythology of its own from the creation to his own day. Ovid is much more interested in ethos than in local detail, making his work a difficult and often not very useful source for the study of Greek myth, religion and society, despite its aesthetic and imaginary triumphs. But his account has been hugely popular from Roman antiquity, through the Middle Ages and the Renaissance, down to modern times. It has been the European artists' first port of call for mythological subjects in painting and sculpture and it has been many people's first introduction to the whole subject of Greek mythology.

We no longer have the work of the Hellenistic prose-writers – not just local historians, but also people like Dionysios Skytobrachion, who in the second century BC wrote books on Amazons and on the Trojan saga. But this was the work which led to important sources who do survive and who transmit local mythical information which is particularly valuable to a realistic study of Greek mythology. One surviving source is the geography of **Strabo** (writing around 20–7 BC). Even more important for us is **Pausanias** (writing around AD 160–80), whose *Periegesis of Greece* is a lavish guided tour to Greece's landscape, towns, monuments and traditions. Apollodoros' information, however, is a canonisation of the work of earlier writers of the Archaic and Classical Ages. The nadir of the mythographical tradition is reached with the mindless work, or summary of a work, of Julius **Hyginus**, the *Fabulae* (or *Genealogiae* – of perhaps the second century AD), which consists of a sequence of genealogies, of stories about particular individuals and finally a *Guinness Book of Records* conclusion: lists of the first people to build temples for the gods (225), people nourished on the milk of animals (252), record-holders for piety (254), for friendship (257), famous inventors (274) and so on. Hyginus largely got his information from a Greek source – though he did not understand Greek too well.

To deal in mythology is to put yourself in touch with ancient classical tradition. Fulgentius, in the fifth century AD, outlined its myths and their (suspiciously Neoplatonic!) meanings, notably in his *Mythologiae*. The ancient world was by now passing away and Fulgentius belongs with people like Servius who wrote the most influential commentary on Vergil, Proclus who wrote with massive erudition on Plato as the Christian world closed in, and with Boethius who a century later preserved Greek learning (for instance on music) for the Latin Middle Ages. Presently the mythology would be laid to rest during the dark era of the church, only to spring back into life in the writing and art of the Renaissance. Boccaccio in his *Genealogie* would take up where Fulgentius had left off 900 years before, renewing the west's subscription to antiquity.

Contents of Greek Mythology

> Nine-tenths of Greek myths are of a quite different type [from the cosmogonical-philosophical]. They play in the particular landscapes of Greece and tell of the earliest men who lived there, of the descent and the adventures of local heroes and suchlike.
>
> (Müller 1825: 72)

So Greek Mythology, as frozen in Apollodoros, is a construct and above all a literary construct – a body of privileged and arranged Greek myths, known widely wherever Greek culture ranged, and constantly alluded to in the work of poets and artists. Meanwhile, myths continued to live more locally and miscellaneously. Not only would locals point out the very place where famous myths had occurred: there were also the myriad also-rans of Greek mythology – those that never made it to the national corpus, though ambitious locals might try to tie them in. Such, for instance, was a tale of Poimandros, the founder of Tanagra, who had been besieged for not wishing to take part in the Trojan War, and such was a tale of Embaros (chapter 7.1) at Mounichia on the outskirts of Athens, who gained a priesthood for his family by (only nominally) sacrificing his daughter.

What, then, does Greek Mythology contain? Frazer divided the work of Apollodoros into 16 sections,[7] which I abbreviate as follows:

1 Beginnings.
  Birth of Titans and monsters from Sky and Earth. Births of the gods ('Theogony'). Offspring of the gods. The gods defeat various enemies – Giants, Python, Typhon, Orion. Persephone seized by Pluto.

2 Family of Deukalion.
  Creation of man, and the Flood. Beginnings of the Greek tribes. Various tales, based mainly in northern Greece: Meleager and the Calydonian Boar, the prophet Melampous, the voyage of the Argonauts.

3 Family of Inachus.
  The Argolid: Io turned into a cow, the daughters of Danaos murder their Egyptian husbands, Bellerophon and Pegasus, Perseus and the Gorgon, Perseus and Andromeda, the Labours of Herakles, the return of the Heraklids.

4–5 Family of Agenor.
Crete: Zeus as bull carries off Europa; King Minos, the birth of
the Minotaur.
Thebes: founded by Kadmos; Aktaion killed by his dogs;
arrival of Dionysos; Niobe turned to stone; Oedipus; the failed
expedition of the Seven against Thebes; the success of their
'descendants' (the *Epigonoi*).

6 Family of Pelasgos.
Arcadia: Zeus kills Lykaon and his sons for impiety; Kallisto
turned into a bear, gives birth to Arkas the first Arcadian; the
trials of Auge, priestess at Tegea; the virgin Atalante defeated
in running thanks to a golden apple.

7 Family of Atlas.
Arcadia: Hermes' early feats.
Thessaly: death of Apollo's son Asklepios; Apollo herdsman
for a year.
Sparta: Helen up to marriage with Menelaos; Kastor and
Polydeukes.
Troy: foundation and famous names before the Trojan War.

8 Family of Asopos.
Salamis: Telamon and his son Aias.
Thessaly: Peleus and the centaur Chiron, marriage to Thetis,
early history of Achilles – and Patroklos.

9–10 Athens.
Kings before Theseus, such as earth-born Kekrops and
Erichthonios. The tribute to the Minotaur.
Theseus: his feats, marriage to an Amazon, descent to hell; his
son Hippolytus dies from an overdose of chastity. Lapiths and
Centaurs.

11 Family of Pelops.
Pelops wins chariot-race by deceit – and the Peloponnese. The
polluted actions of Atreus and Thyestes. Agamemnon marries
Clytemnestra and Menelaos Helen.

12 The Trojan War up to the start of Homer's *Iliad*.
Judgment of Paris, theft of Helen, mustering of the Greek
forces, including Odysseus (pretending madness) and Achilles
(hiding among the girls at Skyros). Fleet gathers at Aulis.
Sacrifice of Iphigeneia. Preliminary tales around Troy, e.g.
Achilles' slaughter of Priam's son Troilos.

13 Homer's *Iliad*.
  Achilles withdraws from the fighting. Achilles comes back, kills
  Hektor. Priam recovers Hektor's body. It's only a matter of
  time now.

14 The Trojan War after Homer.
  Death of Achilles. The contest of Aias and Odysseus for his
  armour. Death of Paris. Theft of the *Palladion* (statue of Pallas
  Athene). The trick of the Wooden Horse. Sack of Troy. Ajax
  rapes Kassandra.

15 The 'Returns' (*Nostoi*) of the heroes from Troy.
  Storm, death of Ajax. Various catastrophes, in particular the
  murder of Agamemnon. Orestes' revenge and madness.

16 The *Odyssey* and its sequels.
  Adventures and return of Odysseus. Slaughter of his wife's
  'suitors'. Stories about Telegonos, a son of Odysseus who kills
  him, marries Penelope and is packed off to the Isles of the
  Blest by Circe. Meanwhile Penelope has born Pan to Hermes.

What immediately emerges is the crucial role of the Trojan War in
Greek mythology – it is this in which mythic 'history' culminates –
and the crucial role of the greatest Greek author, Homer, amidst
this ultimate heroic event. This is the citadel from which he
dominates Greek culture. Sections 13 and 16 are designed to
accommodate him. Sections 12–16 are needed for Trojan and
related material. Sections 7, 8 and 11 are designed to lead into the
Trojan material. Sections 9–10 are intrusions to accommodate
Athens – because our Greek cultural tradition has been transmit-
ted via Athens.

By contrast, the beginnings, dealing with creation, origins of
things and gods (section 1), are very slight by the standards of the
mythologies of other nations. The message is clear: Greek
Mythology is fundamentally about men and women, it is a 'historical' mythology. For the most part it is not the participation of
gods, talking animals or magic that makes Greek myth mythical;
rather, it is the participation of men and women who lived in *illo
tempore* ('yon times'),[8] the times before recorded history began and
beyond reliable oral tradition, in the para-history or proto-
history. They may be referred to as 'heroes', because if their
'graves' are known they will be receiving worship – hero-cult. In
Homer, they are even aware that they are heroes and, especially in
the nostalgic *Odyssey*, are approvingly addressed as 'Hero' – unlike

men of our day.[9] Of course these are not just any men and women of the remote past: as Aristotle pronounced (*Problems* 922b), 'Only the leaders of the ancients were heroes – the people were just men.'

In between the section on gods and origins and the sections on the Trojan War come myths which are sorted genealogically, by descent from famous heroes, but which in fact largely represent the traditions of the different areas of Greece – because so many heroes are designed to project places. This reinforces the lesson that myths are presented mostly as local prehistory, rather than as stories about enduring human concerns (however much they may in fact have to tell about such concerns). They fit tightly into local culture and require a historian's attention.

Chapter 2

How myths work: the theories

All universal theories of myth are automatically wrong.

(Kirk 1977: 293)

The Nemesis of disproportion seems to haunt all new discoveries.

(Max Müller 1873: 252)

What are Greek myths for? Not to tell history, only to masquerade as history. Not just to entertain: they have too much cultural significance for that.

Do they, then, serve a religious purpose? If so, we must beware of thinking of them as scriptures. Greeks did not turn to mythology for guidance on what to believe and how to live. They did not turn to their religion for morals and creeds, either. Of course the Greeks had ideas about the gods and man, and of course they found a reservoir of such ideas in myth and its purveyors (Homer, the tragedians), but these were not articles of faith. Myth is not there to state what must be believed: myth is not dogmatic.

Greek myths are also different from ancient Near Eastern mythologies (Brelich 1977: 7): they were not, at least in the form we have them, propagated by priests. The Greeks did not even have a specialist caste or profession of priests. Their mythology, for all the difficulty that scholars have in relating it to Indo-European tradition (chapter 4.1), at least is faithful to the Indo-European predilection for a rather secular pseudo-historical mythology. Perhaps the closest relatives of Greek mythology are the Sanskrit epics of India, *Mahābhārata* and *Rāmāyaṇa* – though the brahmin caste and its reflective overlay needs to be subtracted.

If not history, not entertainment, not religion, then what? This is the impasse from which the different theories of myth would rescue us. Greek mythology is both enriched and bedevilled by the attempts of modern writers to persuade us of a particular view of myth. Yet there is no escaping from this dilemma. Kirk (in the epigraph to this chapter) is no doubt right that no one theory will explain all Greek myths. But without consciously adopting at each point a theory, understanding what it may achieve and where it might fail, we simply do not know what we are doing. There is no theory-free approach to myth and it is mere illusion to suppose that myths, any more than any other type of empirical data, will somehow, with enough patient research, deliver their own explanations. All explanations are hypotheses, floated in the hope that they will help one's understanding of the world. Of no subject is this more clearly true than mythology.

A book on changing approaches to Greek mythology should be written. But this is not it. Instead, this chapter offers a very brief review of some styles of explanation that have been tried. I hope it catches the flavour of sometimes complicated ideas.

2.1 OLD APPROACHES

Historicism

On this view, myth is actually history, merely damaged and distorted by the passage of time. It is not so much a theory as a mistake to which beginners and those who make only occasional use of myth as evidence are very susceptible. It is also the predominant ancient Greek view, as we shall see in chapter 3. This view is seen quite often in discussions of tribal migrations, where prehistorians frequently mistake the ways in which myth works, supposing it to speak more directly than generally it does.[1] I give a few examples below:

1 Danaos (Ap 2.1.4) can be viewed simply as an historical person who really came from Egypt. But one can be more sophisticated without escaping the historicist fallacy. The myth can be thought to tell of the wanderings of the Danaoi tribe actually in and from the Near East; they are then connected with the 'Denyen' (one of the mysterious 'Sea-Peoples', about whom too much has been written) in an Egyptian inscription of 1186 BC, and with the tribe of Dan in *Genesis* 35 and *Judges* 18 (Roller), or with Danaoi in an Egyptian inscription of *c.* 1380 BC (Faure).[2]
2 Melampous the (legendary) prophet actually introduced the cult of Dionysos (Rohde).[3]

3 Schlieman identified the death-mask of Agamemnon and the jewels of Priam. I have been shown (and doubtless other tourists also have) the actual bath in which Agamemnon was murdered.
4 Gilbert Pilot established the actual route that Odysseus took in the *Odyssey*.[4]
5 Hyllos, leader of the Herakleidai clan, was killed at the Isthmus in single combat *c.* 1220 BC (Hammond: see p. 73 below).

Allegory

Myth is disguised philosophy or theology, concealing its deep secrets from those who do not understand its allegories. This view prevailed amongst ancient thinkers who attempted above all to defend Homer. It was inherited by the Renaissance and last flowered in the immense, influential and wholly mistaken work of F. Creuzer, his *Symbolik* (1st edn, 1810–12) in which he argued that Greek mythology contained deliberately concealed eastern wisdom.

The following sample is taken from a work of the first century AD which seeks to justify Homer through allegorisation:

> Overall, the wandering of Odysseus, if one cares to look at it in detail, will be found to be an allegory. Homer has taken Odysseus as a sort of tool for every virtue and used it to philosophise, since he detested the vices that feed on human life. Take for instance pleasure, the country of the Lotus-Eaters, which cultivates a strange enjoyment: Odysseus exercises his restraint and sails past. Or the savage spirit in each of us: he incapacitated it with the branding instrument of his verbal advice. This is called the 'Cyclops', that which 'steals away' [*hypoklopon*] our rationality . . . .
>
> Wisdom goes down as far as Hades so that no part even of the world below should be uninvestigated. Who, again, listens to the Sirens, if he has learnt the breadth of experience [referring to Odysseus' epithet 'much-experienced'] contained in the accounts of every age? And 'Charybdis' is a good name for lavish wastefulness, insatiable in its desire for drink. Skylla is his allegory for the shamelessness that comes in many shapes: hence she is not without good reason equipped with the dogs' heads that comprise rapacity, outrage, and greed. And the

cattle of the sun are restraint of the stomach – he counts not even starvation as a compulsion to wrongdoing.

(Pseudo-Herakleitos, *Homeric Problems* 70, extracts)

Though it is in the nature of ancient allegory to be wilful, it cannot be denied that this particular passage of moral allegory, though rather mechanical, validly accounts for some of the resonance of Homer's *Odyssey* (Books 9–12). And Aristotle may well have been right that Homer's 350 cattle of the Sun (*Odyssey* 12.129–30) represent the days of the twelve lunar months (Eustathios on *Odyssey* 12.130ff.) But as ancient philosophy developed, the authentic connection with the meaning of a myth in Homer's hands weakened. The philosopher seeks an image to explain his thought and finds one in Homer; Homer is just too authoritative in Greek culture for him not to be credited with the idea as well as the illustrative image. Thus Homer may be perceived as depicting in Kalypso and Circe the pleasures that detain the heaven-bound soul in this material world (Plotinos, *Enneads* 1.6.8).

Natural allegory and comparative mythology

Natural allegory is allegory of events in nature. This view is today associated with F. Max Müller (1823–1900), the son of the romantic poet Wilhelm Müller. He became a formidable scholar in the early days of critical work on Sanskrit literature and, in particular, on the very ancient body of hymns known as the *Rig Veda* ('Correctness–Knowledge'). Oxford created a chair of Comparative Philology specially for him in 1868 and he stayed there for the rest of his life. His influence was considerable, extending even to Queen Victoria, though his ideas were part of a general climate in which scholars propounded various forms of natural allegory.

Max Müller's view of myth was most fully expressed at the outset in his substantial 1856 essay, 'Comparative Mythology'. On this view, myth resulted from the attempts of primitive man to conceptualise the religious awe he felt before natural phenomena – the dawn, the sun and the clouds. Naturally he personalised these abstract qualities, but as language changed the original myths ceased to be understood and their sense could only be recovered by identifying the original meanings of the myths and of the names of the participants in the myths. Comparative philology, the study of (in this case) related Indo-European

languages (see chapter 4.1), enables us to reconstruct these original meanings. The Greeks themselves had, of course, lost the
original sense of these myths, through – and this was his
catchphrase – 'disease of language', though he later emphasised
that 'I have never said that . . . all mythology is a disease of
language' (1873: 252, cf. 259).

Let us start with an example where Max Müller is looking at the
celebration of the deeds of the god Indra in *Rig Veda* 4.30 (1898:
98–102). Indra, on Max Müller's reading, is the 'chief solar deity
of the Veda' and in this passage the dawn flees from his embrace;
elsewhere too the sun follows her – or she is carried away in
triumph by the Aśvins (to whom we will return in chapter 4.1).
But once in the Veda the word for dawn is *Ahanā* and you
sometimes get a variant form of words with a *d- (daśru*, 'tear', =
aśru). A form *Dahanā* would clinch a connection with Germanic
words for 'day' and the Sanskrit root for 'burn'.

> If now we translate, or rather transliterate, *Dahanā* into Greek,
> Dáphne stands before us, and her whole history is intelligible.
> Dáphne is young and beautiful – Apollo loves her – she flies
> before him, and dies as he embraces her with his brilliant rays.
> (Max Müller 1898: 100)

The reader should, incidentally, be warned that Apollo was
wholly unconnected with the sun before mystic inventive speculation of the fifth century BC.

It does not always emerge from descriptions of Max Müller's
interpretation of mythology that it was much more than a dry
philological game conducted with arbitrary etymologies. At times
it rose to a level of romantic splendour admirable for all its
dubiety. Here, for instance, are the last moments of Herakles (Ap
2.7.7):

> From thence Herakles crosses over to Trachys and then to
> Mount Oeta, where his pile is raised, and the hero is burnt,
> rising through the clouds to the seat of the immortal gods –
> himself henceforth immortal and wedded to Hebe, the god-
> dess of youth. The coat which Deianeira sends to the solar hero
> is an expression frequently used in other mythologies [Max
> Müller cites, second-hand, a passage of the *Bhagavat-Purāṇa*
> calling dawn 'the clothing of the god with the great strides']; it is
> the coat which in the Veda, 'the mothers weave for their bright
> son' – the clouds which rise from the waters and surround the

sun like a dark raiment. Herakles tries to tear it off; his fierce splendour breaks through the thickening gloom, but fiery mists embrace him, and are mingled with the parting rays of the sun, and the dying hero is seen through the scattered clouds of the sky, tearing his own body to pieces, till at last his bright form is consumed in the general conflagration, his last-beloved being Iole – perhaps the violet-coloured evening clouds – a word which, as it reminds us also of *ios*, poison (though the *i* is long), may perhaps have originated the myth of a poisoned garment.

(Max Müller 1898: 97)

This type of theory is now wholly abandoned for Greek mythology, though it is rather disconcerting that it appears still to be defensible in Sanskrit and maybe Roman mythology[5] and that the thought of Max Müller appears less preposterous when not read through the words of others.

Cambridge myth-ritual

In the beginning were two formative works. One was W. Robertson Smith's *Lectures on the Religion of the Semites* (1st edn, London, 1889), a seminal work much interested in rituals and particularly in the communal sharing of a 'sacramental' meal – eating the god. The other was Sir J.G. Frazer's *Golden Bough* (1st edn, London, 1890), a massive (and therefore incontrovertible) collection of rituals and customs from around the world, flimsily related to the alleged custom of killing a sacred king so that a new one might replace him and 'fertility' (his commonest leitmotif) be renewed. In later editions, he also pegged to this work an evolutionary theory of the progressive displacement of magic by religion and of religion in turn by science, which shows something of the cosy primitivism with which myth would be viewed. Both writers were based at Cambridge.

From our perspective the interest lies in what Jane Harrison made of Frazer and in particular in her *Themis* (1912). From Frazer sprang her 'year-god' (*eniautos daimon* was the Greek term that Harrison coined), requiring annual renewal and to be discovered for instance (1912: ch. 1) in the worship of the new-born Zeus in Crete and the associated mythology (Ap 1.1.6). At times she thought (1912: 328) that myth was, or had originally been, the words (*legomena* – 'things spoken') which go with the ritual (*dromena* – 'things performed'). All myths are apparently to be accounted for in this way. But her thinking included a rather different view, in which myth was not so much derived from ritual as a representation of the same concerns as the ritual (1912:16), and at the same time her attention shifts from rituals concerned with 'fertility' – Frazer's obsession – to social rituals such as initiation, reflecting the sociological view of religion propounded by E. Durkheim.[6]

Though she was at times rather too imaginative and excessive in her conclusions (and also personally difficult for her era), it is increasingly recognised that seeds for later work, however spurned, lay here. Even the at first rather deviant and implausible construction of a year-god looks forward in a way to the intermittent focus on renewal festivals by Burkert, Graf and others, though I doubt if any of us reached this position as a result of Harrison's work. The same, more importantly, may also be said of her interest in the relationship between mythology and initiation.

Other writers in this Cambridge 'school' included F.M. Cornford, A.B. Cook, and (at Oxford) Gilbert Murray. Cook's major work was the multi-volume *Zeus*, following Frazer in both bulk and, to some extent, theoretical apparatus. Cornford was closer to Harrison, for instance arguing that comedy originated in a New Year ritual (*The Origin of Attic Comedy*, London, 1914, reprinted Cambridge, 1934); and, similarly, Murray added to Harrison's *Themis* an excursus claiming detailed ritual origins and structure for Greek tragedy.

Perhaps the Cambridge school was more a set of friends, a clique with shared interests and views, than a lasting revolution in thought. This might explain why the positions of value which were held by its members tend to be reinvented rather than inherited.

2.2 SURVIVING SYSTEMS

New comparative mythology

Georges Dumézil, from around 1920, saw himself as restoring the comparative study of Indo-European religions after it had become discredited through the excesses of Max Müller and those he influenced. In theory it should be possible to reconstruct Indo-

European myths just as one can reconstruct Indo-European words (see chapter 4.1) and this is in effect how Dumézil proceeded, though etymology became less significant than it had been in Max Müller and structure of myths more significant. By 1938 Dumézil had made his most notable discovery – a fundamental division of Indo-European society into three 'functions' or ideological areas: that of the priest/ruler, of the warrior and of the productive (this is then where both fertility and farmers belong). For Dumézil Indo-European mythologies are concerned to project this tripartition, though others, appreciative of Dumézil's insights, see something less ideological: a social stratification in Indo-European society, naturally reflected in its mythology. Others again find Dumézil's theory exaggerated, but the principal difficulty for us is that, as Dumézil himself has admitted, for some reason the method only works on the rarest occasions for Greek myth, despite many plausible examples in other Indo-European mythologies (Dumézil 1953: 25).

Here are some samples of the three functions at work in Greek myths:

1 The Judgment of Paris (Ap *Ep.* 3.2) is a choice between the three functions: Hera – ruler, Athene – warrior, Aphrodite – productive (e.g. Puhvel 1987: 133).[7] Troy then falls because the choice of Paris has disturbed the hierarchy of the functions.

2 'The Titans are tied to sovereignty; the Giants to war; the Kouretes preside over armed dances and the initiation of youths; centaurs, who also feature as the educators of princes, take part in seasonal masquerades which later became mythical battles; Kyklopes and Telchines are smiths – the former faithful assistants of the Sovereign of the Gods, the latter busy with more workmanlike tasks and playing the role of village magicians' (Vian 1963: 237 f.).

3 Dazzling, if not wholly credible as presented, is Dumézil's account of Herakles (1970: ch. 5). This epitome of 'the warrior function', in his cycle of stories commits a sin against each of the three functions, corresponding to sins committed by what may be identified as his Indian equivalent, Indra, and an old Danish equivalent, Starcatherus:

(i)   he hesitates to accept Zeus' command to perform the labours (at least in Diodoros 4.10–11) and as a result goes mad: he has rejected the sovereign of the gods, and lost the control of his mind.

(ii)   he treacherously kills his guest Iphitos (Ap 2.6.2), thus violating the warrior's code. As a result he loses his physical well-being (or should – I cannot find this in the sources).

(iii)   his lust for two women, Astydameia and Iole, leads to his death by the poisoned cloak of the Centaur unwittingly given to him by his wife Deianeira (Diodoros 4.37-8).[8] He has given way to 'sexual concupiscence' and loses his life.

Psychoanalysis

'Psychoanalysis' is the study and treatment of the human mind, as laid down by Sigmund Freud (1856–1939). Indeed, in the strictest sense, the term refers exclusively to Freud's method. In this approach, dreams possess a special importance because they can disclose the hidden operations of the unconscious mind. Psychoanalysts must understand the ways in which dreams condense and displace unconscious ideas, using symbolism, decomposition or projection. But one can advance from dreams to myths:

> It seems quite possible to apply the psychoanalytic views derived from dreams to products of ethnic imagination such as myths and fairy tales. . . . [Psychoanalytic study] cannot accept as the first impulse to the construction of myths a theoretical craving for finding an explanation of natural phenomena or for accounting for cult observances and usages which have become unintelligible. It looks for that impulse in the same psychical 'complexes' in the same emotional trends which it has discovered at the base of dreams and symptoms.
>
> (Freud 1913: 185)

At this point two problems arise. First, who will take it upon themselves to psychoanalyse classical myths? Psychoanalysts are rarely well equipped: they tend to be amateur classicists (as a sequence of errors in their writings has in fact shown). Equally, classicists are scarcely better – less because they are only amateur psychoanalysts than because they have been hostile to new ideas (an allegation not without some truth) and deaf to the need for psychoanalytical interpretation. The second problem is deeper. You can't psychoanalyse unless there's a psyche to analyse: if you attempt a psychoanalytic interpretation of a Greek myth, whose psyche is it anyway? A repeated and naïve error of psychoanalytic interpreters has been to analyse characters in myth as though they were real, pathological patients on a couch. Can one psycho-analyse a fiction created by an author ignorant of psychoanalysis? The character after all has no life history other than that stated – to think otherwise is to commit the fallacy of 'interpretive supplementation'.[9]

There are only two ways around this latter problem. First, the myth is regarded as a sort of dream of its author. This runs into the difficulty that the force of myth obviously lies in its preservation and value from person to person and time to time. So we reach finally the only tenable position: psychoanalytic interpretation of myth can only work if it reveals prevalent, or even universal, deep concerns of a larger cultural group of human beings ('ethnic imagination' as Freud expresses it above). It is not clear to me whether this would mean just 'the Greeks' (whoever they were) or whether it might extend to us as well, because I do not know how far unconscious anxieties vary from culture to culture. In any case, this idea tends to be dressed up in a rather romantic, mystical way in the notion of not just an indi-vidual's unconscious, but a whole 'collective unconscious' (as though we all shared in a single mind – which some may even want to believe).

If then psychoanalytic interpretation of myth is possible in some way, the final question is: are the particular interpretations offered acceptable? It is here that one notices with dismay the whole battery of themes and symbols which interpreters have received like some Holy Grail from Freud. It is rare indeed that a Freudian interpretation is offered for evaluation: his themes and symbols are too often truths in which neophytes must have faith – the system is not open to challenge, despite Caldwell's claim that the theory is a 'very tentative' model of how the human mind works.[10] But if we were to challenge it, we would have to explain why Freudian psychoanalysis has appeared to work in the social conditions of the twentieth century. I do not have the leisure to do this (though I think others may have done so successfully),[11] but I suspect that there are possible explanations for its success other than that the themes and symbols proposed by Freud are abso-lutely true, scientifically proved and binding. There is surely life beyond childhood psychosexuality.

Freud did not write at length on Greek mythology, unlike Jung (see below), but he is of course responsible for the 'Oedipus complex', the identification of the boy's fear and rivalry of his father and wish to supplant him in his mother's affections. Implicitly this must be the supposed meaning of the myth. The followers of Freud have however turned the Freudian perception of the subconscious to the task of interpreting mythology and a number of examples are given in the course of this book.

Like any other religion, that of Freud has had its measure of heretics and apostates. I mention here only Carl Jung, who developed the 'collective unconscious' by positing a whole series of 'archetypal images' (divine child, mother and daughter . . .) which emerge from the preconscious psyche and find expression in myth. These are collectively possessed and inherited by all of us, just as the shape of our limbs is inherited and common to us all. These shared images may, however, be differently realised in different cultures. Interpretation is in fact rather a limited task, because the core of meaning cannot be laid bare, only re-expressed: 'the most we can do is to *dream the myth onwards* and give it a modern dress' (Jung and Kerényi 1949:79; italics in original). This limit is severe and results in a very slight impact on our understanding of particular myths, despite the occasional insights in the voluminous, rambling and erratic studies of Greek myth and religion by C. Kerényi, who collaborated with Jung during the 1940s. The most that may be achieved, if there is any validity in the theory, is that we recognise just how fundamental and deep-seated are the images that surface in myth. That is all that is left of Freud's revelation of the real processes of the human mind. But it is perhaps philosophically more sound that we have no language in which we can think what lies behind thought.

Structuralism

I do not think Lévi-Strauss has proved anything.

(Burkert 1979: 11)

Claude Lévi-Strauss, too, sought to uncover the workings of the human mind. 'The structural study of myth' goes back to an essay of that title which he published in 1955, and which was reprinted in his *Structural Anthropology* (English translation, 1963). Though his main work had been on South American Indian cultures, he chose the Oedipus myth to demonstrate the application of a structuralist method based on linguistics to the study of myth. Why the Oedipus myth? Perhaps because it was well known and culturally prevalent (largely as a result of Freud).

Myth for him was a sort of language which raised cultural problems and alleviated them. The myth is assembled in all its versions – whoever told them, wherever or whenever. It is then broken down into its elements (motifs, I suppose). The elements stand in some relationship to each other, and by this structure suggest issues. Thus in the Oedipus myth, 'Oedipus marries his mother', like 'Antigone buries her brother contrary to Creon's edict', shows the over-rating of blood relationships; whereas, 'Oedipus kills his father' and 'Eteokles slaughters his brother Polyneikes' show the opposite. The myth proceeds, as structuralist myths tend to, by antithesis, by the presentation of opposite poles ('binary opposition'). In the end the presentation of opposites leads to some sense of resolution. In their most 'scientific' form structuralist discussions can easily be identified by the construction of diagrams reminiscent of algebra or formal logic in order to represent the intersection of different pairs of opposites ('logical quadrangles').

Beyond this, it becomes almost impossible to state what should be understood by the term 'structuralism' in the study of Greek mythology. 'Structuralism' itself became a buzz-word in the 1960s and 1970s, understood in different ways by different workers in different fields (linguistics, in particular, adopted the term). Lévi-Strauss' own application of the method to the Oedipus myth (back in 1955) became in retrospect not entirely satisfactory, even to those who generally admired his work, and his methods certainly became more refined in later work, which however was not concerned with *Greek* mythology. Thus, on the one hand, critics attacked Lévi-Strauss for a part of his output which had been overtaken by later developments, and, on the other hand, in order to view a revised, corrected structuralism, one had to believe that successors to Lévi-Strauss were applying his method to Greek mythology both faithfully and better than he had himself.

A truly scientific way of interpreting myths has been the target of mythological alchemists (and most of us are) since K.O. Müller's *Prolegomena zu einer wissenschaftlichen Mythologie* ('Prolegomena to a Scientific Mythology') (1st edn 1825). Lévi-Strauss's approach was particularly alluring in this respect, even for those whom one might have expected to oppose it. E. Leach, in criticising the method, in fact extended it to other examples (1974: 68–83). And G.S. Kirk, doyen of Anglo-Saxon empiricism, deployed something rather like it on his own account – if not too much (1970: ch. iv, 'Nature and culture').

Lévi-Strauss on principle disregarded chronological and strictly historical factors and included in his analysis all motifs of a myth, no matter when or where attested. Perhaps because of our training, classical scholars have found this hard to accept and the rejection of this aspect of Lévi-Strauss' approach has been a noticeable feature of the digestion of his thought. In any case it is a general, if not invariable, characteristic of Greek myths to name their location (Brelich 1977: 9) and therefore to invite a more specific treatment than Lévi-Strauss was prepared to allow.

2.3 MODERN TENDENCIES

Now that we have scanned a range of nineteenth- and twentieth-century approaches, we can see that a number of different directions remain possible. With the exception of the comparative mythologists, the trend now is towards an eclecticism, slightly differently balanced in different groups of scholars. At this point I highlight the following strands: (1) the acknowledgement of the usefulness of specific and distinctive historical data, thus rejecting part of the Lévi-Strauss view; (2) the sensitive and systematic exploration of themes and their place in the map of Greek culture, thought or ideology; (3) the confrontation of myth with ritual.

Modern myth-ritual

Some myths are tied by their motifs to local rituals, especially initiation-rituals. Harrison had in effect reached this position, but it is hopefully by now better grounded. What is striking is the convergence of scholars of different traditions towards the recognition of this type of interpretation. In France, Jeanmaire as long ago as 1911 (in the age of Frazer) had written a careful article identifying the Spartan *Krypteia* as an initiation-ritual; and in 1939 he used his deep ethnographical knowledge to advance to a larger study of boys' initiation rituals (*Couroi et Courètes*). This embraced a particular view of the relationship of myths, for instance of Theseus, to this type of ritual. The major amplification of this approach came with Brelich's 'Rome school' (see below) work of 1969. Meanwhile, the work of Burkert had begun, leading to his provocative exploration of the significance of ritual in his 1972 *Homo Necans*. The prevalence of interest in myth-ritual matters independent of the scholar's academic tradition has led to some astonishing instances of mutual ignorance of each other's work: Brelich and Burkert were unaware of each other around 1969–70, for all their many similarities in method; and Pierre Brulé and I, as he has said (if rather in jest), practically wrote the same book as each other. Perhaps I should cite the words of Calder in a different case: 'A conclusion that is independently reached by two expert investigators working without knowledge of each other is far more than twice as certain to be correct.'[12]

Several examples of this type of interpetation will be found above all in chapter 7. But an initial example may help: Burkert, in an article that has proved something of a watershed (1970), argued that the murder of their husbands by the women of Lemnos (Ap 1.9.17) corresponds to a ritual separation of the sexes in a New Year festival which must have been held on Lemnos. The arrival of the Argonauts corresponds to the ritual arrival of a ship bringing new fire, and denotes the restoration of the state of marriage. Incidentally, the foul smell of the Lemnian women may correspond to a ritual chewing of garlic such as we find at the Athenian Thesmophoria.

The principal limitation of the method is that it delivers explanation at an antiquarian level, but does not always explain the continuing interest and force of the myth in, for instance, classical Greek society.

'Rome school'

This term has been applied to those scholars of the history of religions that work or worked in the Istituto di Studi storico-religiosi at the University of Rome. In Greek mythology one thinks immediately of Brelich and, too slowly, of those whose work has not readily reached the English-speaking market: D. Sabbatucci, G. Piccaluga, M. Massenzio, I. Chirassi-Colombo.

Brelich (1977: 5) identified two principles which these scholars had learnt from the founder of the Institute, R. Pettazzoni: (1) the importance of comparing information from different fields, in particular, 'ethnological' information – i.e. information from traditional cultures around the world; and (2) the need to set religion in an historical context. They look at particular myths and myth-types and seek to identify various layers relating to specific historical, social and religious data.

Brelich (1977: 16 f.) offers the following example. One version of the error of the great hunter Orion was excessive enthusiasm for slaughtering animals.[13] The error of Agamemnon was his boast over the slaughter of a deer (Ap *Ep.* 3.21). These errors reflect necessities in the life of pre-agricultural, hunting peoples (ethnology!) and have their roots in an unusually ancient layer of Greek myth and society (history!), which nevertheless, to judge by the amount of hunting in Greek myth, remains extensive.

The style and area of discussion will depend greatly on the strata being examined. So, for instance, where the data pertain to religious ritual, modern myth-ritual conclusions will emerge: one of Brelich's major works, *Paides e parthenoi* (1969), links myths to initiation rituals, having carefully established the ethnological background for comparison. But Piccaluga's *Lykaon* (1968), though considering the linkage between myth of Lykaon and cult of Zeus Lykaios important, regards cult alone as an insufficient basis for understanding the myth. So she looks, for example, at the place of the unsavoury Lykaon in the intertext of Greek Mythology, evoking such figures as Busiris (Ap 2.5.11) and Tereus (Ap 3.14.8), and explores the ambivalent theme of water – water as deluge and water as a necessity for agriculture after the rupture of relations between man and god. Her view becomes all-embracing: botany, animal-life and meteorology all find their place. This influx of data from usually discrete fields is perhaps what Brelich meant to derive from Pettazzoni.

Yet Brelich was reluctant to identify an unduly distinctive 'Rome school', and in practice the emphasis on history or varied cultural data is obviously not exclusive to their work. Brelich himself was a good deal more eclectic than his reluctant description suggests and it is surprising that his careful and humane scholarship was so little understood at the time in the Anglo-Saxon world.

'Paris school'

The term 'Paris school' refers above all to J.-P. Vernant, P. Vidal Naquet and M. Detienne. The crisis for them has been to state their relationship to the work of Lévi-Strauss. In effect, they stand much closer to concrete historical data and thereby close the gap between 'structuralism' and other approaches, though they may be tarred with the 'structuralist' brush, despite their protests: 'People christen us "structuralists" without my knowing exactly what they mean by the term when they stick this label on our backs' (Vernant in Gentili and Paioni 1977: 398). In any case, it is clear that Vernant's approach owes more to the historical, anthropological approach of L. Gernet than to Lévi-Strauss. On the other hand, Detienne has been prepared to view himself as deploying the method that Lévi-Strauss really intended.

If there is anything that these scholars have in common, other than being French, it is perhaps a great sensitivity to the issues, ambiences and tensions expressed in myth and the ability to construct a picture piece by piece. Thus, though Vidal Naquet's analysis of the Athenian ephebeia – initiation-ritual and myths – in terms of its propositions and conclusions could have been written by Burkert or Brelich, a feeling, for instance, for the role of the colour black or for the meaning of hunting by oneself and with nets is evoked over and above the need to drive home an explicit ritual or social conclusion. This is even more evident in the case of Detienne's work on Adonis, where, for example, the sexual ambience of perfumes and the frigidity of lettuce contribute not only to a systematic understanding of the mythical environment of the Adonis myth and cult, but also to its place in the Athenian – and Greek – imagination. Vernant could never be mistaken for Burkert. His essays explore, realise possibilities, capture the feel and the imagination, but defy summary. Here he is concluding a study of themes of lameness, tyranny and incest in the Oedipus mythology and in the stories about the tyrants of Corinth, Kypselos and Periander:

> Despising the rules which preside over the ordering of the social fabric and which, through the regular inter-crossing of sons, determine the positions of each in relation to the others – or, as Plato puts it more crudely, ready to kill his father, sleep with his mother, eat the flesh of his own children – the tyrant, at once equal to the god and equal to a ferocious beast, incarnates in his ambivalence the mythic figure of the lame man, with his two opposing aspects: a gait beyond the human because in rolling, faster and more agile in all directions at once, he transgresses the limitations to which walking straight must submit; but also this side of the normal mode of locomotion

because mutilated, unbalanced, vacillating, he advances limp-
ing in his singular fashion all the better to fall in the end.

(Vernant 1982: 34)

We can all drift towards thinking that our approach solves all
problems and displaces all others. Yet it is obvious enough that
many of these approaches are mutually compatible. A myth may
trace something of its construction to history, may be used in a
superficial way to explain a ritual, may, when more deeply
probed, tell us something about that ritual, may – viewed together
with other myths – form part of a systematic, even unconscious,
way of dividing up and thinking about the perceived world.
Historicism, myth-ritual, structuralism all have their dangers, but
they lie chiefly in exaggeration. I must confess to greater doubts
about the role of psychoanalysis, though these relate more to how
it should be applied and what sort of statements might validly
result than to whether there is a valid role at all. It is fascinating
that Caldwell has recently produced a structuralist look-alike of
the psychoanalytic approach with tables that would do credit to
Lévi-Strauss.[14] We live in syncretistic times.

Chapter 3

Greeks on myth

3.1 THE SIXTH AND FIFTH CENTURIES

Greek culture valued its traditions. There is little sign in Homer or Hesiod of criticism of myth – except when Hesiod allows that the Muses could on occasion tell plausible lies (*Theogony* 27). Criticism only begins with two intellectual developments of the period 550–450 BC. The first, and earlier, was the emergence of philosophical and scientific thought in a series of individualists today generally labelled the 'Presocratic' philosophers (i.e. those before Socrates). On both scientific and moral grounds these thinkers found it difficult to continue to accept traditional theology and myth. The second development was the beginning of geographical, ethnographical and historical writing, which resulted from an increase in travel – and better observation. Yet, though much enthusiasm has been expended on these developments, neither really had much impact on the public at large.

The thought of the Presocratics perhaps seeped through the cautious theology of the tragedians to mass audiences, but a much greater pressure was exerted by tradition, ritual and the poems of Homer. Historians and travellers may to an extent have improved the range of knowledge before audiences, but, as we shall see (e.g. chapter 8.2), they created mythologies of their own and often served only to move the ends of the earth or the times of legend a little further away. In addition, our view of history-writing suffers from the iceberg fallacy: we see Herodotos and Thucydides, but they are part of a larger prose tradition which as a whole was very receptive to traditional myth and even their relationship to this body of traditional knowledge is something which divides them from our notion of what it is to be an historian.

Some Presocratic thinkers

Any speculation about the nature of god is liable to lead sooner or later to the abandonment of literal belief in mythical pictures. Yet few Greeks felt ready simply to jettison their cultural heritage. It was not until around 500 BC that **Xenophanes** ridiculed the idea that gods were man-shaped – oxen would have an ox-shaped god, he observed. But he is less dismissive than he seems: he, too, names a shape for his special god – spherical. And even this rotund god, though apparently single, remains 'one god amongst gods and men', confusing modern monotheists who cannot easily understand why ancients with all the materials ready for mono-theism persist in accommodating polytheism. He proceeds, how-ever, to reject (fr. 14) the idea that gods are born (the basic motif of theo-*gonies*, '*births* of gods') and, in particular, challenges the morality of myth:

> Homer and Hesiod have ascribed to the gods
> Everything all the disgraces and shame that mortals have
> – stealing, adultery, and cheating each other.
>
> (Xenophanes, fr. 11)

Thus the traditional presentation is false and improper: as with the shape of god, it needs correction.

Xenophanes' contemporary **Herakleitos** similarly does not wholly reject the name Zeus, commenting with characteristic obscurity that 'the Wise in its unity is alone not prepared and is prepared to be called by the name of Zeus' (fr. 32). But all the same he thought 'that Homer was fit to be thrown out of the games and beaten' (fr. 41).

The very fact that Xenophanes and Herakleitos can see any way of keeping in touch with traditional religious concepts must mean that they can envisage a relationship between a traditional, mythically conceived world and the new philosophical–scientific world. Others began a more methodical defence of traditional myth, and, in particular, of Homer by supposing that what Homer said was not literally meant but allegorical. This method begins, we are told, with one **Theagenes** of Rhegion around 525 BC, as a method of finding an acceptable interpretation of Homer for the new age. An ancient commentator on Homer refers to Theagenes in explaining what is meant by Homer's battles be-tween gods which so shocked thinkers:

In fact, they say that it is [i.e. represents] the dry fighting the moist and the hot fighting the cold and the light fighting the heavy. Furthermore, water is what quenches fire and fire is what dries out water. And in the same way all the constituent elements of the universe display conflict and to an extent simply suffer destruction, whilst all remain eternally. He [Homer] laid out battles, calling fire 'Apollo' and 'Helios' and 'Hephaistos', water 'Poseidon' and 'Scamander', moon 'Artemis', the air 'Hera' and so on. Similarly on occasion he applies the names of gods to dispositions – 'Athene' to good sense, 'Ares' to insanity, 'Aphrodite' to desire, and 'Hermes' to reason – and makes them conform to these. This kind of defence, a very old one which goes back to Theagenes of Rhegion who first wrote about Homer, is based on diction.

(Scholiast B on Homer *Iliad* 20.67 (= Theagenes 8T2))

It should not be thought that every equation here goes back to Theagenes, but some of them will, and a sort of common interpretation gradually builds up, which, for instance, will be dear to the hearts of Stoic philosophers in the Hellenistic Age. This is *physical* allegory – the figures of myth represent facts of what we would call science.

This type of physical allegory is evidently being drawn on by **Empedokles** in the middle of the fifth century. He represents the four elements by god names: Zeus is fire (though in some places Hephaistos serves just as well), Hera is air, Aidoneus (i.e. Hades) is earth and an idiosyncratic 'Nestis' ('Starvation') is water. However, as is the way with physical allegory, these have become mere physical elements and the real work in Empedokles' universe is done by two counterbalancing principles – Philotes ('Love') and Neikos ('Strife').

Around the same time, **Anaxagoras** is credited with an important development, if it is true. According to the second-century AD polymath and hermaphrodite Favorinus, Anaxagoras (59A1 para. 11) was the first to state that Homer's poetry was about virtue and morality. This would be the beginning, then, of *moral* allegory, of which we saw a sample in chapter 2.1 (p. 24). His follower **Metrodoros** of Lampsakos, on the other hand, took to a more physical allegory of sophistic bravado, but little plausibility:

Agamemnon was the aether, Achilles the sun, Helen the earth, Alexandros (Paris) the air, Hektor the moon and the others were named on the same lines as these. As for the gods, Demeter was the liver [i.e. as a seat of emotions], Dionysos the spleen, and Apollo the bile.

(Metrodoros (61T4) reported by Philodemos)

Response to traditions

These avant-garde thinkers were in no sense typical even of writers. A much more conventional and mainstream tradition is represented by **Akousilaos** of Argos, who in his *Genealogies* of around 500 BC retold the traditional accounts that most later authors knew from Hesiod. Sometimes he added an Argive perspective, telling, for instance, the tale of the First Man in local Argive tradition, Phoroneus (*FGH* 2F23).[1] Sometimes he improved on Hesiod by producing more 'knowledgeable' variants of these traditions (T6). So, for example, when Ouranos (Heaven) was castrated, the drops of semen that fell to earth begat not giants but the Phaiakians – for Odysseus to meet in the *Odyssey* (F4); Iris (Rainbow) is the messenger not just of Zeus, or alternatively of Hera, but of all the gods (F9); and all biting creatures come from the blood of Typhon, Zeus' most dangerous enemy (F14). Beyond this, there are a number of revisions to genealogical chains for reasons rarely apparent to us.

Akousilaos displays no historical sense: he does not reach beyond Greek mythology (i.e. any later than the Trojan War) and his sense of accuracy is restricted to corrections, for instance, of the genealogy of 'legendary' Argive kings. Disbelief is simply suspended. Yet the historical character of Greek mythology can create special problems for those Greeks more concerned with historical accuracy. On the one hand, they can see as plainly as we can that the traditions about, for example, Pelops and Agamemnon are on a different footing from recorded history. But, on the other hand, these are the only traditions relating to times which otherwise would be blank – only myth can fill the historical vacuum. The compromise position generally reached is that myth is indeed historical evidence, but it is rather special or distorted. Those that are particularly scrupulous or confident will adjust myths to make historical sense. This adjustment is known today as 'rationalisation'.

'Rationalisation of myth' usually conjures up the name of **Hekataios** of Miletos, a politician active, as we can see from

Herodotos (5.36, 125f., 6.137), during the failed revolt of the
Ionians from Persia (499–494 BC). A contemporary, maybe, of
Akousilaos, he was as interested in tradition as in geography and
ethnography and he wrote a *Genealogies* of his own about the
origins of Greek (and other) tribes and places. A distinctive
critical attitude is the keynote of his opening: 'Hekataios of
Miletos gives this account [*mytheisthai*, archaically?]: I write this in
the way which seems true to me – because the accounts [*logoi*] of
the Greeks are, as they seem to me, numerous and laughable'
(Hekataios, *FGH* 1F1).

One's expectations should not be unduly raised. He tells a story
of the origins of wine in Aitolia: a pregnant bitch gives birth to a
rooted vine-stock; Orestheus, the son of Deukalion (the Greek
Noah), orders it buried; and that is where grapes come from
(F15). Or take the story of how the ram with the golden fleece (Ap
1.9.1) actually spoke to Phrixos, urging him to escape on its back:
'the story that the ram spoke is in Hekataios' (F17). It was left to
others to rationalise this one: Phrixos sailed off in a boat with a
ram-shaped prow, or perhaps, as Dionysios Skytobrachion
thought (32F2, second century BC), 'Ram' was the name of the
slave who had brought him up and this man sailed with him to
Kolchis. Herakles' fight with the Hydra of Lerna is especially
disappointing: Aelian gives 'poets and composers of ancient
myths' a licence to tell this story 'and Hekataios the logos-writer
belongs with them' (1F24).

So what of the rationalisations of Hekataios? He had traced the
actual route of the Argonauts (F18) – a persistent fascination of
misguided books down to our own days. He knew the tale of the
Danaids and how the sons of Aigyptos pursued them to Argos:
'Aigyptos himself did not come to Argos – only his children.
There were 50 of them according to Hesiod but to my mind less
than 20' (Hekataios, *FGH* 1F19). Geryon and the cattle Herakles
stole were nothing to do with Spain and that region, but belonged
to north-west Greece (F26). And Herakles did not bring the dog
Kerberos from Hades: he brought back a fearsome snake which
lived at Tainaron, the reputed entrance to the underworld, and
the snake was called 'dog of Hades' because its bite was so deadly
(F27). So Hekataios makes adjustments to these traditions to allow
for distortions in the course of transmission. There is no notion
that these traditions were never designed to tell a literal truth;

they have simply gone wrong and the damage time has done, man can repair.

Akousilaos was perhaps the dominant influence on **Pherekydes** of Athens in a rather more extensive genealogical work which was apparently entitled *Histories* (meaning, as in Herodotos, 'Researches'). He wrote uncomfortably late (maybe 460–450 BC) for those who wish the Greeks to advance from *Mythos* to *Logos* ('more primitive impression . . . practically no fundamental myth-criticism', remarks Nestle (1941: 141)), and serves to demonstrate how utterly the Greeks remained committed to myth despite enlightenments. His is the path that ultimately leads to Apollodoros.

At much the same time as Pherekydes, or possibly a little later, **Hellanikos** of Lesbos was himself writing rather thorough genealogy–mythology (up to and including the Trojan War). But he is also the first 'universal historian', i.e. the first man to attempt to write a total history from the beginning. His framework for this is a chronology supplied by the list of the priestesses at Argos, which of course went back indiscriminately to the times of myth, and he used the list to specify the events during each priesthood. His book was far from historical, being full of population movements led by fictional bearers of tribal and local names: 'Nisaia [one of Megara's ports] was captured by Nisos son of Pandion [king of Athens] and by Megareus from Onchestos' (Hellanikos, *FGH* 4F78). He is, however, the first to put dates on myths – for instance dating the Trojan War in relation to other events that did not happen. A characteristic passage is reported as follows:

> The author who put together the *Priestesses in Argos* and what was done under each priestess says that Aeneas came from the Molossians to Italy and became, together with Odysseus, the founder of the city, naming it 'Rome' after one of the Trojan women.
>
> (Hellanikos, *FGH* 4F84)

Tagging this sort of event to a particular priesthood makes it history, for in Hellanikos' mind there was no difference between myth and history. In fact it must be said that despite the impression given by many books, there is precious little historical writing or sense in Hellanikos. According to Thucydides (1.97.2), he touched briefly and inaccurately on the Athenian rise to power in the period 479–432 BC in his work on Attica, but this is an exception, if an important one: his was the first in a very popular genre of Athenian local histories, of which little remains today. As in his other local histories, in this case too he was interested in places, institutions and mythical colour, laying the foundations for Pausanias in the second century AD and the Michelin *Guides Verts* in the twentieth.

Such writers do, however, differ in their propensity for 'improving' myth. One who was very much so inclined was **Herodoros** of Herakleia, who around 400 BC wrote a number of works devoted to mythological subjects. One was on the Argonauts, one a *Pelopeia* (matters connected with Pelops), one on Orpheus and Mousaios (famous prophets both), but the most influential was the work on Herakles in a staggering 17 books. He was clearly a virtuoso in precision, if he could actually put a name to the boy (Eunomos) that Herakles accidentally cuffed to death (*FGH* 31F3). Or you might learn that Herakles taking over the pillars of the world from Atlas signified the acquisition of knowledge of the heavens by learned study (F13), or that there were in fact eight Herakleses (and two Orpheuses) – to account for what legend tells of them (F14, F42). I call this last process, so popular amongst Greek scholars and biographers ('n of the same name'), **differentiation**. Herodoros' moral allegory could be elaborate: to win the three apples of the Hesperides Herakles had to kill the dragon of desire with the club of philosophy, clothed in the lion-skin of noble spirit. And the three apples? – refraining from anger, money-grubbing and the life of pleasures (F14).

'Historians'

History is the priestess of Truth.

(Dionysios, *On Thucydides* 8)

It is against the background of these writers that we should understand other writers that we (but not the Greeks of the time) starkly distinguish with the label of 'historian'. Traditionally the label is first applied to **Herodotos**, maybe a younger contemporary of Hellanikos. His focus is on the great achievements and interest of men of the past: if he does not register them, then they are likely to be forgotten (1.1). So his primary task is actually the preservation of worthwhile tradition. Greek Mythology is by his time in no danger of being forgotten: his subject is therefore later

and for that single reason historical. His achievement is to understand that we can learn as much from more recent tradition as
from the ancient mythical traditions that everyone knew and
could read about.

His opening pages appear neatly to separate myth from history. First we see myth. Io, who in the Greek myth wandered cow-
shaped over the earth from Argos to Egypt thanks to the lust of
Zeus and its detection by Hera, is given a new, rationalised story:
now, implausibly, it is studious (*logioi* – Detienne 1986: 56)
Persians who tell how Io was an Argive princess abducted by
Phoenician merchants. There follow the abductions of Medea,
and of Helen (with recriminations between east and west) – and
the Trojan War, with which myth ends. Constant rationalisation,
with competing accounts from Persians and from Greeks, gives
the illusion of history. It is hard to tell whether Herodotos means
us to take it seriously – it is certainly a good story. Then he draws
the distinction:

> Personally, on this subject I am not going to say it happened in
> one way or the other. Rather, I will proceed with my *logos* by
> indicating the man I know for myself to have been the first to
> begin unjust action towards the Greeks.
>
> (Herodotos 1.5.3)

This is Kroisos, the last king of Lydia, who lost his kingdom to the
Persians in 547 BC. But Herodotos' distinction is not ours: for
us, Io, Medea and Helen are myth, Kroisos history. For Herodotos, Io, Medea and Helen are the distorted remnants of history,
where one cannot say that it happened this way or that: the
evidence only becomes strong enough for personal assurance
with Kroisos. Interestingly, Io is where history begins for
Hellanikos too: she is the first Priestess at Argos.

Not even **Thucydides** seems to know the difference between
myth and history:

> Before the Trojan War Hellas [Greece] clearly did nothing
> jointly: in my opinion, it did not yet have this name as a whole:
> before Hellen ['Greek'] son of Deukalion [= Noah] this name
> did not exist at all . . . but when Hellen and his sons gained
> power in Phthiotis [part of Thessaly] and people invited them
> in to the other cities for assistance, group by group they now
> gradually were called Hellenes by association.
>
> (Thucydides 1.3.2)

In this section of his history, the so-called 'archaeologia', Thucydides recovers as far as he can the style and scale of earlier expeditions, in particular the Trojan War, in comparison with his own subject, the Peloponnesian War. Yet for all its insights, brilliant arguments and ingenious hypotheses, Thucydides is writing another rationalisation of myth. Hellanikos did not hesitate to talk of Nisos founder of Nisaia and Megareus of Megara; nor does Thucydides flinch at 'Greek, son of Noah' who with his 'sons' gave the Greeks their name. Thucydides' Homer is rather a documentary writer too:

> There is no reason to be distrustful . . . one must accept that this expedition [the Trojan War] was the greatest hitherto, though small by modern standards, if one can trust the poetry of Homer on this point – where in all likelihood, being a poet, he exaggerated for effect.
>
> (Thucydides 1.10.3)

Is this really so different from Hekataios reducing Hesiod's estimate of the number of the sons of Aigyptos from 50 to 20 minus? Thucydides displays superb handling of evidence, but not even he challenges the basic historicity of myth.

3.2 PLATO ON MYTH

It is natural that Plato (428–348 BC) reacted adversely to what were accepted as facts about the gods and heroes when he came to envisage education and society in his *Republic*. He does not specially object to myth as fiction, though this is not a point in its favour as Greek uses the same term, *pseudos*, to cover both fiction and falsity: 'At first we tell myths to children. This, as a general rule I suppose, is *pseudos* ['false/fictional'], though there is truth in amongst it' (Plato, *Republic* 377a). However, there are good and bad myths and most of the present myths, says Socrates, must be rejected (377c). Homer and Hesiod are particularly culpable because they misrepresent the nature of 'gods and heroes' (377e). It is not so much that what they say is false as that they are bad fictions, and Plato cites the castration of Ouranos by Kronos (Hesiod, *Theogony* 180–1) and that area of the mythology altogether (378a). Likewise, Plato cites the long-criticised battles and conspiracies of the gods against each other; and he specifically rejects the allegorical solution because the young are in no position to make that adjustment (378d). Plato's replacement mythology would stress how gods are responsible for all that is good in the world but for none of the evil (379c), how they are consistent and unchanging even down to their physical appearance (382e). When it comes to heroes, the basic rule is that they must be represented in a way which will support, and not undermine, the cardinal virtues. So the expedition of Theseus and Peirithoös to abduct Helen is intolerable (391b–d) and so is Achilles' behaviour in dragging Hektor's corpse around Patroklos' tomb (condemned even by Homer, *Iliad* 22.395).

Plato's condemnation of existing myth is instigated by its educational context, but it is scarcely restricted to that context. Because these myths provide clearly unacceptable models of behaviour, they fail absolutely. Whilst it is true that he offers no opinion about the general validity of allegorical interpretation, he does leave the impression that the works of the poets are false/fictional anyway and that allegory is therefore pointless.

Yet he still recognises a place for myth, both within his proposed educational system and – in a new development – as a form of presentation of ideas in his own literary works. For one thing, he envisages a replacement mythology within the educational system. Then there is what is traditionally translated as the 'noble lie' – though the word at issue is again our fiction/falsity word (*pseud-*, 414c) and Plato casts it as a *mythos* (415a). In any case this perpetuates Plato's proposed caste system by viewing individuals as having various metals – gold, silver, bronze, iron – in their make-up, carrying forward Hesiod's metaphor of the progressive degradation of successive generations from the Golden Age to the Age of Iron (*Works and Days*, 109–76). Finally there is that most glorious of inventions, the extended myth used in Plato's works when ordinary language and reasoning can carry him no further. This is where he turns to stories of the soul and what happens after death in the manner of the Pythagoreans. In this use lies an extraordinary recognition of the possibilities of understanding that lie beyond ordinary language and that are accessible through a medium which is the bearer of a different truth. Ironically, the approach of some modern scholars to the traditional mythology supposes it to be nearer Plato's heart than he thought.

Plato's view of his own myths is a mystic one and was taken up by more erudite mystics throughout antiquity. For such intellectuals the problem of the old mythology remained, though few followed Plato in wishing its abolition. Instead the path of allegorical reinterpretation, begun by Theagenes, was blended with Platonic ideology and produced in the fullness of time the notion of Homer the Theologian. This is what we find in Pseudo-Herakleitos (from whom we cited a passage on p. 24) and in the middle Platonic and Neoplatonic tradition, but that leads us too far from our more grass-roots concerns.

Plato is the prism through which the light of the Presocratics is refracted into the schools of philosophy that dominated the Hellenistic and Roman ages. In mythology perhaps myths about conflicts between gods would never be quite the same again. But in the case of heroic myths the tragedians were every bit as persuasive as Plato feared.

3.3 THE FOURTH CENTURY AND BEYOND

Universal history

A generation younger than Plato, **Ephoros** (c. 405–330 BC) wrote antiquity's most celebrated universal (i.e. complete) history. He made an interesting decision: 'He dispensed with the telling of the ancient myths and adopted as the starting-point for his history an account of events after the Return of the Herakleidai' (Diodoros of Sicily, *Historical Library* 4.1.3). The 'Return of the Sons of Herakles' is of course itself a myth, defining the populations and dialect structure of historical Greece. It may reflect an actual arrival in mainland Greece of the Dorian and north-west Greeks at the beginning of the Dark Age, though this is disputed (chapter 4.4). Regardless of whether it does, this alleged movement of peoples opens the next chapter after Greek Mythology, which had finished on the Trojan War and its aftermath, and in some way Ephoros recognised this.

Diodoros, writing his own universal history during the stormy transition of Rome from Republic to Principate (c. 50–30 BC), viewed Ephoros' decision as resulting from practical difficulties. I paraphrase:

1 The time gap: the modern writer is too far removed from these events.
2 Dates cannot be established accurately and readers find this irritating.

3 In practical terms it is very difficult to organise the details of all those heroes, demigods, men.

4 Above all, there is no consensus in existing authors on 'the most ancient deeds and myths'.

These are the concerns of historians with difficult, but historical sources, recalling Herodotos' decision to start with Kroisos. Diodoros himself, interestingly, is undaunted, showing perhaps an increased dependence of later writers on a sense of tradition and antiquity and a corresponding weakening of the historical spirit which we attribute to a Herodotos or Ephoros:

> In fact, an enormous number of major deeds have been accomplished by the heroes, demigods and many other fine men. Because of the benefit society has derived from their actions, later generations have introduced worship, with sacrifices, to some as gods and to others as heroes. And the record of history has hymned them all with appropriate praise for all time.
>
> (Diodoros of Sicily, *Historical Library* 4.1.4)

For Diodoros, as for most Greeks, the heroes of the past were real and so, if somewhat distorted, were the stories about them. Perhaps there had in fact been more than one Dionysos (the method of Herodoros has taken off), but no one would doubt his reality.

Amongst Diodoros' sources was a curious writer of around 300 BC, one **Euhemeros**. This man had composed a fiction, the *Hiera Anagraphe* 'Sacred Record', in which a column recorded the achievements of notable kings of the past – Zeus, Kronos, Ouranos – who, by a distortion of memory, were thought of as gods. This was the ultimate historicism and is known today as 'Euhemerism'. The shock of Euhemerism is that it reduces even the most distanced mythology to history: Zeus becomes a man just like Achilles or Perikles. This should alert us to the gradations in reality which Greeks, or at least some Greeks, were capable of perceiving in mythology. This is outstandingly revealed in Artemidoros' second-century AD book on dream-interpretation, which dissects myths as closely as all the other things we dream of:

> But remember that you [i.e. the dream-interpreter] must only pay attention to stories that are believed to be wholly true on the basis of extensive valid evidence, e.g. the Persian Wars and,

before that, the Trojan War etc. In these cases you can see their quarters, the locations of their lines of battle, the sites of their camps, places where cities were founded and altars erected and everything else that goes along with this.

Also, you should pay attention to stories which are constantly told and believed by most people, e.g. about Prometheus and Niobe and the various heroes of tragedies – because even if these were not so, all the same because they are accepted by most people, they turn out in accordance with their outlines [i.e. once dreamed, they offer a basis for prediction].

But as for all the faded stories, full of nonsense and rubbish, like the Gigantomachy business [Ap 1.6.1] and the Sown Men in Thebes [Ap 3.4.1] and again in Kolchis [Ap 1.9.23] etc., either they will not turn out accurately or as we were saying above they nullify every rationale and defy expectation; they suggest vain and empty hopes, except insofar as any of these mythic elements allows physical allegory.

(Artemidoros, *Dream Interpretation* 4.49)

Tablets of stone

Finally, it may help our understanding of the historical view of myth to see it written in tablets of stone – and that is just what the so-called **Marmor Parium** ('Marble of Paros') provides. This remarkable inscription records one man's chronological table of history from the first king of Athens, Kekrops (chapter 5.6), to his own day, namely 264 BC. In the table below I have made a selection and paraphrased a little:[2]

Table 3.1 A selection from the Marmor Parium

1581 BC	Kekrops becomes king and names the country Kekropia – it had previously been called Aktike after Aktaios the *autochthon* [for autochthony see p. 75 below].
1528 BC	Deukalion's flood.
1531 BC	Contest between Ares and Poseidon over the future 'Areopagos' ['Hill of Ares'] at Athens.
1520 BC	Hellen ['Greek'] becomes king.
1510 BC	Arrival of Danaos from Egypt in the first ever *pentekontoroi* ['50-oared' ships].
1505 BC	Erichthonios becomes king. Panathenaia festival first held.
1462 BC	Minos [the elder] becomes king of Crete. Iron is discovered on Ida by the Idaian Dactyls.

1397 BC	First mysteries at Eleusis.
1259 BC	Theseus brings about the synoikism of the 12 cities into one Athenian state and introduces democracy.
1256 BC	Campaign of the Amazons against Athens.
1251 BC	Campaign of the Seven against Thebes.
1218 BC	Trojan War begins.
1209 BC	Troy captured, on the seventh day of the waning moon of the month Thargelion.
1208 BC	Orestes acquitted at the Areopagos.
1077 BC	Neleus founds Miletos and other places in Ionia.
937 BC	The poet Hesiod emerges.
907 BC	Homer emerges.
? 790 BC	Archias founds Syracuse.
683 BC	Archonship annual.
645 BC	Terpander revises the musical modes.
605 BC	Alyattes becomes king of the Medes.
603/596 BC	Sappho escapes to Sicily.
581/562 BC	Establishment of the comic chorus at Athens.
561 BC	Peisistratos becomes tyrant at Athens.
490 BC	Battle of Marathon.
485 BC	Aeschylus' first victory (in the tragedy contest), Euripides born.
324 BC	Death of Alexander the Great.

Although this is only a selection, I should emphasise, even in the complete text, a sudden loss of detail after Orestes in 1208 BC. Until then there had been 25 entries; it only takes a further seven entries to get from 1208 to 683 BC. There are two reasons for this phenomenon, both of which are revealing: first, real historical information just peters out in the Dark Age and the quantity of what precedes is a measure of the success with which myth masquerades as history of the prehistoric period. But second, this period of beginnings, firsts and legend has a magic aura about it, luring the Greeks into their mythology. That is what it is for.

3.4 THE CULTURAL PREVALENCE OF MYTH

Myth was deeply embedded in Greek culture. Most factual writers in all ages, even whilst questioning details, accepted the claim of myth to report a past era. It is not hard to understand this. Today, we have the consolation of a long literary tradition and of a well-developed science of archaeology to compensate for man's lost history and to free Christians from the over-dependence on the genealogies of the Old Testament that shackled centuries not so distant from our own. The Greeks had nothing but their mythology. Nor were they exceptional: it was the fate of several Indo-European mythologies to be or become viewed as history. Persian 'history' contains a whole mythic dynasty of kings, the Kayanids (Puhvel 1987: 122f.). And in Rome, traditional stories preserved by Livy and others as its history are probably largely mythological to the fall of the Kingdom ('509 BC'). The stories of the early Republic, too, must often be viewed with great suspicion, even if the Roman annalist historians can assign events to years – giving an even better illusion of historicity than by assigning them to priesthoods in Argos.

Meanwhile, Greek poets, who so often avoided the individual, the personal and the contemporary, lived from the beginning to the end of antiquity in a world of myth: Homer and Hesiod at the beginning, Nonnos' 48-book epic celebrating Dionysos at the end. And understandably: Greeks were taught myths from the cradle by their mothers and nannies – a practice which Plato had identified as one which it was necessary to subvert in the interests of the propaganda of morality – and they were educated to regard Homer and the Tragedians as closer to the Bible than to Shakespeare. Wherever they turned, expensive works of art in public and prestigious places reinforced the lesson that mythology was at the heart of their culture and its values. Wherever a Pausanias sought explanation of a landscape or its customs, mythology was at hand. And whenever it was time for serious theatre, not just in classical Athens, but throughout antiquity, the old myths were there to be recycled.

During the Empire it became a matter of social one-upmanship to know utterly obscure mythical names or to have views on what the names might be – even for Romans. And Roman poets signed up for cultural recognition by retelling and alluding to the mythology of the Greeks (for they had none left to call their own). In Petronius' *Satyricon*, Trimalchio, an appalling upstart and *nouveau riche*, reveals his inadequacy through his disgraceful failure to command the facts of mythology. This would disgrace him by the standards of culture which the court of Nero might recognise and for which Petronius was a trend-setter. Nero himself subscribed to this Greek culture by his devotion to their mythological art: had he not, muttered the disaffected aristocrats, sung his very own *Fall of Troy* as Rome burned?

Part II

Myth and the past

Chapter 4

Myth and prehistory

4.1 THE WELL OF THE PAST

> Very deep is the well of the past. Should we not call it
> bottomless?
> (Thomas Mann, *Joseph and his Brothers*, trans. H.T. Lowe-
> Porter)

Does human society evolve? Are its various features and aspects
organisms like man himself, that are born and grow till they are
what we see today? Maybe, but to think so is to surrender to a
metaphor. Perhaps the metaphor is useful for political systems or
the history of engineering, but other aspects are so deeply in-
grown in human nature that their beginnings seem untraceable
or even implausible. The origins of religion fascinated speculators
in the nineteenth century, but no evidence takes us to a time
before men became religious. Equally, few theories are more
entertaining than those which tell how language first developed,
but there is no evidence for a *Homo sapiens* who did not speak. If,
then, we cannot reach a time when man was without religion or
speech and if we cannot find societies so primitive that they have
no traditional stories, how can we believe that mythology had a
beginning which we can conceive? The well of mythology is to all
intents bottomless.

We cannot imagine, either, that Greek mythology was invented
as a whole new set of stories to replace what had gone before and I
do not think that, in so traditional a society, stories were constantly
being invented and discarded. The Greek mythology that is
known to us is a late stage in a millennia-long series of adjustments. Not evolution, not development, just change – in reaction
to social environment.

The Greek language, as we know beyond reasonable doubt, descends in large part from an earlier language, which we call Indo-European (purists like to call it 'Proto-Indo-European'). This language was perhaps spoken in the fourth millennium BC across a wide area north of the Black Sea. Indo-European has left no undisputed remains except the languages and cultures derived and descended from it. These include most of the languages of Europe (e.g. Latin, Russian, German, English, Welsh) and others further east (e.g. Sanskrit, Persian, Hittite). They exclude, for instance, Hungarian and Finnish (Finno-Ugrian group), Akkadian in Babylon, Phoenician, Hebrew and Arabic (Semitic group), and Old Egyptian (Hammitic, related to Semitic). Different nations may share similar words and similar myths because they have inherited them from their common ancestors; they may also share similar words or myths because their different ancestors came into contact during the course of history and one learnt from the other. So both words and myths may be either (a) inherited, or (b) taken over from other cultures.

I do not have room in this book to deal with the borrowing of myths, though it is of particular importance in the study of Hesiod's mythology. There, connections with Near Eastern myths look strong and lead readily to the supposition of borrowing during the Dark Age. However, it is worth reflecting that it is the early use of writing in Near Eastern cultures which allows these discussions. To our joy, their writings – unlike the dreary account-tablets of Mycenaean Linear B – include strange and captivating mythology. Though Greeks must have shared myths with other cultures (perhaps Phrygians, or Illyrians), we are only going to discover examples when they are actually written down. Hence discussion of borrowing will privilege the connections of Greek myth with the Near East.[1]

Inherited myths are less easily identified than inherited words. A word combines a meaning or application with a sequence of arbitrary and quite complicated sounds, whose development is sufficiently regular for us to state almost scientific 'laws' of sound-change. For instance, our word 'daughter' can be identified as the same word in origin as the Greek 'thygatēr' and Sanskrit 'duhitár-', which allow the reconstruction of an Indo-European *$dhug_{H_2}tēr$, delivering more or less what is expected in each language where it survives. Myths, however, are narratives consisting of sequences of often obvious motifs, which can be found the world over in traditional stories ('folk-tales', see chapter 7.3). So it is hard to say that this or that myth is sufficiently distinctive and sufficiently like another to derive from a common ancestor.

Yet it does happen on occasion. One example, which has been thoroughly tested for coincidence by Ward (1968: chapter 1), is the Indo-European myth of horsemen twins who must rescue their sister/wife. In the Sanskrit tradition, the twin Aśvins ('horsemen'), *Divó nápātā* ('sons/descendants of Dyāuḥ'), jointly woo and marry Sūryā, daughter of the Sun Sūrya. Meanwhile, in Latvian songs, two or more horsemen, *Dieva dēli* ('sons of Dievs'), woo *Saules meita* ('the sun's daughter', sometimes just Saule herself). The comparison is the more interesting for the fact that the Indo-European sky god, **Dyēus*, the principal god of the Indo-Europeans, like his Greek manifestation, Zeus, has lost his significance in both these cultures. We do not, however, have to go far to find the corresponding Greek twins: the *Dioskouroi* ('sons of Zeus'), the twin horsemen Kastor and Polydeukes (Castor and Pollux in Latin). The figure corresponding to Sūryā/Saule, the sun maid, is almost as clearly their sister Helen, whose name might just, as Puhvel has argued, be related to *hēlios* ('sun') and that in turn to 'Sūrya' and 'Saule' (Puhvel 1987: 59f., 225f., 141–3). In general, ancients turned to the Dioskouroi for rescue – especially if they were mariners in distress; but myth presents them as the rescuers of Helen, seized (in one descendant of this Indo-European myth) by Theseus.

But there is another, more familiar, descendant of this Indo-European myth. It obviously lies behind the twin Atreidai, Agamemnon and Menelaus, going to recover Menelaus' wife – Helen – from Troy. The story of the Trojan War is not quite as historical as it seems.

This is a rare example of the visibility of Indo-European myth in Greek myth.[2] Greek myth, like Greek religion, is very hard indeed to associate with other Indo-European cultures. The names of Greek gods, with the exception of Zeus and his faded feminine counterpart Dione (replaced by Hera), cannot readily be compared with those of other nations. What can be responsible for this alienation from the Indo-European inheritance? The answer must lie amongst the non-Indo-European nations whose cultures some Indo-Europeans absorbed on their way to becoming the Greeks that we know. Scholars used to talk freely of a

substratum, a 'layer underneath', implying that the Greeks themselves were a *superstratum* (a 'layer on top'). But these are antiseptic
images: they belie the merging of cultures which took place over a
period of time in ways which are not easy for us to understand.
Apart from mute archaeological remains, we have little useful
knowledge of the cultures which preceded the 'Greeks' in Greece
(and even less of what cultures these embryonic Greeks met on the
way to Greece). Indeed we do not even know for a fact when the
'Greeks' arrived in Greece or whether we should talk of anything
so definite as an 'arrival'. Changes in pottery styles suggest an
emergence around 1900 BC, but no one has refuted Palmer's view
that 1600 BC is the more likely moment.

4.2 MYTHOLOGY AND THE MYCENAEAN AGE

The Mycenaean world

What is clear, however, is that the Mycenaean Age of Greece, the
age of the great palaces, played a decisive role in the formation of
Greek Mythology. This was first clearly seen by Nilsson (1932),
long before the decipherment of the Linear B tablets (in the
1950s) proved that the Mycenaeans were Greeks. In *The
Mycenaean Origin of Greek Mythology* Nilsson argued that 'the
mythical importance of a town corresponds to its importance in
the Mycenaean age and civilisation' (1932: 130). This thesis, of
course, has a corollary too: 'the great mythical cycles also which
are attached to the Mycenaean centers go back into the
Mycenaean age' (1932: 34). The importance of this thesis cannot
be overstated: there was a cultural continuity from the Mycenaean
Age to the Historical Age, regardless of the disturbances and
silences of the archaeological record.

Nilsson's thesis can easily be illustrated, whether we turn to
Eurystheus of Mycenae sending Herakles on his labours or to
Proitos of Tiryns, whose walls the Kyklopes built. Whichever
Pylos Nestor ruled over (I do not believe it was the one in
Messenia, despite modern enjoyment of its remains – Dowden
1989: 97f.; Nilsson 1932: 83f.), it was uninhabited by historical
times. Despite a few problems, as we shall see, the basic theory
must be accepted. It may even be true in a more systematic sense
than Nilsson contemplated.

Greek Mythology, as organised by location, tribe and genealogy at the end of the Dark Age, at some level represented, mapped, registered, even justified Greece at the end of the preceding age – at the time when it had last been settled and, if you like, authentic. It also expressed the passing of this world, mythologically deconstructing it through the stories of the Theban and Trojan Wars. Was the mythology, maybe, an expression of insecurity in the face of changes in tribal distribution and dislocation of populations during the Dark Age? Did it mediate between the equally impossible alternatives of acceptance and rejection of the new order? In any case, this was the version of the mythology that went on the record thanks to the epic tradition. And epic was strong amongst those who had migrated from a disturbed world to Asia Minor whilst clinging to the traditions (and even place names – Dowden 1989: 56 and n.13) of the mainland. It was a version of mythology with which historical 'Dorians' would find it difficult to cope: Kleomenes of Sparta, when the priestess of Athene barred him from the inner shrine on the Athenian acropolis in 508 BC, was driven to the remark, 'Madam, I am not a Dorian: I am an Achaian' (Herodotos 5.72.3).[3]

Any state endorsed by myth must be ruled by a king. In the historical period kings were few and political power was more a matter, on however restricted a basis, of community and solidarity, rather than of autocratic direction. Myth, however, is a prehistory and the Greeks thought (rightly, so far as we can see) that 'there were kingdoms everywhere in Greece in ancient times, not democracies' (P 9.1.2). So from our point of view, myth shadows the Mycenaean palace-based societies and indeed is often sited in their centres. But kings also make effective heroes of stories, and because they personally direct events have more explanatory power. Aetiology is therefore likely to privilege them regardless of the political institutions prevailing at the time (see further chapter 9.1).

So it is an open question whether the prevalence of kings leads us straight into the institutions of Mycenaean Greece (Brelich 1977: 20). And it may have been a rather different kingship from that which people of classical times might envisage. The Mycenaean kings ruled from palaces which presupposed a different economic and social landscape. Nor can their rule have been as tidily absolute as myths would lead us to believe: the seeds of the later oligarchies must already have been planted by the dependence of kings on the consent of other leaders of clans and groups. Myth does not present us with a Mycenaean *wanax* – the institution of the great 'lord' running his palace economy is displaced by a projection of a classical image of autocrats.

Mycenaean history

There is of course no Mycenaean history. There is Mycenaean archaeology and there is Greek Mythology. Archaeology has its limits as an historical tool: I do not think we can use it to distinguish between various Greek tribes; and we certainly cannot discover much about named important individuals of the past. There is no narrative.

Greek Mythology purports to tell about the remote past, which must on chronological grounds be set in the Mycenaean age, but to believe it is to misunderstand its purpose (chapter 2.1, pp. 23–4), however desperate we may be for such information. Myth is treacherous because its accounts of peoples and individuals are usually designed to construct identities and make statements, as we shall see in chapter 5. Indeed, given the propensity of myth for creating eponyms, figure-heads and persons on whom to focus key events in 'history', I think it is not going too far to say that *there is not a single individual in mythology in whose actual existence we can believe*. Apart from names of purely administrative importance on Linear B tablets (and maybe, in the Hittite archives, a certain Eteokles disrupting Hittite foreign policy at Miletos – if that is what lies under the name *Tawagalawos*)[4] we know nothing about any Greek until 'Homer' and Hesiod themselves. Even Lykourgos at Sparta and Theseus at Athens are, I think, myths (pp. 112, 88 below).

On the other hand, myth embeds material which may result from the actual history and self-definition of the Mycenaean Age. Myth may teach us something worthwhile about places and peoples, though it must always be cross-questioned for its motives in doing so. Following up Nilsson's thesis, we can view myth as confirmatory evidence for the prominence of some centres. It was worth looking for Mycenae, if not for Agamemnon's death-mask or Atreus' personal treasury. Tiryns, Argos and a 'Pylos' mattered, and so did Sparta, Orchomenos, Thebes and Iolkos. The importance of Ithaka has been inflated by Homer's focus on Odysseus and someone's mysterious decision to site him there

(Nilsson 1932: 99) – his association with Penelope in fact belongs in the southern Peloponnese. Conversely, the indisputable palace at Gla (on Lake Kopais in Boiotia) seems to have sunk without trace in the mythology, and Midea in the Argolid is almost as bad. Nilsson (1932: 128f.) put this down to the relatively short period for which these sites were occupied; evidently, they did not survive long enough into the Dark Age to secure their place in the mythological tradition. More accurately, the absence of a major site in Arcadia is matched by the absence of any major centres in the mythology.

Other places can be discerned as late arrivals: Corinth only gets in by a spurious identification with a rather minor town of 'Ephyre' somewhere 'in a corner of Argos' (*Iliad* 6.152 – that is where Bellerophon came from). Argos was hyped during the Dark Age, taking over the authority that had been Mycenae's, and so was Athens, a very minor place in traditional myth. Places like Mantinea in Arcadia, or Tanagra in Boiotia (was it perhaps Homer's 'Graia', *Iliad* 2.498 – and would it matter anyway?) are nowhere. Beyond the mainland, one feels the presence of Crete, maybe in the form of Knossos or the cave on Mt Dikte, or maybe in the person of King Minos.

Out in the Aegean islands, it is curious that Homer is interested in Aeolic sites like Skyros, Lesbos, Tenedos, Lemnos and, of course, Troy, but not in Ionian Chios or Samos (Nilsson 1932: 54). Perhaps not quite a question about mainstream mythology, but interesting anyway, is how closely Homer's *Catalogue of Ships* (*Iliad* 2.484–760) reproduces the geography of Mycenaean Greece at such a distance in time (400–500 years). Certainly Hope Simpson and Lazenby have demonstrated a surprising degree of accuracy.[5] But here we become aware that Homer filters Greek tradition and that Nilsson's thesis only works because the oral traditions propagated above all by the epic poets were concerned to preserve a particular Mycenaean map. My guess is that the epic preserved the traditions of Aeolic Greece – of old Thessaly, Boiotia, Argos, Triphylia (Pylos), maybe even Lakonia – and of the Aeolic migration towards the Troad.

All these sites are places where history happened, though (apart from archaeological clues to destructions and depopulations) we do not know what that history was. Beyond sites, however, we can also discern peoples and in particular tribes who

have disappeared or faded in the face of the population movements and the social changes that brought about the historical
Greece that we know.

One case is the Danaoi. So important was this tribe that Homer
uses their name to denote 'Greeks' in general in the Trojan War,
yet by historical times the tribe has vanished. Its eponym has not,
however: the tomb of Danaos was sited where only the tombs of
founders might be, in the centre – of Argos. He had founded the
Argive acropolis, and displaced the Pelasgians.[6] Argos is where he
and his daughters, the Danaids (prototype maidens for the community of the Danaoi), 'arrived', pursued by 'Egyptians' (Ap
2.1.4). Clearly Pausanias was right to state that 'Danaoi' had been
the particular (local tribal) name of Achaioi at Argos (P 7.1.7). But
the name is also found in the feminine as Perseus' mother Danaë
and Perseus appears to be based in Mycenae (Dowden 1989: 112,
117). Another scene again is supplied by the tradition that the
Danaids founded the temple of Athene Lindia on Rhodes – on
their way from Egypt of course (ibid.: 149–51). So once we dismiss
the idea that myth is telling us directly about the movements of
historical persons, we can see that it implies the existence of the
Danaoi tribe and institutions at Argos and Mycenae, and also at
Rhodes. If we then ask what genuine historical explanation can
account for this distribution, we will surely speculate that Rhodes
is a Mycenaean colony from the Argolid – and we will discover a
tradition reported by Strabo (14.2.6) that colonists set out for
Rhodes from Argos and Tiryns.

Similarly, we can perceive something of the Minyai, another
tribe which had disappeared by historical times – except for some
living near Olympia who were dispossessed by the people of Elis
during Herodotos' own lifetime (4.148). But, for myth, the major
associations of the tribe are with sites further north. Minyas
himself is the 'founder' of Orchomenos in Boiotia, rather echoing
the role of Danaos at Argos (though Danaos arrives bearing
identity for a town already in existence). Like Danaos he is kitted
out with daughters, though these 'Minyads' form only the custom-
ary trio. In addition, the Argonauts are described as 'Minyai' and
their base, Iolkos, is either founded from Orchomenos or vice
versa. Once again, behind these patterns we can glimpse the
distribution of a real tribe. Perhaps, following the general north–
south progress of Greek migrations, they descend from the port
of Iolkos in Thessaly to Orchomenos in Boiotia and, as

population expands or as they are pressed by new waves of migration from the north, some move south to the Peloponnese. In Arcadia we find another Orchomenos, and Minyas is specified as a grandfather of Arcadian Atalante (Ap 3.9.2 – there was a Boiotian Atalante too). A final group reaches out of Arcadia into Triphylia, the land around Olympia. This is, of course, only the mainland and the existence of a port and a mythical voyage seem made for a distribution of Minyai further afield – Teos, Lemnos, maybe Thera, Kyrene. Myth is just one part of the evidence we can use to follow their movements.[7]

So myth gives us some clues to the centres and populations of the Mycenaean Age and tells us something about population movement. Does it tell us anything about the *events* of the Mycenaean Age?

4.3 MYTHIC WARS

The Trojan War did not take place

Perhaps we, too, are tempted by the romance of discovering where myth actually happened. Where did Argo actually sail? Where did Noah's ark actually reach land? Where did Atlantis sink? Where was King Arthur's castle, and where was Homer's Troy? We have got to recognise that there is a deep yearning in us to make contact with the world of myth, as we can see from the Turin Shroud, the countless fragments of the True Cross and the multiple heads of St Peter.

Clearly there was a city which we may refer to as 'Troy'. The excavations of (and demolition of much of) Troy by Schliemann at least showed it existed. We know that it was inhabited from the early third millennium BC up to the sixth century AD, maybe continuously. We know also that in the earliest historical times it was inhabited by Aeolian Greeks, a branch of the Greeks who had been expanding eastwards at least since their settlement of Lesbos maybe as early as 1400 BC.[8] The correct name of the city is in fact *Ilion* (earlier *Wilion*), its inhabitants are *Troes* ('Trojans'), named naturally after *Tros* (compare Danaos and the Danaoi) and its territory is theirs, the *Troia* or *Tro(i)as* (Troad). It looks as though these names occur in Hittite records. In the records of King Tudhaliyas I (*c.* 1440–1410 BC), we find names which could be those of a town or a district and could be realised as *Trōiša* and

Wilušiya, apparently referring to places which could well be in this region of Asia Minor. In addition, in a later record of King Muwatallis (1296–1272 BC), we find a kingdom *Wiluša* being ruled by one *Alaksandus*, and this instantly recalls the other name of Priam's son Paris – Alexander.[9] This is heady stuff for those who wish to convert myth to history, but it really does not add up to much. At most the epic tradition has preserved, in Greek dress, the real name of a ruler or rulers of pre-Greek Troy.

What is perhaps more interesting is the instability of western Asia Minor in Hittite records in the thirteenth century and the involvement of some Greeks. If the Hittite word *Ahhiyawā* refers to the land of the Achaian Greeks, then it is plain that there is a lot of trouble in the Miletos area, over which the Achaian king is thought able to exercise control. The same king and the Hittite King Hattusilis also appear (*c.* 1250) to be in dispute over *Wiluša*. Meanwhile a former subject of the Hittites, one Piyamaradus, appears to be getting support from the Achaians in Miletos and even to have attacked Lazpas (Lesbos?). What we seem to be seeing is an encroachment of the Greeks and an extension of their influence. Looking from the other side of the Aegean, we would talk about Mycenaean colonisation of western Asia Minor in the face of opposition from natives and from those who consider the natives to be in their power-block. In this unstable context, it is no surprise that Troy was massively fortified and suffered a number of destructions, though as often from earthquakes as at the hands of invaders – it can be difficult to tell.

Greek tradition, as we can see from Homer's *Iliad* and *Odyssey*, asserts that Mycenaean Greece united behind the Lord of Mycenae, Agamemnon, to wage a just war against the Trojans, which ended after 10 years in the capture of Troy. This of course plays up the righteousness of the defeat of Troy and plays down the wider context, making it seem that this was a single, exceptional expedition after which Troy is left a blazing ruin and everybody goes home again. The few glimpses we get of the wider context are, of course, presented as diversions which happened during the expedition, heroes enjoying a weekend off from the siege to go and sack a few neighbouring cities – something which Thucydides (1.11), rationalising, puts down to the need to obtain provisions. One of these *obiter victa* is Lesbos (*Iliad* 9.129–30).

The Agamemnon, Menelaus, Helen framework is an Indo-European myth (p. 59 above). Individual instances of combat in

Homer (and elsewhere) are plainly not historical evidence and sometimes belong to traditions located elsewhere than at Troy: Tlepolemos of Rhodes fighting Glaukon of Lykia points to a local tradition of conflict between these two neighbouring areas; the Pelasgians from Larisa that figure in the *Catalogue of Ships* (*Iliad* 2.840–1) on the Trojan side are surely just a transposition from the Larisa in Thessaly, even if there is a Larisa in the Troad (cf. Sakellariou 1977: 152f.). The tomb of Hektor at Thebes (Boiotia) is believed by some (including myself) to indicate that he began as a mainland hero. The tale of Troy has acted as a magnet for traditional combats and conflicts and Homer's exceptionally huge *Iliad* offers 'everything under one roof'. The Wooden Horse is clearly mythical (though I doubt if it is yet fully understood). And Achilles, in my opinion, is a conquering hero that follows Aeolian Greeks wherever they go – for instance to Lesbos, taken over as much by Aeolian Greeks as by Achilles. The Trojan War is a shell.

The very unity of the Greek world in attacking Troy is a mythic construct, perhaps correctly interpreted by Herodotos as comparable with the Greek v. Barbarian conflict perceived in the Persian Wars of 490–480 BC – more than a little mythological themselves, as can be seen both in Herodotos' epic polarisation of the world between Greek and Barbarian and in the Parthenon's sculptures of Lapiths and Centaurs (chapter 9.2). The *Catalogue of Ships* in *Iliad* 2 is central to this Trojan myth, because later Greeks were desperate to have been involved in the united force of Agamemnon: the mention in this *Catalogue* (2.546–58) of Athens and Salamis, for instance, is a heavy-handed Athenian addition. In effect the campaign defines Greekness in a positive, warlike way and justifies its encroachment on mainland Asia Minor. There is no wonder that this was a major myth for the bardic culture of the Greek colonists of Asia Minor, both the earlier Aeolic colonists and the later Ionian colonists. Its message is to justify them and that seems to me to be the reality of the myth's relationship to history.

Perhaps indeed Troy fell to a Greek force: for a fact, Greeks at some point took it over. Perhaps, even, a substantial party did set out from Aulis, traditionally (Strabo 9.2.3) the embarkation point for Aeolic colonists. But I doubt if Aulis was where an Agamemnon of distant, southerly, Mycenae collected his forces. In any case we should beware of thinking that a stable Mycenaean world suddenly broke up and splintered into countless migrations.

Obviously, migrations may occur out of desperation and displacement, but they also occur when economies are strong and when the land can no longer support this prosperous, increased population. De Polignac has shown how the colonisation at the beginning of the historical period was the outcome of the economic turn-around of the later Dark Age. The Mycenaean Age had already had its own colonisations, for instance in Lesbos, Miletos and Rhodes. The Trojan War, despite its sense of end-game, reflects that continuing process. Is Troy anything more than just a representative of all those towns and hamlets that fell to the Greek colonists? Maybe it was, or once had been, more remarkable than average and maybe its scaling-up is not quite as inaccurate as the amplification by the *Song of Roland* of a defeat of Charlemagne's rearguard at Roncesvalles.

The Theban War did not take place, twice

Back on the Greek mainland similar problems of historicity arise in the case of two mythical campaigns against Thebes. These are: (a) the story of the Seven against Thebes, the principal mainland battle epic (Ap 3.6); and (b) the successful attack on Thebes 10 years later by the 'Epigonoi' ('descendants', sons in fact of the original Seven – Ap 3.7). A historicist approach might easily draw on archaeological data: a rather reduced palace in Thebes re-placed an earlier one destroyed by fire in the mid-fourteenth century (the Seven?) and was itself destroyed around 1300 BC (the Epigonoi?). With that destruction the importance of Thebes came to an end and Thebes is as a result absent from the *Catalogue of Ships*.

Yet there remains the nagging doubt that the second campaign is a duplication of the first, contains figures no less mythical and is separated from the first by the Trojan and initiatory interval of 10 years (see p. 111). A duplication also exists in the case of the Trojan War, though we tend only to remember Homer's. Had not Herakles, cheated of the immortal horses promised by King Laomedon, led his own expedition against Troy? This Troy is as guilty as the Troy that harboured Paris, and Laomedon's sons are all killed, just like Priam's, save only one, Podarkes – left to change his name and become 'Priam' for the next bout (Ap 2.6.4). So far no clubs or lion-skins have been found in the deposits of Troy VI.

Returning to the Seven against Thebes, Burkert has shown it to be stridently mythical, whatever the *Cambridge Ancient History* may say.[10] The seven heroes are required in order to attack the seven gates of Thebes, but there is not the slightest sign that the real Thebes had or could have had seven gates. What is more, the principal characters apparently have what Germans call *redende Namen* ('speaking names'): the twin who holds Thebes is called *Eteokles* ('True-glory'); the twin who invokes foreign help to take Thebes is called *Polyneikes* ('Much-strife'). So the story is originally told from the Theban point of view, which fits a tale of how the city is *not* captured – rather an odd subject for an epic, one might think, in comparison with Troy. The force is led by the king of Argos, *Adrastos* ('Inescapable'), who rides the divine horse Arion (P 8.25), and in whose party is Tydeus, who is found later in the story eating a fallen opponent's brains. This is talking some other language than history. Burkert has even suggested that what is represented is an attack by demons and he has found some Akkadian (i.e. Babylonian) material offering tempting comparisons, for instance an eighth-century tale of an attack of seven demons of plague and death on mankind, aborted after much suffering. He has also found in an Akkadian exorcism a motif of conflicting twins involved in an attack of seven demons.

Personally, I am not convinced that this story is borrowed from the Near East at a late date, as Burkert thinks: borrowings from the Near East are dated too automatically to the late Dark Age period and the Theban legend has roots which seem too deep. The story seems to require that it is initially told in Thebes and in a Thebes which has sufficient influence for the story to gain currency. This is admittedly not a strong argument, but it points, for what it is worth, to a date before 1300 BC. It is impossible to say what its original purpose was, though it became in the context of Greek mythology a demoralising venture showing the fabric of the mythological world under stress, in some ways the beginning of the end. All we can say for certain is that it is nothing to do with history. And because it tells how nothing after all happened (Thebes remained untaken and Adrastos flew back on a magic horse), it cannot be archaeologically confirmed – until we find the crater where Zeus' thunderbolt hit Kapaneus.

Conclusion: *mythology tells us nothing of value about wars in the Mycenaean period*. Even if it is based on a kernel of truth (Troy was taken, Thebes destroyed), it adds nothing to that kernel. It is simply not what myth was for.

4.4 ACCOMMODATING THE DORIANS

The Dorian Greeks stand, largely ignored, on the fringes of Greek Mythology. The traditional view amongst scholars, echoing the Greek myth of the 'Return of the Herakleidai' (see below), is that though in historical times the Dorians were notable for their occupation of much of the Peloponnese, they had only entered the Peloponnese at the beginning of the Dark Age. Like all other Greeks, they had arrived from the north, and in fact the little area of Doris (north of Delphi, south of Thermopylai) owes its name to them – or they owe theirs to it. They had been geographically and culturally marginal to the Mycenaean world – like the later Macedonians.

More recently (see the Topic bibliography, p. 182) it has been suggested that the Dorians were in the Peloponnese all along, though subjected to Mycenaean overlords (rather like Norman barons). This view marginalises them socially rather than geographically. It is then envisaged that, for instance, in the wake of the economic collapse of the Mycenaean world they overthrew their masters and asserted their native culture. So the 'Return of the Herakleidai' becomes even more purely metaphorical and mythical – and it is a neat thought of Chadwick's that the subjugation of their hero Herakles to Eurystheus reflects that of the Dorians to their Mycenaean masters (though in fact Herakles was not a Dorian at all).[11] There are indeed difficulties with the traditional view, but personally I am convinced that in some form it is the right view, and I feel that much of the impetus to the second view results from unrealistic demands that archaeology should be able to identify a Dorian arrival by new styles of remains, the failure to find such remains and the dubious deduction that there had therefore been no arrival. In what follows I take the traditional view and leave readers who judge differently to make their own adjustments.

The mythology concerning the Dorians is complicated and remarkably propagandist. Overall, it is designed to legitimate their power in mainland Greece through association with Herakles. At the beginning of the story (Diodoros 4.37.3) we see Aigimios, a pale man without significance for Greek mythology, as king of the Dorians in Hestiaiotis (north-west Thessaly). The systematic genealogies will tell us that Aigimios is son of Doros (Diodoros 4.58.6), the eponym of the Dorians, and that Doros, son of 'Greek' (Hellen), had established the Dorians there (Herodotos 1.56). The Dorians start, then, in their proper Mycenaean place: outsiders to civilised tradition, confined where they belong, far off in northern Greece. They have no impact on Greek mythology except to come into existence as a branch of the Greeks. They have no cities (chapter 5.3).

But now in Diodoros' story there is trouble: a neighbouring tribe, the Dryopes (if Greek, evidently belonging to a pre-Dorian group such as the Aeolian), is fleeing southward from this region and the Dorians, Herodotos (1.56) reveals, are occupying their land. But Herakles is responsible and in any case, the Dryopian king Phylas had done something awful at Delphi, disqualifying him from sympathy. Now, however, King Aigimios fights the Lapiths, people of mythological standing and of only mythical existence, unlike the poor Dryopes. It is hard fighting mythical tribes, but fortunately Herakles comes to Aigimios' assistance, gaining as his reward a third of the Dorian kingdom for his son Hyllos – eponym of one of the Dorian tribes, the Hylleis. The other two eponyms are sons of Aigimios: Pamphylos of the Pamphyloi – 'All-tribes', perhaps originally designed to mop up the rest – and Dymas of the Dymaneis (Ap 2.8.3). Thus, tentatively, the Dorians acquire a 33 per cent stake in mainstream Greek mythology. It is tentative because only one eponym gains any validity and that through an outsider: Aigimios is no son of Herakles or Apollo – and Doros son of 'Greek' is a routine invention to deal with an empty tradition.

Herakles, on the other hand, was a good choice for a tribe which had in fact ousted the traditional rulers of the Argolid. Not only is he an important hero there, he is also an enemy of the established ruler of the land – Eurystheus of Mycenae – and one who has been cheated of the kingship. Furthermore, it is a question no longer of Dorians invading land that is not theirs, but of the sons of Herakles *returning*. This propagandist presentation, originally invented in Argos, ensures that what we might refer to as the 'Dorian invasion' is known to myth, and therefore to Greek history, as the 'Return of the Herakleidai'.[12]

The story that follows is, however, peculiarly contorted. The Dorian invasion, though propelled by slights on Herakles, cannot safely take place until after the 'Trojan War', because (a) that (in a sense) is when the invasion actually occurred and (b) there are no blank slots in the myth-history of the Argolid till then. So we must wait while Eurystheus dies, Atreus takes over, Atreus' son Agamemnon rules, campaigns at Troy, returns and is murdered, Agamemnon's son Orestes returns, rules (acquiring Sparta and most of Arcadia (P 2.18.5), usefully for Dorian territorial claims) and dies, and his unprestigious son Teisamenos comes into existence, in order to be expelled. To cover this gap there is nothing to match an ambiguous Delphic oracle: Hyllos is told the Herakleidai must wait for the third crop before they return (Ap 2.8.2). Mistakenly he returns in the third *year*, only to be killed in single combat at the Isthmos (Herodotos 9.26). In fact the return was to be in the third *generation*: this is when Temenos, great-grandson of Hyllos, and Kresphontes, with the aid and deaths of Pamphylos and Dymas (prodigiously old, one would have thought, by now), must complete the task. Argos, Sparta and Messenia are now Dorian and by right.

By right? Will anyone believe this sort of myth? Listen to Pausanias:

> As for Argos and the throne of Argos in my opinion they [Temenos and company] were absolutely correct in their claims, because Teisamenos was [only] a descendant of Pelops [father of Atreus], whereas the Herakleidai are ultimately descendants of Perseus [earliest known king at Mycenae, off-spring of Zeus].
>
> (Pausanias 2.18.7)

Pausanias also accepts the claims on Sparta and Messenia, exhibiting once again the inability of the Greeks to reject myth as history. The same is shown when Herodotos (9.26–7) presents the Tegeans and the Athenians arguing over who should command one wing at Plataia by appeal to the role they played in these mythical events: it was a leader of Tegea who killed Hyllos in single combat at the Isthmos; it was the Athenians who received the Herakleidai and assisted them in battle against Eurystheus. These myths filled gaps and were designed to be believed. There was nothing else to believe.

And what of us? Can we find history in these myths? Maybe, to an extent. The myths relate to a real enough Greek tribe, the Dorians, and their real movements from northern Greece,[13] doubtless including Hestiaiotis, to the Peloponnese – though we will need evidence beyond myth if we are not to follow the more recent view in rejecting the Dorian migration as mere historicism. But if it is accepted, the expulsion of the Dryopes is plausible and looms large enough to receive an explanation mitigating the guilt of displacing them. Shall we, then, construct from the story of Hyllos and his defeat in single combat at the Isthmus an initially successful repulse of the Dorians from the Peloponnese by the Mycenaean Greeks? It is not impossible and could make sense of the well-known Mycenaean wall across the Isthmus. But it is also, as I have observed, a mytho-chronological necessity to separate the Return of the Herakleidai by some generations from the immediate son of Herakles – Hyllos.

It is, however, unwise to believe in the named characters of these stories too much:

> In the previous generation the Heracleidae, a clan of Achaean stock, originally native to the Argolid but then in exile, had been the ruling power in Epirus, and members of the clan had led settlers overseas to Rhodes and the Dodecanese. The head of the clan, Hyllus, had led a large force against the Peloponnese but had been killed in single combat c. 1220 BC.
>
> (Hammond 1976: 141)

I fear that this type of writing does fail to understand how mythology works and regresses to primitive Greek standards of understanding the remote past. Even the distribution of lands between rulers in these myths may reflect no historical situation. Yet these secondary myths, which are products of the Dark Age, not of 'Mycenaean origin', are historical in a particular sense: they are all too visibly tied to historical changes and shamelessly attempt to justify them.

Chapter 5

Myth and identity

Myth establishes people, places and things. More than that, it identifies them and gives them some sort of conceptual place, by associations or by contrasts. Indeed the whole of Greek Mythology may be viewed as an enormous text in dialogue with that other text, the world in which we live. It has, after all, no other function than to address the task of existing in the real world in its various oblique and suggestive ways.

5.1 THE ORIGIN OF TOWNS

To establish an entity, myth often turns to the **eponym** – the person after whom something is named. Take, for instance, the following explanation of towns in Arcadia:

> In the opinion of the Arcadians, Thyrea in the Argolis and the 'Thyrean Gulf' got their names from this [man] Thyraios. Mantineus and Tegeates and Mainalos founded the following: Mainalos founded Mainalos, in ancient times the most famous city in Arcadia; Tegeates and Mantineus founded Tegea and Mantinea. And Kromoi was named after Kromos and Charisia had Charisios as its founder and Trikolonoi was founded by Trikolonos and Peraitheis by Peraithos and Asea by Aseates.
> (Pausanias 8.3.3–4)

This splendidly dreary list supplies eponymous heroes, so that towns may simultaneously gain names and existence. We should not, perhaps, underrate the magic in a name for a pre-critical age and the power of a poem, such as that of Asios, listing this type of information. Yet Pausanias can tire of eponyms and we can see that they are hollow shells until placed in a context. In this case, the vital detail is that this is a list of the sons of Lykaon. And his significance in turn emerges from the following passage: 'Lykaon, the son of Pelasgos, introduced all the following – things cleverer than his father did: he founded the city Lykosoura on Mt Lykaion and he named Zeus 'Lykaios' and established the Lykaian games' (Pausanias 8.2.1). Lykaon is the key figure in southern Arcadia. He is an original figure, but not too primeval: he is the son of Pelasgos (chapter 5.5), not Pelasgos himself. In this story, Pelasgos' achievements are half-measures, surpassed (as Pausanias notes) by Lykaon. Lykaon founds Lykosoura, the world's first city (P 8.38.1). The mountain which bears his name affords a view (supposedly) of the whole Peloponnese (P 8.38.7), thus beginning to look like some world-mountain at the centre of the earth. On this mountain Lykaon introduces the region's major cult and its associated games, which unite all the local cities, just as their eponyms are united in being 'sons' of Lykaon. Solidarity is thus expressed through participation in ritual and through kinship in myth. The tribal cohesion is maintained despite the division of the tribe into autonomous cities.

5.2 THE ORIGIN OF GREEK TRIBES AND PEOPLES

Mythology personalises: an eponym supplies a personal version of a more abstract entity; a founder focuses the elements of civilisation on himself. The eponym may even be the founder: Danaos at Argos, eponym of the Danaoi (chapter 4.2), founded the key temple of Apollo Lykeios, introduced writing, built the first ship – and so on. King Minyas, eponym of the Minyai (chapter 4.2), founded Orchomenos.

Accounting for tribes by eponym had clearly once had significant currency. The Dryopes, scattered around Greece by the movements and expansion of other tribes, remained locally identifiable and distinctive. The focus of their identity was naturally the eponymous hero Dryops. For Dryopes in southern Thessaly, Dryops was the son of the River Spercheios. To be the son of a river is a statement of **autochthony**, of belonging to the land from the beginning and therefore having full rights to the land (such a person is an *autochthon* and the adjective is 'autochthonous'). Other instances are the Argive first man, Phoroneus, who is the son of the River Inachos and (P 7.2.7) 'Ephesos' the son of the River Kaystros. But in Arcadia Dryops was an Arcadian who married a daughter of Lykaon (so expressing affiliation with the southern Arcadians) and it was one of his daughters in turn that bore the god Pan to Hermes. Asine in the Argolid, turned into a ghost town by the Argives, had been a settlement of Dryopes (Strabo 8.6.13) and Asine in Messenia, founded by the refugees, honoured Dryops in cult – because he reminded them who they were. And to judge by the word *drys*, they were the Men 'of Oak'.

Enough tribal names end in *-opes* (plural) to make it worth wondering about any hero in Greek myth whose name ends in *-ops* (singular). Dolops was a brother of the centaur Cheiron (who lived in a cave on Mt Pelion) and was a hero good enough to receive cult in Magnesia. No prizes for realising there were Dolopes – who lived in southern Thessaly, reaching the fringes of Epeiros in the west and reaching past Magnesia to Skyros in the east. But what of disreputable Pelops, father of Atreus, with his criminal trickery in chariot races? A trickster (chapter 7.2) would not be out of place at the beginning of a tribe, obviously the 'Pelopes' (as suggested by West 1985: 157–9), though there is no trace of them in historical times: did they live incognito as citizens of one of our well-known city-states? Quite different are our final -opians, the 'Blazing' Men in the remotest south, the purely mythical Aithiopes (Ethiopians), though increasing geographical knowledge made it difficult for them to stretch from the real Ethiopia to India as had been hoped.

The name of Lykaon may point this way too: perhaps he is the 'Wolf'-man, in reference to his myth – and to the ancient Indo-European wolf-pack (chapter 7.2). But perhaps too the *-aon* ending should be compared with area names in *-aonia* and we should think of a former tribe of *Lykaones*, a 'Wolf'-tribe (Dowden 1989: 101, 192).

5.3 TRIBES, PEOPLES, PALACES AND TOWNS

These examples come largely from tribes that have disappeared or fallen by the wayside of Greek culture. A pivotal example is that of Argos, where it can seem that the death-knell of local, tribal mythology was sounded during the Dark Age and archaic period: in historical times there were no Danaoi, only inhabitants of Argos. Whether this resulted from new additions to the local population during the Dark Age (Argos comes out speaking the new-wave, Doric dialect) or from economic and social changes, their new sense of themselves as a city extending its power over their neighbours leads to a propagandist mythology.

Figures called 'Argos' now appear. One Argos (P 2.16) enters mythology as the grandson of Phoroneus, the Argive 'first man'. This Argos is the eponym and his descendants (and therefore juniors) include:

1 Peirasos (or Peiras), a hero responsible for the key religious symbol at Tiryns, the pearwood statue of Hera;
2 Iasos, apparently a figure once of tribal importance, maybe in origin an eponym;
3 Iasos' daughter, Io, the first priestess at the Argive Heraion, a temple used by Argos as the focus of its domination of the Argolid;[1]
4 Danaos (of course);
5 the warring twins Akrisios (of Argos) and Proitos (of Tiryns), between whom the Argolid had been divided.

Perhaps, too, one should add in Perseus, son of Danaë, grandson of Akrisios, who seems to be specially linked with Mycenae (P 2.16.3; cf. Dowden 1989: 117). The effect of this genealogy is to subordinate other powers in the Argolid to Argos himself and itself. This direct control of the Argolid parallels Sparta's direct control of Lakonia and Messenia. Beyond that, both had to tread more gently and Arcadia was crucial. Sparta took to shifting bones to remind Arcadians of Orestes' rule over them (chapter 5.7 below). But Argos found that another hero 'Argos', the same it seems as the many-eyed watchman over Io, had (switching to Herakles/Theseus mode) killed a bull that ravaged Arcadia and killed some Satyros or other who 'committed crimes against the Arcadians' (Dowden 1989: 137). The story invites the acceptance by Arcadians of Argos' watchful eye.

The arrival of a *polis*-based mythology was not unprepared. The very word *polis* can be found in other Indo-European languages (Sanskrit *pūr*, Lithuanian *pilis*) showing that some sense of fortified settlement goes back to Indo-European times. There is a tendency to project our (mythological?) ideas of evolution on to prehistory and create wandering, pastoral Indo-Europeans and unsettled, migrating Greeks. Neither is wholly real. The Indo-European language had its words for 'field' and 'plough', had its social structure with king and head of household, had households which were sufficiently extended to produce words for 'village' in some descendant languages but 'house' in Greek (*oikos*) and it had the *polis* word for a settlement. Even the backward Aitolians in north-west Greece, who are revealed by Thucydides as possessing a political structure based on 'villages' (*komai*) rather than the *polis*, had cities to their name – Kalydon and Pleuron.

The issue here is the degree of centralisation and unification of the state. We think in terms of Athens and Sparta, cities holding undisputed power over their territories. Other such city-states obviously existed: Argos, Corinth, Megara, Miletos and so on. But in classical times there was also a significant number of states where power was more evenly spread and where the focus of identity was more on a population (*ethnos*) than on a single city (*polis*). Examples include Arcadia, Achaia, Aitolia, Thessaly and, in a rather more precarious sense (as Thebes struggled for the single-city model), Boiotia. These are the states that produce leagues or federations in the fullness of time.[2] Mythology should cope with both models, but there is a considerable leaning towards the single-city model. This has a historical origin in Mycenaean culture, where the palaces, readily understood and operated by incoming Greeks, clearly concentrated a territory's wealth and power, and in so doing created the economic conditions for the celebration of their traditions in poetry. Thus another reason emerges for the Mycenaean imprint on Greek Mythology.

This balance of mythological power is summed up in the Aitolian case: the Aitolians have relatively little impact on mythology, but their (Mycenaean) city of Kalydon finds its place comfortably in the index of Apollodoros. The Arcadians are not so very different. They were confined to the mountainous centre of the Peloponnese by population movements at or after the end of the Mycenaean age. Though well enough endowed with towns, Arcadia displays no sign of any depth of local history or any great, Mycenaean centre. The exception is Tegea, which figures in myth as the place where Kepheus rules (but he and his army are killed by Herakles – Ap 2.7.3) and as the site of the temple of Athene Alea where the story of Auge begins (Ap 2.7.4) – in whose vicinity there are Mycenaean remains. Otherwise Arcadia is about people not cities: their identities are shaped globally by their common ancestor Arkas, born to Kallisto, and, in the more southerly part by the ensemble of myth and cult which we have seen surrounding Lykaon and Mt Lykaion.

5.4 TRIBAL GROUPINGS

It was part of their view of themselves that Greeks of the historical period belonged to tribal groups. These followed the major dialect divisions (Dorian–Aeolic–Ionian) and found their place in mythology, though it must be said that, like Greek political practice, Greek Mythology has much more interest in parochial boundaries than these large-scale affiliations. The groupings are presented, as might be expected, through eponyms:

> The sons of Hellen ['Greek'] the war-loving king were Doros, Xouthos and Aiolos enjoyer of horsemanship.
>
> (Hesiod, *Catalogue of Women* fr. 9 M-W)

> The sons of Hellen and the nymph Othreis were Doros, Xouthos and Aiolos.
>
> (Apollodoros, *Library*, 1.7.3)

> After Hellen died the other sons of Hellen expelled Xouthos from Thessaly, alleging that he had misappropriated some of his father's belongings. He fled to Athens and was thought fit to take the daughter of Erechtheus in marriage. He had his sons Achaios and Ion by her. . . .
>
> During the reign of Ion, the Eleusinians were at war with the Athenians and the Athenians invited Ion to command them in the war, but he met his fate in Attica and there is a tomb of Ion in the deme Potamos. But the descendants of Ion ruled over the Ionians until they too and their people were driven out by the Achaians. Then it was the Achaians' turn to be driven out of Sparta and Argos by the Dorians.
>
> (Pausanias 7.1.2, 7.1.5)

The genealogies tell us that Dorians, Aeolians, Ionians and Achaians are to be regarded as part of one big Greek family, but that the Ionians and Achaians are to be regarded as closer to each other than to the rest. This analysis cannot and perhaps should not be falsified, but it does leave some questions, in particular about the Arcadians, who are excluded from this genealogy. Their Lykaon is less distanced from autochthonous, primeval Pelasgos than one might expect; and generally Greek myth and genealogy grants them special rights to autochthony. This may be worth taking seriously: our conception of the Dark Age leads too readily to a division of Greeks into those who arrived before and those who invaded after; but Greek mythology more realistically stresses the multiplicity of conflicts and arrivals. On that model, Arcadians are there first; Achaians, even before they are displaced by Dorian arrivals, are displacing Ionians. Some facts of history, however general, may underly this mythology.

There are lessons, too, in how these stories are fleshed out. On a matter of detail, misappropriation of paternal property may seem a feeble narrative motivation for a population movement, but it is conditioned by the genealogical ambience in which inheritance is important. But more important, the tomb of Ion looks like a feature of the cultic landscape which has been drawn into the story. This would have its origins in an identity which Athenians wished to display, maybe in order to enhance claims to rights over land. And the version of Hesiod (fr. 10a) had evidently received some Athenian touches: Xouthos was the father of Achaios and Ion, but their mother was Kreousa, daughter of autochthonous Erechtheus (chapter 5.6 below), thus asserting Athenian primacy over both Achaians and Ionians (Parker 1987: 206). Indeed Euripides, as Parker (ibid.: 207) notes, appears in his *Ion* to have developed the myth in an even more patriotic way: Ion becomes the son of Apollo imposed upon Xouthos, whilst Achaios *and Doros* become sons of the mere mortal Xouthos himself.

The tribal groupings are themselves subdivided; the Dorians, for instance, into Hylleis, Dymanes and Pamphyloi. These tribes do not play an important role in myth, suggesting that by the time of Greek Mythology as we know it their significance was limited – as indeed the reforms of Kleisthenes at Athens (509 BC), if not those of his grandfather Kleisthenes at Sikyon (Herodotos 5.66), would suggest. The three Dorian tribes obtain rather transparent, late eponyms, as we have seen, of which the most substantial is Hyllos son of Herakles. The Aigikoreis, Hopletes, Geleontes and Argadeis of the Ionians have no significant mythology.[3]

5.5 PRE-PEOPLES

Greek Mythology did not restrict itself to Greek populations. But it is extremely dangerous to suppose that its account of non-Greek peoples conveys genuine information about them. Non-Greek peoples, just like centaurs and giants, are there to speak about hypothetical, alternative orders of things, by contrast with which the essence of the Greek culture may be understood. This way of thinking still pervades Herodotos' account of barbarian customs – or that of his sources. And it will not die out, even today, until 'foreigner' becomes a mere objective term. Foreigners in Greek myth exist in order to define Greekness and are usually found in the slot of the earlier population, the pre-people.

Greeks used several terms to describe previous, non-Greek speaking, inhabitants of Greece, the islands and Asia Minor, above all 'Leleges' and 'Pelasgoi'. Obviously there were tribes in Greece before the speakers of what became Greek arrived, but the Greeks themselves had no accurate or carefully defined idea of who these tribes were and how they differed from each other. Thus references to Leleges and Pelasgoi are, in our terms, at best casual and at worst imaginative and as a result any attempt to discover where either 'tribe' lived is doomed to failure – and so is the attempt to demonstrate whether 'they' were speakers of an Indo-European language (though some of the pre-Greek peoples may indeed have been).

The word 'Leleges' looks like an onomatopoeic word to describe those who speak unintelligibly (like the – later? – term *barbaroi*) – a similar term, *lulahi*, is used in Luvian, a language of western Asia Minor, to denote just that.[4] Most appearances of the 'Pelasgoi' too serve mythical rather than directly historical purposes. It is true that the term sometimes appears more substantial: something lies behind the region 'Pelasgiotis' in eastern Thessaly, 'Pelasgic Argos' – a place or a plain somewhere in Thessaly (*Iliad* 2.681), and Zeus 'Pelasgikos' – so addressed by Achilles (*Iliad* 16.233). Yet the freedom with which the term is applied suggests that it denotes 'foreign tribe', like the shifting Germanic term which appears now as 'Welsh', now as 'Vlach', now as 'Volcae' according to where it freezes. I suspect it may even *be* the Greek version of that term.[5] In that case it has simply frozen at the point of entry for Greeks into a settled culture, namely the Thessaly that is so prominent in their myths, where their 'Olympos', home of the gods, is frozen too.

In the Spartan genealogy reported by Pausanias (P 3.1; cf. Calame 1987), all begins with an autochthonous king, Lelex, the eponym of the land's first inhabitants, the **Leleges**. This is a world of which we learn nothing, it is a pre-world, before known features are established. His son Myles, whose name points to the corn 'mill' that he invented (P 3.20.2), thus begins civilisation. Meanwhile, his brother Polykaon exists solely to marry Messene, in effect laying down Sparta's claim to Messenia. Myles' son, Eurotas, drains the plain, creating the river of that name, blending civilising achievement with the creation of the known landscape. Eurotas marries Sparta, their son is Amyklas – and two more towns, Sparta and Amyklai, are placed on the map. Only with Tyndareus, some generations later, do we reach mythic characters of flesh and blood. Lelex and the Leleges, whatever their historical significance, have acted as a blank sheet on which to draw Lakonia and all it means. They appear elsewhere too: the Lokrians too had had their Leleges – the people who grew from the soil, from the stones which Deukalion sowed; only later did their leadership pass to 'Lokros'.[6]

In Arcadia it is Pelasgos and **Pelasgians** that begin the story, in Pausanias' source, Asios of Samos (*c*. 600 BC, if genuine):

Godlike Pelasgos on the high-leafed mountains
The black earth yielded, so that the human race might exist.
(Asios fr. 8 Kinkel, in Pausanias 8.1.4)

He is an *autochthon* and, like the generations immediately succeeding Spartan Lelex, makes certain basic, if limited, steps towards settled civilisation. He invents huts, the wearing of sheepskins and the eating of acorns of the edible oak. All are half measures (huts not houses, skins not clothes, acorns not corn). This blank sheet land was of course called Pelasgia. The great leap forward comes with his son Lykaon, as we have seen.[7] This sort of mythology appears also in the puzzling passage of Herodotos (2.52) in which he reports that, according to the authorities at Dodona, the Pelasgians had not yet heard of naming gods. They certainly worshipped (so, limited first steps), but the divine apparatus (which identifies Greeks as Greeks) had not yet been installed. Yet Pelasgos is also perceived as making some use of the land which is so specially his. At Argos he is even credited with the invention of bread,[8] which of courses civilises the product (raw corn) of settled agriculture. Meanwhile, in Thessaly he is responsible for a festival in which the normal barriers of society between free and slave, between native and foreigner, are suspended:[9] masters serve their slaves. This is, of course, a suspension of the defined society by Pelasgos, the personification of the pre-society. At Athens, the equivalent festival is the Kronia, equally attached to a displaced figure of prehistory, Kronos, whose reign came to an end with the arrival of the definitive world-order of Zeus. These festivals implicitly dismantle the social order which has been superimposed upon the land and its produce. Pelasgos, himself yielded like a plant (Sakellariou 1977: 110) by the earth, is associated with acorns or even bread, but that is only a beginning, a foundation, for society.

As Diller (1937: 37) observes, 'The Aeolians, the Athenians, the Arcadians, the Ionians in the Peloponnesus, all the pre-Doric Peloponnesians, were originally called Pelasgians.' Diller draws this information from Herodotos and traces it to his inventive predecessor, Hekataios. But I think that Hekataios was building on a fairly widespread use of the label 'Pelasgian' to fit the mythological moment before Greek identity is fully assembled. The Pelasgoi, when real, seem to belong around Thessaly or not too far from it. But already Asios (if our fragment above is genuine) has Pelasgos in Arcadia.

Karians are intermittently associated with Leleges by ancient writers. Philippos of Theangela, writing a work *On Karians and Leleges* (*FGH* 741, third century BC), claimed that the Leleges were the serfs of the Karians (which sounds too specific to be true), whilst Herodotos (1.171) had simply stated that Leleges was an old name for them (which of course fits the mythic slot of pre-identity and is therefore of doubtful historical value). However this may be, we know the Karians as a real non-Greek people, known for instance to the Persians by this name. They lived in historical times in south-western Asia Minor (including Halikarnassos), but they could once have been more broadly spread across both Greece and Asia Minor. If the Greeks had encountered them in mainland Greece, it would explain how the mythical founder of raw, pre-Greek, pre-political Megara could be named Kar (son of Phoroneus, the first man) and how Athenians could expel 'Keres' (= 'Karians'?) at the end of the Anthesteria. The story at Megara reinforces the time-depth by including not only Kar, but – in the twelfth generation after him – Lelex, whose arrival from 'Egypt' turns the (Karian) Megarians into Leleges (P 1.39.6). The founder of the real Megara, by contrast, is Alkathoös, son of Pelops.[10]

Something similar to this Greek way of thought is found in our own discernment of earlier stages of our civilisation in 'primitive' cultures (the term 'primitive' itself indicating that they are at the first stages and we have moved on). Foreigners had strange un-Greek, pre-Greek customs – like promiscuity and, as we shall see in the case of the Lykians (p. 152 below), matrilinearity. These foreigners also made up the substratum (chapter 4.1) beyond which Greek culture had developed. Thus to these foreign and prehistoric populations are ascribed the negatives of Greek culture. Our version consists of remote tribes, preferably living in a jungle, clad in skins, consulting witch-doctors, recreating the life of Stone Age man, who lived in caves, hunted and, strangely, wasn't contemporary with dinosaurs. For 'Pelasgian', read 'in the Stone Age'.

The **Thracians** are less different than one might hope. Writers allege (we cannot tell whether it is true or false) that there had been Thracians in Greece in prehistoric times. Ephoros said they had been in Boiotia (though this same account has Leleges, Pelasgians and Phoenicians wandering around there for good measure) and told a strange story about a treacherous Thracian attack at night, a prophetess who is a Pelasgian sympathiser recommending sacrilege (and being burnt alive) and a finely-balanced conflict between judges of different sexes on the acquittal of those (Greek) Boiotians who burnt her alive (Strabo 9.2.4). This is not an historical record or an allegory of tribal movements. There has got to be a ritual behind this story: here is a nocturnal event with typical inversion of normal rules of behaviour, prominence of pre-people (reversion to Stone Age), crisis over the division of duties between the sexes and resolution through trial. The women of the story are classed with the pre-people (as in the Roman myth of the 'Rape of the Sabine Women' or in the Women of Lemnos), not with the Greeks: only men, it seems, can define Greek identity and avoid chaos. Something, if not much, of a ritual survives: the Boiotians must annually by night steal a tripod dedicated in a shrine (where?) – just as in another, nearby, myth Herakles steals the Delphic tripod (Ap 2.6.2). The Boiotians send their tripod to Dodona, and, uniquely, it is men, not women, who deliver oracles to Boiotians at Dodona. So what of the Thracians? They are mythical shadows of the Pelasgians, enmeshed in a partner-myth for a ritual. It just shows how careful we must be before supposing that Greek mythical reports of for example, Thracians in Boiotia should be taken as genuine.

In Athens there is a puzzling case of Thracians (Diller 1937: 51f.). The distinguished prophet Eumolpos, ancestor to the hierophants at Eleusis, is presented as a Thracian – and even invades Attica with an army of Thracians to challenge Erechtheus (e.g., Ap 3.15.4). Here lies a key. Eleusis is to be absorbed into the Athenian state, but the myth first disqualifies its independence by associating its resistance to absorption with 'Thracians', so confining Eleusinian autonomy to a preliminary and incomplete stage of development. We will discover a further reason for Eumolpos' Thracian nationality below, but in our present context, the disqualified state might as well have been Karian, Lelegian or Pelasgian. Other Athenian stories also include Thrace: Boreas who snatches Oreithyia from the banks of the Athenian River Ilissos, as befits a north wind, lives in Thrace. And Tereus in the tale of Prokne and Philomela (Ap 3.14.8) is king of Thrace, though maybe only by association of his name with Teres, name of several real kings of Thrace. The scene for this story is apparently set in Phokis in any case.

Mythology's most famous Thracian is of course Orpheus. Graf (1987b: 99–101) has asked why he was depicted as a Thracian. Music and poetry hold an answer: they come from outside into the daily life of the Greek polis; and these mythical religious poets have a quality of otherness. Other singers are Thracians too: Thamyris, Musaios, even maybe Eumolpos whose name at least means 'Good-singer'. But Orpheus also exists in Thrace in order to be killed there by manic Thracian women (whose behaviour has displaced their nationality) and so that his head may arrive, floating, from Elsewhere to found his oracle in Lesbos.

So the account of pre-Greek tribes in Greek mythology is not objective or historical. Its purpose is to define those tribes relative to a sense of Greek identity. They therefore play the only role they can: to have existed, once; to have preceded the things that make Greece Greek; to have had a worrying right to the land through having always been there (from the point of view of those who newly arrive) – a right which needs to be transferred somehow to the Greeks; perhaps to have made some initial progress as a result of being settled on the land; but otherwise, to have made little valued or lasting distinctive contribution to culture – that needs Greeks (whose presence must be justifiable and who must be content with their part in things).

5.6 ATHENS

Now a case history: Athens, as always an exception. There is no hero 'Athen' – they have the goddess Athene for that, and for once they may be right: Athens could be named after the cult of Athene. Pausanias does not roll out an extended genealogy at the beginning of this, his first, book, perhaps because he has not yet defined his method, or maybe because his old genealogical authors had not assembled the traditions of Athens.[11] But Athens did have a mythological setting.

Athens' story starts with a double dose of autochthony, because the traditions of different clans have been merged. First there is **Kekrops** (eponym of the clan Kekropidai), born from the soil like Arcadian Pelasgos, but half-man half-snake. The snake again points to autochthony (cf. p. 122), but it is also a recurring theme at Athens, appearing in a chest with the baby Erichthonios and in cult as the sacred snake in the Erechtheion. Later tradition, based on the work of fourth-century antiquarians, maintains, as in the case of Pelasgos, a sense of half-formed achievements (Parker 1987: 197). He worships Zeus the Highest with cakes, rejecting blood-sacrifice; he co-ordinates Attic identity, in the fight against land-based Boiotians and ship-based 'Karians' (Strabo 9.1.20), but only as far as the 'dodecapolis', a sort of federation of 12 towns (notably including the actually disputed Eleusis), but not as far as synoikism; and in any case he is only half a man! But in his reign, all the same, comes the invention of marriage (ending primal promiscuity)[12] and, above all, the identity-creating dispute between Poseidon and Athene, with primal flood (Poseidon's revenge). Athene's success names the city and establishes its principal cult (just as Inachos, the River-Father of first man Phoroneus, created the cult of Hera Argolis and Lykaon created the cult of Zeus Lykaios). Kekrops, like any good founder, has his tomb in the heart of the city, in the Erechtheion.

Erechtheus (eponym of the clan Erechtheidai) is a shortened form of 'Erichthonios' and both mean 'Very earth(born)'. There is a fluidity between the two, one the grandfather (usually 'Erichthonios'), the other the grandson (always 'Erechtheus'). As the name suggests, the first (under whatever name) is born from the earth, as lines found in our text of the *Iliad* recognise (2.547–9), and he is nursed by Athene herself. In essence, Athene is his mother – and the story, at least in historical times, was that the seed from which he sprang was that of Hephaistos, fended off by the virgin goddess. The Athenians thus, as Parker has observed (1987: 195), have it both ways: their race is autochthonous, but they also are the children of gods. But details of the deeds of either this Erichthonios (did he found the Panathenaia, putting Athens' major festival on the map, as they said in the fourth century?) or the other Erechtheus (did he sacrifice his own daughter to win his battle against the Eleusinians?) are sparse, as with any of these remote figures in genealogy (take, for instance, the Spartan Eurotas). They are flat, one-dimensional, for whom it is enough to exist at a certain point in genealogy, caught in a snapshot. Local genealogy is the illusion of a continuing story, but in fact it is the description of a static situation, how it is now. Incidentally, this snapshot of the stage before true identity is not unique to Athens: Erechtheus is also the name of the father of Thespios (of Thespiai in Boiotia – P 9.26.6) and Erichthonios of the father of Tros (eponym of the Trojans – Ap 3.12.2).

Somewhere in this early mythology, sandwiched maybe between Erichthonios and Erechtheus stands **Pandion**, who having married the daughter of the king of Megara was expelled from Athens and fled there: he died in Megara and his tomb is there too; but his children returned from Megara to Athens (P 1.5.3–4). One of Pandion's sons, Nisos, becomes king of Megara and gives his name to its port Nisaia. Athens always resented Megara's independence and had bitter disputes with it, in early times over Salamis, and maybe Eleusis; in later times one has only to think of the Megarian Decree that began the second Peloponnesian War. I do not claim to know precisely what this myth of Pandion sets out to do, but it does both register the hostility of Megara and Athens and in some way attempt to resolve or deny it. Pandion's other son, **Aigeus**, becomes king of Athens but is overshadowed by his son Theseus. In origin he must, like Aigeus son of Oiolykos ('Lone Wolf') at Sparta (Herodotos 4.149), be the eponym of the Aigeidai – a tribe or clan found at Thebes, Sparta, Thera and going back perhaps to Mycenaean, non-Dorian times.[13] The Aigeidai have faded away at Athens, leaving behind only their eponym, positioned in the genealogy at a suitable time-depth.

Kekrops and Erechtheus/Erichthonios belong to pre-mythology, like Lelex and Pelasgos. 'To pass from Cecrops or even Erichthonios to Theseus is to breathe another air' (Harrison 1912: 316). **Theseus** organised the unification of the Attic state, the synoikism. Synoikism, the centralisation of power in a single city, sometimes even a new one, is something which happens during the course of recorded Greek history and which was supposed to have happened earlier in some other states. It is not

clear to me that it is anything more than mythical in the case of
Athens, but in any case its attribution to Theseus is a way of
entrenching the unity of Attica in the Athenian identity. As time
progresses he becomes to an unusual extent a model of Athenian
character: he saves Oedipus and his daughters from Kreon's
Theban army; he defeats the same army to recover the bodies of
the Seven against Thebes; he limits the authority of kingship
(Aristotle, *Constitution of the Athenians* fr. 4, 41.2) and asserts the
values of the free city against presumptuous foreign heralds
(Euripides, *Suppliants* 404f.). In Pausanias' day there are even
paintings of Theseus, Democracy and Demos – facing Zeus of
Freedom . . . and the Emperor Hadrian (P 1.3.3). Theseus and
Peirithoös the Lapith are a paragon of friendship, and meanwhile
he defeats the Amazons, keeping dangerous women in their place
(chapter 8.3). Simultaneously he is the Athenian Herakles, with a
set of labours ridding the world of trouble – notably around the
Isthmus. Presumably its inhabitants, such as Megarians, were
meant to be as grateful to Theseus as the Arcadians were to Argos,
the Argive bull- and satyr-slayer (p. 77 above). And when, in the
wake of the Persian Wars, Athens' vision of her influence grew
larger, it was good to retrieve the bones of Theseus from Skyros (*c.*
475 BC).

Transparent eponyms existed at Athens as elsewhere.
Mounichos founded Mounichia with its temple of Artemis
Mounichia. Not much here. Phaleros founded Phaleron. He was
an Argonaut, the Athenians allege, and Phaleron was their port
before the Peiraieus (P 1.3.4). Aktaios was the first (eponymous?)
king in Attica (P 1.2.6) and Kekrops married his daughter. Which
Kekrops? The earth-born snake? Someone has been improvising
here. But look, here is Aktaios' granddaughter Atthis – and she, it
turns out, is the eponym of Attica (P 1.2.6)! It is obviously difficult
to say how far any of these inventions go back, but we can see that
they had their uses in the culture of a Greece interested in its
heritage, the Greece of the Atthidographers (writers of local
history of Attica) and of widespread literacy.

More striking than these are the 'Eponyms' ('for that is what
they call them' – P 1.5.2), chosen for the 10 new tribes that
replaced the original four in 508 BC. Supposedly 100 names were
put to the Delphic oracle and 10 chosen. This reform of local
government was clearly concerned to present a traditional face to
the world and the 'eponymous heroes', as they are generally called

in modern books, served that function. Thus the tribe Erechtheis was named after Erechtheus (II) and others were named after Aigeus, Oineus (bastard son of Pandion), Akamas (son of Theseus), Kekrops, Pandion (Pausanias does not know which Pandion or Kekrops!).

This eponymous way of thinking did not die out. In a new interpretation, favoured kings could be given the standing of the heroes of legend: Attalos of Pergamon and one of the Ptolemies of Egypt were chosen to be eponyms of new tribes – and so, in Pausanias' own time, was the Emperor Hadrian (P 1.5.5).

Heroes were also chosen as founders for the new demes of 508 BC. These were to be the necessary focus of each one's identity, though the extent to which they caught on was rather variable and many were perhaps as shadowy to the demesmen as they are to us. The Athenian authorities, however, found eponyms a most useful device. They even had a cycle of 42 years, each with its own eponymous hero, under whose name you were registered as at the age of 18 you became an *ephebe*. After 42 years of eligibility for military service the eponym of your year passed to the incoming 18 year olds (Aristotle, *Constitution of the Athenians* 53.4, 53.7). It is probably thanks to this sort of Athenian enthusiasm that we have the word 'eponym' at all. Overused, however, they are spread thin and mythless – and cease to be of interest to us.

5.7 ARGUING WITH MYTHOLOGY

No matter how fictional or artificial local myth seems to us, it is always capable of being treated as strict history by interested parties. Myth, like propaganda, is worthwhile because people will believe it. Enemies must be prepared to counter it within the rules of the game it establishes. Mythic argument is accorded the same respect as historical argument would be in our day – that is, it is persuasive within the limits allowed by the more pragmatic concerns of self-interest and practical politics.

On the road from Eleusis to Megara are graves of those who fell in the mythic war of the Seven against Thebes (P 1.39.2–3). The Seven (cf. chapter 4.3) were Thebes' enemies and they had come from Argos. Kreon of Thebes sought to deny them burial. Adrastos of Argos had approached (good) King Theseus of Athens, who fought the Thebans and recovered the bodies, burying them in the territory of Eleusis (also, Herodotos 9.27.3).

Bodies produce a visible monument, the grave. The message is of unreasonable, maybe impious, behaviour by Thebans and of principled Athenian intervention. Athens' hostility with Thebes underlies the tale, as does a claim to the friendship of an Argos perceived (to the exclusion of Sparta?) as the prime power of the Peloponnese. These long-standing views can be seen, for instance, in the history of the Peloponnesian Wars. It is interesting that this demonstration of Athenian beneficence is sited in the land of Eleusis, over which Athens had not always exercised undisputed control, and like other, more personal, feats of the hero Theseus seems designed to justify expanded borders. Meanwhile, how seriously is this taken by those whose interests are at variance with Athens'? Will the Thebans denounce the fiction? 'The Thebans say they voluntarily granted the recovery of the bodies and deny that they joined battle', notes Pausanias. I do not know which Thebans Pausanias refers to, but their attitude amply reveals the literal-mindedness of Greeks towards myth.

The Argolid is a principal site of Greek Mythology and Argos itself was clearly pressured by an inherited mythic view of its importance. The Argos of historical times, after all, had no access to real knowledge of the Mycenaean period, only to what mythology told. Yet that was enough. Invited to join the Greeks against Persia, Argos demanded, according to Herodotos (7.149), a 30-year truce with Sparta (a pragmatic concern) and joint leadership of the campaign, claiming that technically Argos was entitled to sole leadership. This claim, related to Herodotos by Argives, can only be based on the mythology that fossilises the non-Dorian world. No less interesting is a different version ('told throughout Greece' – Herodotos 7.150) in which the Persians claimed kinship with the Argives because of their descent from Perses, son of the famous Perseus and Andromeda. At first sight, real Persians seem as unlikely to have propounded this view as to have told how Io was seized by Phoenician sailors from Argos (Herodotos 1.1). But Greeks who can regard their myth as history and therefore not culture-specific do not see why Persians should not so argue. Furthermore, if Persians understood their Greeks, then might they have felt free to argue according to Greek rules? Their own view of myth was probably little different.

If Argos was strong in myth, Dorian Sparta might seem weak.[14] We have seen King Kleomenes of Sparta claiming he was an Achaean not a Dorian (p. 61 above). In the Spartan king list, some remedial action is taken. After a run of eponyms (Eurotas, Lakedaimon, Amyklas) and one Oibalos, Tyndareus (accredited grandson, on his mother's side, of Perseus) only gains his throne through the intervention of Herakles (P 3.1ff.). The throne passes to Menelaos and then to Orestes. Orestes' son Teisamenos is then (as we have seen) displaced by the 'Return of the Herakleidai', who are themselves descended from Perseus. By a mixture of good work and blue blood, the Herakleidai – or Dorians as we call them in the real world – are established. The weak point is clearly the succession after Orestes and this casts interesting light on events, apparently, of the 550s BC.

At this time the Spartans were attempting to extend their power over Arcadia and were having difficulty overwhelming the first major city in their path, Tegea. An oracle told them that what they needed was the bones of Orestes and a further oracle, so the story goes, told them where to find the bones: Tegea (Herodotos 1.67). The bones are then by trickery removed from Tegea and Sparta's military difficulties are overcome. It is a good story, but it may also be based on real policies. Scholars have connected it with the revised, less confrontational policy (attributed to the ephor Chilon, 556/5 BC) on which Sparta now based the expansion of her influence over the Peloponnese. The Peloponnesian League led by Sparta replaces military conquest. The bones of Orestes then make a necessary ideological statement about entitlement to leadership, marked by his new grave in Sparta (P 3.11.10), and their removal from Tegea reflects a transfer of authority. To this period, too, must surely belong the amplification of mythology, according to which

> Orestes the son of Agamemnon held Argos, and, living nearby, though his father had not ruled them, he added most of the Arcadians and acquired the throne of Sparta, constantly having at hand an allied contingent from the Phokians ready to assist.

> (Pausanias 2.18.5)

This allied contingent from Phokis, a Doric homeland, is plainly the Dorians transfigured. Perhaps, too, we should remember Orestes' stay in Phokis and his Phokian friend Pylades. This is the man who stands at his side as he kills his mother in the three tragedians and who, in an Athenian painting, slaughters sons of

Nauplios (eponym of Nauplion) as they attempt to aid Aigisthos (described at P 1.22.6).[15]

Orestes is more than just a figure of tangential importance in Greek mythology and is often commemorated in the landscape. He was tried for the murder of his mother at the Athenian Areopagos (Aeschylus *Eumenides*, P 1.28.5); at Troizen is the Tent of Orestes where he underwent cleansing (P 2.31.8) and the Holy Stone on which nine men of Troizen purified Orestes of matricide (P 2.31.4); half a kilometre out of Gytheion was the unwrought stone of Zeus *Kappotas* ('downfaller', presumably a meteor) on which Orestes sat and was released from his madness (P 3.22.1); at Keryneia in Achaia is a temple of the Eumenides founded by Orestes (P 7.25.7); the influence of his name changed one-time Oresthasion in Arcadia to Oresteion (P 8.3.2); 1.5 km out of Megalopolis, heading towards Messene, is a place called after its goddesses, the Maniai ('Madnesses') – here Orestes was seized with madness as a result of his matricide, bit off a finger (view now the Tomb of the Finger), and adjoining is a place Ake ('Cure') where, yes, he was cured (P 8.34); and the Tegeans show the Tomb of Orestes (whence the Spartans stole the body – P 8.54.4). His influence even seems somewhat disproportionate and may go back to an earlier age when this 'Mountain-man' (*Ores-* means 'mountain') had not yet been associated with the house of Atreus and displayed wildness in his locale and behaviour.

Part III

Myth and religion

Chapter 6

Arrival at the cult-site

Cult-sites need to be accounted for even more than landscape, towns and peoples. Here the sacred intrudes into an otherwise profane world and disrupts the uniformity of the land and its people. The explanation is a *logos* ('account') and in particular a **hieros logos** ('sacred account'). They tell us the circumstances which led to the cult-site's foundation, they give its 'reason', its **aition**, and are therefore said to be **aetiological**. The *hieroi logoi* I look at in this chapter talk about the 'arrival' of various gods in order to achieve this explanation, but as they are not historical accounts we may find that in telling us how the site was supposedly founded they tell us something of what the site is actually about.

6.1 ARRIVAL AT DELPHI: APOLLO AND PYTHON

Our first site is Delphi – in poetry also known as 'Pytho'. Strange though an alias is, even Pausanias tires of invoking genealogy to explain it: 'Those that like to genealogise everything consider that Pythes was the son of Delphos and that it was as a result of his reign that the city got the name [Pytho]' (Pausanias 10.6.5). In fact this name (as well as the name of Apollo's priestess at the oracle, the 'Pythia') must go with the root *pyth-* ('ask questions'). But as we shall find with the winding River Snake (chapter 8.1), the prosaic explanation is not enough. Various stories are told, but much the most influential in later times is the tale of the monstrous snake known since Ephoros (fourth century BC) as Python. Originally Gaia ('Earth') or Themis ('Correctness', in a religious sense) had owned the oracle and it was guarded by the huge snake which Apollo kills to win ownership of the oracle. One way or another the snake gives the name: in earlier writers its body 'rotted' (*pythesthai*) hence the place 'Pytho' ('Homer', *Hymn to Apollo*, P 10.6.5). Later, the name 'Python' becomes established, blending Pytho, place of 'rotting', with Zeus' opponent Typhon (chapter 8.3).

There are several ways to approach this myth, but one must be ruled out immediately: this is not an historical account of changes of ownership of the oracle. The purpose of the myth is not to deliver factual information to the effect that before the cult of Apollo at Delphi there was a cult of Gaia or Themis. Rather, we should read it in the light of the genealogies we have explored. Earth and snake stress autochthony and land-rights, the intimate association of the oracle with the place and its authority from being there since the beginning; Themis stresses its absolute standards in a different way. However, like the autochthons Pelasgos, Lelex and even Kekrops, the initial autochthonous regime is there to be overwritten by something mapping the detailed sense of the phenomenon dissected by myth. Apollo is the defining stage and arrives with the supreme strength of male youth (which will also be seen in Delphi's Pythian Games), turning back the monstrous, female, undefined.

The myth can also be viewed in the light of 'divine succession myths', the sort that tells how one god replaced another in control of the world and which is found not only in Hesiod's *Theogony* but also in several Near Eastern mythologies. Here, too, we note the same rhythm in defining the current world. A prior, unsatisfactory stage must be enunciated before our real world can be defined: the life under Kronos, a golden age of freedom from toil and of spontaneous generation, must be overwritten by the age of Zeus in which we actually live.

The connection of the Python myth with different myths, the monster-slaying myths of Greece (Zeus and Typhon) and the Near East, has been explored in great detail by Fontenrose. For him this type of myth ultimately represents the success of a creative god over the dark forces of chaos and destruction (1959: e.g. 473). Again we are dealing with the establishment of the world in which we live.

So, different approaches but same destination: establishment of the order of the world in which we live.

6.2 ARRIVAL BY BIRTH: ZEUS

Gaia had always been there, but Apollo arrived. No Olympian god is autochthonous (itself a fact inviting explanation).[1] Consequently, a myth designed to explain a cult readily calls it into existence by the arrival of the god.

The most extreme form of arrival is birth. Zeus can be born on Mt Lykaion in Arcadia, as we shall see – though Rhea's girdle was loosened at a certain Mt Thaumasion, also in Arcadia, where her cave was (chapter 8.1). According doubtless to Cretans, Zeus was born in a cave on Mt Dikte (Ap 1.1.5), and he was reared on Mt Dikte – or in another tradition Mt Ida (depicted in Apollodoros as Rhea giving him to the nymphs Ida and Adrasteia to rear).

What becomes clear from this is that Zeus was worshipped on mountains, preferably with caves, and that cult on various mountains was explained by a tale of Zeus' birth there. Some centres are however less influential than others, and so will only bid for a girdle-loosening or a rearing, thereby allocating themselves a subordinate but recognised place in a religious system. Those who later put together whole histories will be grateful for a tale of Zeus' birth to begin his biography. But they will need to make decisions as to the best claim on his birthplace. Here in Greek Mythology Dikte won. But the grave of Zeus in Crete is a different matter, being wholly inconsistent with the known historical fact that Zeus is immortal: his death is either a monstrous Cretan lie, or, by Herodoran differentiation (p. 45 above), the grave belongs to another Zeus, a king (Diodoros 3.61.2).

6.3 ARRIVAL *EN ROUTE*: APOLLO AND ARTEMIS AT SIKYON

Arrival demands travel, which can serve in myths as a linkage between different centres. Apollo and Artemis arrived at Sikyon after the slaughter of Python (P 2.7.7). The priority of the cult at Delphi is thereby recognised. They were seeking purification for the slaughter. Feeling afraid, at the place called Fear (aetiology), they diverted to Crete where they were purified by one 'Karmanor' – originally, Müller (1825: 159) suggested, *Katharmanor* ('purification man'). This story allows that Cretan Karmanor's purification is more 'correct' or authoritative than the Sikyonian.

But the function of the Cretan story is duplicated by a story of the flight of Apollo to the vale of Tempe (at the bounds of

Thessaly) to seek purification. This story of flight and purification is mobile because people migrate, as Müller understood long ago (1825: 159f). Delphians could retain the Thessalian story and maybe ritual that they brought with them. Migrants to Crete set up a new shrine and a new story in the remote west at Tarrha. But Apollo cult, especially as viewed from Delphi, navel (*omphalos*) of the world, is a system: thus Karmanor is organised into providing a son, Chrysothemis, to be the first victor in the hymn-to-Apollo contest of the Pythian Games (P 10.7.2). We may also deduce from this that the establishment of the Pythian Games is in its way connected with the acceptability of the slaughter of Python – a slaughter celebrated in these very hymns.

Meanwhile, the arrival of Apollo and Artemis at Sikyon has been inserted into an approved myth of the purification of Apollo. This gives the arrival a certain momentum: the Sikyonians failed to give the requisite purification, and somehow their country inspired fear in the gods. For this they pay: seven boys and seven girls must annually persuade the gods to look kindly upon them, bringing the gods from the margins of the River Sythas to the heart of the citadel – the Temple of Peitho ('Persuasion'). This is actually an instance of *aphosiosis* – the discharging of religious obligations, incurred in this case by exiting the condition of youth (in order to enter adulthood). The arrival myth motivates the impurity (almost contagiously) and the wrath, which must be expiated and propitiated and it also sets up a tension for return to the centre through the gods that are fleeing the centre. The purity of the gods is renewed and the adult community is refreshed by new entrants.

6.4 ARRIVAL WHILST WANDERING: DEMETER

Demeter, too, must arrive and the occasion for her arrival is straightforward: she was searching for her daughter, her *Kore* ('Daughter/Maid' – where named she is Persephone or Phersephatta; in Latin, Proserpina). For Kore has been abducted by the king of the underworld, Hades (or Plouton), and Demeter has been searching everywhere where there later turns out to be a cult-site. She learnt from the people of Hermione (in the Argolid) that Plouton had taken Persephone (Ap 1.5.1); at Argos she was received by Pelasgos (shows how long ago it was) and Chrysanthis told her about it (P 1.14.2); in a suburb of Athens on the road to

Eleusis, Phytalos ('Plant'-man) received Demeter and the goddess gave him the (first?) plant of the fig-tree (P 1.37.2). More colourfully, at Onkion in Arcadia (founded, of course, by Onkios son of Apollo), the temple of Demeter *Erinys* ('Avenging-fury') commemorates how, when searching for her daughter, she turned into a horse to avoid the attentions of Poseidon, but he just did likewise and the result made her very angry (P 8.25). Hence also the cult of Poseidon *Hippios* ('Horse'-Poseidon) in those parts.

How then did the Eleusinian mysteries come into existence? We have an early source for Demeter's arrival at Eleusis. This is the *Hymn to Demeter*, an early work (perhaps 600–575 BC – Richardson 1974: 5–11), supposedly by 'Homer'. Demeter was looking for her daughter (what else?), and took temporary employment as a wet nurse in the royal palace. Here she attempted to make her charge, the royal prince Demophon, immortal, but was interrupted by the prying curiosity of his mother. In response to this failure Demeter prescribes the setting up of a temple and demonstrates the rites to the local heroes, secret rites which may not be divulged. The prying reflects the secrecy of the ritual; and the more limited policy benefits after death, which the rites offer, correspond to, and console for, the failure to achieve complete immortality. They also shadow the incomplete return of Kore/Persephone for whom initiates will search annually.

6.5 THE ARRIVING GOD: DIONYSOS

No arrival has been more misleading than that of Dionysos. The myths about him can be particularly insistent on his arrival from elsewhere and this led scholars into a mythology of their own. Nietzsche (1872) had analysed the particular quality of Greek culture as resulting from a combination of two opposing spirits, the restrained inspiration of Apollo and the wild enthusiasm of Dionysos. Rohde (1890) then transposed this, in a historicising way, into a thesis of the invasion of the Hellenic consciousness by a genuinely foreign and even barbaric cult of Dionysos, thus preserving the Greeks for a purity such as scholars of the day might applaud. The myths might now be read as recording the essentially non-Greek nature of the side of Greek civilisation which did not fit preconceived ideas of the Greek achievement. This modern myth has been a long time dying in books on Greek religion.

In Euripides' *Bacchae*, Thebes is presented as the first place in Greece where Dionysos arrives to demonstrate his powers. He has come from Lydia, Phrygia, Persia, Baktria, Media, Arabia and the whole of the Asian seaboard. It is perhaps therefore curious that his late mother Semele, before her incineration (Ap 3.4.3), was a resident of Thebes and that its founder Kadmos (the Erechtheus of Thebes) was her father and his grandfather. He arrives in Thebes fully equipped with Maenads ('Raving Women') as his worshippers and represents an irresistible force which it is folly to oppose. In fact the three remaining daughters of Kadmos, Agaüe, Autonoë and Ino (*Bacchae* 681f.), are leading the three *thiasoi* (ritual dance-groups of Dionysos) out on the mountains. The reversal is extreme: matrons who should be in the city, weaving clothes, peaceably looking after children, are out on the wild mountain, wearing animal-skins (from animals which they have torn apart alive, in an un-sacrifice with no cooking), suckling snakes and wild creatures in mighty, possessed bands. Woe betide any baby they come across!

This – or something like it – is what actually happens in Dionysos cult, in Boiotia though not in Athens (where there was no ecstatic cult). The myth which Euripides is setting and exquisitely elaborating is in fact the *hieros logos* of the Agrionia festival at Thebes. It depicts a force sweeping in from Outside and Abroad, beyond the well-ordered male-dominated Greek polis, and inverting the behaviour of decent Greek womenfolk. It depicts the three groups in which the women are organised (which we know of from elsewhere). And it depicts Dionysos, impossibly, as both the force of the Outside, thus an outsider, and as specially associated with Thebes. He has, in any case, come to Thebes first. Thus Thebes becomes the premier location of the Dionysos-cult, in keeping, one suspects, with its claim to the leadership of the cities of Boiotia.

With the development of Greek culture and, in particular, the impetus given by the expeditions of Alexander the Great, knowledge of a once distant world increased and so too did the travels of Dionysos. Notably, he reached India – or maybe he even was an Indian – or at least one of the many Dionysoses which history confuses (differentiation) was an Indian with a long beard, as Diodoros tells (3.63). This was of course not the one born of Semele in Thebes, though that one travelled too, notably to a Mt Nysa which someone had managed to identify in Arabia (3.64.5).

And there were those who thought he travelled from India to Thebes by elephant (3.65.7). It took two years – which just happens to be the interval between Dionysos festivals.

Other cities, however, who did not persuade the Greek tradition, stuck to their own version of the birth model. Dionysos was born in Elis or Naxos or Eleutherai or Teos – but, if we may trust 'Homer' in his *Hymn to Dionysos* (Diodoros 3.66), this is all lies: Zeus gave birth to him on Mt Nysa in Phoenicia. Teos just isn't exotic enough.

If therefore in a myth a god is born or arrives at a place, however temporarily, it is worth thinking in terms of an aetiology of a cult-site, perhaps expressing a view of the cult or of its relationship to other cult-centres. The exception is when the place is clearly designated as a distant land, a 'beyond' – a margin to go to, be out of circulation at, or return from. That, I think, is the role of India and Thrace in the Dionysos story and of Karmanor's Crete in the Sikyonian or Delphic view. We will see more of beyonds in chapter 8.2.

Chapter 7

Myth and initiation ritual

It is time now to delve into some of the myths which gain their shape from association with rituals. As I write there seems to be a growing acceptance that this approach to myth is delivering results. But the reader should be warned that the acceptance is not universal, despite the enthusiasm of the author (my *Death and the Maiden* (1989) is devoted above all to the area outlined in chapter 7.1 below). There are, I think, two objections. The first is that the method involves too much speculation and guesswork.[1] The second is that, even if the method does deliver results, it tells us about the prehistoric significance of the myth and not what it meant to Greeks of classical times. Of course, I myself think it makes sense, reaches a sufficient level of proof and coherence and explains much, but readers will have to judge for themselves the plausibility and interest of this approach.

I have chosen in this chapter to concentrate on initiation rituals. The stories that emerge from the period of expulsion and seclusion tend to be colourful and to ensure disproportionate survival. But of course there were myths associated with other festivals too, for instance the myths that Burkert (1970) explored associated with a renewal-festival on Lemnos and forging a link between that and the Thesmophoria (p. 35 above) – well enough known for its own mythology of Demeter and Kore.

7.1 THE INITIATION OF THE MAIDEN

Bears and 'Bears'

At two sites in Attica – Brauron and Mounichia – and maybe at many more, a ritual called the *arkteia* was performed by selected

Athenian girls before marriage, in the 5 to 10 age bracket at the start (so comfortably before marriage). They were said to *arkteuein* during this period of service to the goddess Artemis, or to be *arktoi* ('Bears'). We know little of the detail of this ritual, though drawings on special small pots which we call *krateriskoi* and a few other sources give us glimpses. We see girls running in races, clad in tunics or naked. Young women direct the races. Sometimes a person dressed as a bear is present. On one occasion a real bear is present! We hear of a special costume called the *krokotos* ('saffron'-robe), perhaps meant to present the skin of the tawny bear in a more civilised mode. At some stage, each girl was to sacrifice a goat.

A myth is told in connection with this ritual, with differing versions for the two sanctuaries involved. At Mounichia:

> A she-bear appeared in the shrine and was killed by the Athenians; as a result there was a famine. The god gave an oracle that they would gain relief from it if someone sacrificed his daughter to the goddess. Embaros alone agreed to, provided his clan held the priesthood for life. He dressed his daughter, but hid her in the *adyton* [restricted room] of the temple and, dressing a goat in clothes, sacrificed it as though it was his daughter.
>
> (*The Souda*, under *Embaros eimi* ('I'm an Embaros'), slightly corrected)

At Brauron we are told that there was a wild bear in the region, that it was tamed and (according to one authority) given to the shrine of Artemis:

> But a girl poked fun at it, with her lack of restraint upset it, and it scratched her face. This annoyed her brothers and they shot the bear, as a result of which a plague befell the Athenians. The Athenians consulted an oracle and it replied that their troubles would end if, to pay for killing the bear, they made their maidens perform the *arkteia*. And the Athenians voted that no girl should be married to a man without performing the *arkteia* for the goddess.
>
> (*The Souda*, under *Arktos e Brauroniois* ('I was a Bear at the Brauronia'))

There is a particularly transparent connection between these stories and the ritual of which we know some details at Brauron.

Both stories supply a bear which is killed, for which a girl in myth, or girls in ritual, must compensate. The two versions even suggest, when put side by side, that the girl that is 'sacrificed' at Mounichia is equivalent to the girls performing the *arkteia* at Brauron. In ritual the girls compensate for the dead bear by becoming Bears themselves. They also sacrifice a goat, which is portrayed by the Mounichian myth as a substitute for themselves, to the point of being dressed up as them.

It is not wholly clear why the goddess is so upset at the death of the bear. We are simply left to suppose that it was in some way sacred to her or under her protection, just as young maidens are. But maidens must pay for their exit visa from maidenhood and we perceive that the momentum of this myth has become comparable to that of the myth of Apollo and Artemis at Sikyon (p. 98). This is another myth of *aphosiosis*, discharge of religious obligations, on leaving youth for adulthood.

There are other themes to note too. The 'sacrifice' by the father fits well with the termination of maidenhood, during which the father is responsible for the daughter. Once she becomes a full matron, the husband will be responsible instead. But the girl is not immediately married – far from it. First she must pass into a sort of limbo, an area of transition outside the normal bounds of society – in this case, the seclusion of the shrine of Artemis. This corresponds to an analysis of rites made by Van Gennep in 1909: in a large category of rites, which he termed 'Rites of Passage', participants transfer from one social status to another. These rites, he argued, exhibited a tripartite structure (Van Gennep 1960: 11):

1 rites of 'separation', from the former status;
2 rites of 'transition', a 'liminal' or 'marginal' period, time out, cut off from society altogether;
3 rites of 'incorporation' (*agrégation*), returning the person(s) to the society but in a new capacity.

The *arkteia* corresponds to the liminal phase. The myth, whilst appearing to narrate the aetiology of the *arkteia*, in fact establishes the tensions that precipitate the crisis and transfer maidens out of maidenhood into this period of seclusion.

Implications: myth and ritual

The Attic bear-myth is a specially useful example of the inter-relationship between myth and ritual and can serve as a model. At this stage two misconceptions about the relationship should be cleared away.

First, it has not been necessary to claim that the myth is the words spoken over the ritual, the *legomenon* over the *dromenon*, as Jane Harrison on occasion did (p. 28 above). Second, I have not claimed that the myth derives from the ritual or that the ritual derives from the myth. As we have no knowledge of how either the myth or the ritual is initially established (this is the well of the past, chapter 4.1), we cannot pretend to know that one originated from the other (on this point see Burkert 1970: 14; Versnel 1990: 59f.). Indeed to claim that one derives from the other seems like an intellectual tidying-up operation, a form of reductionism, an explaining away. One might as well explain away 'heroes' by claiming that they were originally gods or originally men.

What we may say in this case is that the myth and the ritual are two media operating in partnership. They explore, alleviate, accommodate moments that are felt difficult or significant. The society has been mapped in the minds of its members as consisting of several groups according to sex and age. In the case of female members these are: maidens, matrons, old women (widows). The bear-ritual and the bear-myth show how the map is preserved but individuals must be shifted. In fact, the myth will be told within its society when it seems interesting or relevant and such occasions are liable to increase in number as the moment of transition approaches. Perhaps it will be welcomed into hymns to the goddess, like the foundation-myth of the Eleusinian mysteries in the Homeric *Hymn to Demeter*. Myths, however, are stories and good stories have a life of their own. By the time they reach us, many of the surviving myths that have at one time been associated with a ritual have become detached and become part of a common Greek stock of stories, used above all by poets. Even so, when we look at one of these myths, we may realise from its shape and motifs that it belongs to this category.

To recognise a myth as belonging to this category is one form of interpretation of myth. It gives a reason for it to be constructed as it is. It will not, however, show the full range of possibilities inherent in the story – which a tragedian might extract or amplify. And it will not show the significance assumed by the myth within the context of a broadly systematic mythology, perhaps revealing the ways of thinking of its locally-based society. But it is a start and has the benefit of relating myths to particular peoples of particular places with particular ceremonies: the Attic bear-myth casts a light of its own on a specific context.

Ramifications: Bears

The Attic bear-myth itself has to be hunted out: it is not part of the standard Greek Mythology. But other myths which are part of Greek Mythology do take on a different hue once we have looked at the Attic bear-myth.

To return to Arcadia, a myth here cries out for attention, that of Kallisto. There are several variants of her story (e.g. Ap 3.8.2), but it is at least clear that she is the leading figure in a group of girls/nymphs that accompany Artemis in hunting and that she is under a duty as a result to remain a maiden. However, Zeus has sex with her. And she is transformed into a bear.

We can immediately see a cluster of Attic bear-myth motifs: focus on the maiden (like the daughter of Embaros, the girl who provokes the bear, or the Athenian maidens who must henceforth be Bears); a moment of crisis brought on by sexual maturity (the Athenian maidens must perform the rite before marriage, and the mythic girl hints at sexuality in her attitude towards the tame bear); Artemis (as at both Brauron and Mounichia); a segregated – single-sex, single-age-group – community of Artemis (like the Bears, and as implied by the *adyton*). The wrath of Artemis is implicit in the story and is worked out in different ways in different versions: it is Artemis who turns Kallisto into a bear, or Hera does and Artemis shoots the bear. In any case, this anger is associated with the end of maidenhood (Zeus, Athenian girls before marriage) or the end of the maiden ('sacrifice' of Embaros' daughter). Together with this goes the clinching detail, metamorphosis into a bear, which is what Brauronian ritual is all about. This is not to deny that there are differences, most notably the intervention of Zeus, or problems, most notably the wavering variants and the lack of a clear location of the myth, other than 'Arcadia'. But it does seem irresistible to identify the Kallisto myth as a partner-myth displaying ample indications of association with a lost passage rite of maidens who must become matrons.

Iphigeneia and the deer

A different myth is evoked by focusing particularly on Embaros' 'sacrifice' of his daughter. This is, of course, Agamemnon's 'sacrifice' of his daughter Iphigeneia at Aulis (e.g. Ap, *Ep.* 3.22). It starts with the death of an animal: Agamemnon shoots a deer, as a bear was killed at the beginning of the Attic bear-myth. Again the wrath of the goddess Artemis is the result, and again it requires the sacrifice of a daughter. Iphigeneia is summoned as though for marriage to Achilles – maybe a romantic invention of a poet, but not out of place as it stresses the moment at which these myths must happen. A realistic account would now demand that Iphigeneia was actually sacrificed, but this does not seem to be the usual outcome of the myth: rather, Artemis substitutes a deer for Iphigeneia, whilst she herself is whisked off, secluded we might say, and – in some versions, at any rate – becomes a priestess. The story has undergone some modifications: Iphigeneia becomes a priestess of Artemis Tauropolos (a title in some way associated with *tauroi* – 'bulls') amongst the Tauroi, a Scythian tribe identified as a result of increased acquaintance with the wider world, just like Dionysos' Mt Nysa in Arabia (p. 100 above). Aeschylus in his *Agamemnon*, for his own black purposes, leads us to think Iphigeneia was actually sacrificed (though interestingly his witnesses look aside at the last, terrible moment). But the type of the myth looks very close to the Mounichian.

This looks like a partner-myth for a rite of maidens in the cult of Artemis at Aulis. And to judge by the prevalent animal, it looks as though they should become not Bears, but Deer. A deer-rite is in fact suggested by three inscriptions from two sites in southern Thessaly and it does seem to be preliminary to marriage: a man who on one inscription pays a 'release-fee' to Artemis Throsia at Larisa for a female who has *nebeu*-'d (cf. *nebros*, 'deer') turns up on another inscription as her husband. Perhaps a deer-rite, apparently demanded at Aulis by the myth, is not entirely imaginary.

This local myth has been swept up into Greek Mythology – by travelling poets, striving to entertain audiences with their fund of stories, putting this myth to a different, though scarcely new, use. But it still bears the marks of an earlier social and ritual function based on a firmly categorised, traditional society.

Cows

Metamorphosis is a theme of sufficient extent to hold together Ovid's 15-book collection of myths, and it has several applications. Most notably it can be used to bring things into existence, to account for them, to provide an *aition*. But the purpose of the myths I now present is not to account for the existence of cows.

The daughters of King Proitos of Tiryns, the Proitids, have grown to the age for marriage and in one version poke fun at the statue of Hera – surely, in her shrine (story: Ap 2.2.2). This is described by Hesiod as an act of *machlosyne*, a word with sexual overtones ('raunchiness' perhaps goes too far). So: right age, dangerous adolescent behaviour (like poking fun at bears), angry goddess. Result: madness. They think they have become cows (a delusory metamorphosis, surprisingly tentative for myth) and are afflicted by a whitening skin disease and hair loss, reminiscent of ritual daubing of the body and shearing of the hair (like that which Achilles was growing for the River Spercheios – *Iliad* 23.142). For a period of one year they wander, expelled from Tiryns, in the wilds: we glimpse caves and mountains in the myth and cult of this stage.

The Tirynthian ending to the story has not survived. Instead we have a number of places where they were supposed to have been cured of their madness, usually by Melampous, the celebrated wandering (cf. chapter 6.4) seer. The best-known endings are (a) at a temple of Artemis at Lousoi after a year in the mountains above, and (b) somewhere in Sikyon after a colourful chase by a band of youths led by Melampous. There are hints here of Rhea's girdle (p. 97 above): Tiryns is accepted by all centres as the authentic home of the Proitids, but they feel free to stage the release of the Proitids at their own site. The case is particularly strong at Lousoi, perhaps reflecting the population movements from the Argolid to this part of the world at the end of the Mycenaean Age. This would imply transfer of rites without rejection of the point of origin. Tiryns itself was depopulated by the Argives after the Persian Wars and its local traditions lost except for some mythology; but we can use this myth to envisage the rite. Girls, probably select, at the age for marriage undergo service to Hera, goddess presiding over marriage. At the start Hera is hostile and must be won over. The girls start in the shrine, then leave the city daubed white and hair cut. They are the Cows of Hera. After a period of seclusion in the wild, they return to assume their new role in the community, that of matrons.

No mention of cows is complete without Io (Ap 2.1.3). Her story belongs only a few kilometres away from that of Proitids, at the temple of Hera known today as the 'Argive Heraion' (but, I think, originally a sacred site of Mycenae). She is a priestess of Hera, unmarried and still therefore in the control of her father, though authorities differed on who he was. But Zeus has sex with her. And she is transformed into a white cow. Now she is a prisoner in the precinct of Hera and is tied to a sacred olive-tree in 'the grove of the Mycenaeans', guarded by the many-eyed Argos. But Hermes kills him with a stone and Io wanders away from the shrine, across the face of the earth until finally in Egypt she is made human again, gives birth to Epaphos and . . . becomes Isis.

The Egyptian adventure is late: depictions of the Egyptian goddess Isis with cow's horns (which originally belonged to another Egyptian goddess, Hathor) has led to the identification of Io with her. And Egypt, instead of being a 'beyond' (chapter 8.2) to which people may wander, has become real and specific. But the kernel of the myth fits our pattern: Io's bovine metamorphosis belongs with that of the Proitids; the goddess is the same, Hera (known as 'cow-faced' in Homer, though literary people prefer to translate 'ox-eyed'); and the temple is once again in the foreground. Unlike the Proitids, Zeus ushers in the age of sexuality (as for Kallisto) and a period of seclusion in the shrine is indicated by the myth (as in the case of Embaros and the *adyton*). After this, the cow shape is again associated with wandering and we look forward to a release. The Io myth is, however, complicated by a second layer of ritual allusion – to the priestess of the Argive Heraion. Io is not just in the service of Hera, she is the first priestess of Hera, beginning a succession that led down to historical times – the same list that provided the backbone of Hellanikos' work (p. 44 above) and was considered by Thucydides. But the priestess at Argos was not a young maiden: she was a woman, presumably a virgin, who held the post for life. Had this once been a post held, as others were (Dowden 1989: 130–3), by a select maiden until she reached the age for marriage? Or did the priestess continue indefinitely the condition entered only as a liminal phase by the girl-initiands? We cannot know. All we can observe is the pattern which the myth forms beside that of the Proitids and other related myths.

7.2 THE INITIATION OF BOYS

It looks as though a female who no longer belongs to one group in human society and does not yet belong to another is depicted in myth as not human at all. What then of males? Immediately cult provides 'Bulls' (*Tauroi*) at Ephesos and 'Herds' (*Agelai*) in Crete and at Sparta – there they are directed by 'Ox-leaders' (*Bouagoi*). At Halai (Attica) we hear of a rite involving a mock-killing of a man, supposedly because Orestes was almost sacrificed by the barbarous Tauroi (Eur. *IT* 1458-61). Had there been a mock-sacrifice preceding entry into the liminal class of Bulls, marking the end of the previous condition? Such a suggestion is perhaps supported by the mock-killing which preceded entry into the Roman brotherhood of the *Luperci* ('Wolf'-men).

Wolves

It is at this point that we return to Lykaon. So far we have only seen him as a mythic tool for establishing Arcadian unity in the cult of Zeus Lykaios and for grounding city life (chapter 5.1 above). But his name is more often associated with an unsavoury story. Ovid tells in his *Metamorphoses* how Lykaon, as part of a package of impiety towards Jupiter (Zeus), slaughtered a hostage and served him up for a banquet for the god; for this he is turned into a wolf. Pausanias claims that his account has been 'told by the Arcadians since olden times' (P 8.2.4), plainly in books, but he does seem closer to ritual. Here Lykaon sacrifices a human baby on the altar of Zeus Lykaios (that, after all, is how you give food to a god); immediately, he turns into a wolf. This, it turns out, is an *aition*:

> 'How, then, does the change from protector to tyrant begin? Is it obviously when the protector begins to perform the same action as the man in the myth told in connection with the shrine of Zeus Lykaios in Arcadia?'
> 'Which one?'
> 'The one about the man who tastes human entrails, chopped up among the entrails of other sacrificial victims, and how he must turn into a wolf. Or haven't you heard the story?'
> 'Yes, I have.'
>
> (Plato, *Republic* 8 565d–e)

They say that ever since Lykaon there has been someone who changes from a man into a wolf at the sacrifice of Zeus Lykaios. But it does not happen for his whole life: if he abstains from human flesh whilst he is a wolf, nine years later he turns back from a wolf to a man; but if he doesn't, he stays a beast for ever.

(Pausanias 8.2.6)

But what is it an *aition* for? People don't actually turn into wolves. And it is not clear that there was actually human sacrifice at the Lykaia, though this has been believed both by ancient authors who have a weakness for myth ('I thought it unpleasant to look into the matter of the sacrifice. Let it be as it is and as it always has been' – P 8.38.7) and by primitivising scholars ('the savage and cruel rites . . . cannibal banquet . . . the awful sacrifice' – Frazer 1921: i 391–3).

The answer appears to lie in Indo-European tradition. There are traces in various cultures descended from Indo-European (Germanic, Celtic, Persian) of a custom whereby pre-adult youths of noble birth form roaming bands, typically involved in warfare (in the service of some important person), outside the normal structure of society. It is this violent, semi-outlaw union in bands that evokes the image of the 'wolf' – so prominent in men's names, tribal names and werewolf stories.[2] The metamorphosis into wolves, fierce enemies of man, is accomplished through a rite of at least supposed human sacrifice, as with bulls and *luperci* (the same inheritance), and is a way of presenting warrior-initiation in myth and in ritual.

Nine years as a wolf may seem a long time, until we look at Troy. The Greek warriors spent nine years besieging Troy (I presume the counting is inclusive). Who were they? According to Homer, the *kouroi Achaiōn*, the 'youths of the Achaians' – the young nobility who form a band, complete with their *hetairoi* (close comrades). None of the Achaians, apart from Nestor, have sons in battle. Some of the most important are married (the mark of adulthood): Agamemnon, Menelaos, Odysseus. These are the eminent chieftains whom roving bands of *kouroi* choose to assist. Diomedes and Achilles are not married – and they have *hetairoi*. Nine or ten years is, I suppose, about how long the physical peak of modern sportsmen lasts, who by the age of 30 must wonder whether they are past it. And in the Spartan system, a preliminary adulthood is reached in the twentieth year (i.e. at 19, the age of Telemachos) – now they become *eirenes* – but full adulthood with marriage only around the thirtieth. These are the nine or ten years at Troy or transmuted into wolves. I should perhaps mention for completeness at this point the preliminary two-year stage begun in the eighteenth year (i.e. at age 17) by Ephebes at Athens, *Melleirenes* at Sparta and also, for good measure, the age at which Herakles killed the lion of Kithairon in Apollodoros' source (Ap 2.4.9).

The Greek for *lupercus* is *lykourgos*, the name of the Spartan lawgiver. It is hard to see how there can be much history in what we are told of him: those Spartan institutions which seemed odd elsewhere in Greece are largely put down to him, though they had their parallels in Crete and are plainly survivals from an older way of life, requiring no Lykourgos to invent them. Even the definition of constitutional arrangements enshrined in the 'Great *Rhetra*' ('Decree') and its later codicil, both authorised from Delphi, leave him out of the picture. Historically, there is little room for there to be a Lykourgos, but mythically there is plenty. Some of what is told of him looks like a displaced version of the Lykaon story: reading Plutarch (*Lykourgos* 2–3), it becomes clear that he could have been king (if he had wished), he could have had a child killed as he ate (but refrained). Indeed, a recent writer (Kunstler 1991: 201–5) has even tried to connect this not-slaughter of a nephew to the maddened slaughter of his own son by the Thracian Lykourgos (Ap 3.5.1), in that case put down to the hostility of Dionysos. It obviously requires a lot of speculation, but the tattered evidence points to a Wolf-figure in charge of a wolf-pack of youths (hence the attribution to Lykourgos of the initiatory system at Sparta), united around a supposedly human sacrifice and cannibalistic meal.

'Boy'-snatching

Greek attitudes to homosexuality were rather different from those of most modern societies. But only one form had any degree of social approval: an upper-class relationship between a young adult and a pre-adult. The pre-adult, the *eromenos* ('beloved'), is not, in our sense, a 'boy' but a youth making the transition to adulthood. And the adult, the *erastes* ('lover'), is one who himself has recently made that transition. This institutionalised relationship goes back to Indo-European times, but in classical Greece it was disintegrating and unevenly preserved. In

Athens it remained as a custom, rather than a ritual, among the upper classes: hence all those vases pronouncing that so-and-so is *kalos* ('nice') or depicting youths as objects of interest, particularly when accompanied by a cockerel – a traditional present for an *eromenos*. Sometimes the *eromenos* is Ganymede himself, the nice son of King Tros ('Trojan'), taken by Zeus to be his cup-bearer and thereafter the archetypal passive male (Etruscan and Latin, *catamita*).

But the institution remained at its strongest and most associated with ritual in parts of Crete:

They have a unique custom regarding love-affairs: they win their *eromenoi* not by persuasion but by kidnapping. Three or four days in advance the *erastes* announces to the [boy's] friends that he is intending to do the kidnapping. For them it is a particular disgrace to hide the boy or not to allow him to travel on the arranged road, because in effect they would be admitting that the boy did not deserve an *erastes* like this. When they meet, provided the kidnapper is of equal or superior status to the boy, they chase him and lay hold of him only in a restrained way, satisfying the custom, but otherwise are happy to let him take him away. If he is not suitable, they remove the boy. The pursuit ends when the boy has been brought to the *andreion* ['men's (dining-)room'] of the kidnapper. They consider most worth loving not a boy of exceptional beauty but one of exceptional manliness and composure.

After giving him presents he takes the boy to some place of his choosing in the country; and they are followed by those who were present at the kidnapping, who feast and hunt together for two months (that is the maximum time for keeping the boy) and then come back down to the city. The boy is released after receiving presents – military costume, an ox, a drinking-cup (these are the regulation gifts) and other, expensive gifts besides, so much so that the friends contribute because of the expense. He sacrifices the ox to Zeus and feasts those who came back with him. Then he reveals whether he actually enjoyed the intercourse with his *erastes* or not – something for which the rules make provision so that if any violence was employed against him during the kidnapping, he can then and there avenge himself and be rid of him.

It is a disgrace for those of attractive appearance and who have distinguished ancestors not to get an *erastes*, because this failure is put down to their character. But the *parastathentes* ['stood-by'] – for that is what those kidnapped are called – receive honours: they have the most privileged positions in dances and races, and they are allowed to dress in a way that marks them out from the others, in the costume given to them by their *erastai* – and not just then, but even when they become adult they wear distinctive clothing by which one can tell in each case that they have been a *kleinos* ['famous'] – they call the *eromenos* a *kleinos* and the *erastes* a *philetor* ['lover']. This, then, is their custom regarding love-affairs.

(Strabo 10.4.21)

Sergent has unravelled the institution along the following lines. The *eromenos* is specially privileged amongst his age-group to be abducted. The *erastes* trains him in appropriate skills, for instance hunting, during their time out, which is of course the liminal period we have looked at before. During this period he is a sort of squire and, presumably, cup-bearer. (And there is a good parallel for the reality of the sexual relationship in notorious inscriptions found on Thera certifying consummation.) At the end, the 'youth' is a qualified adult, receiving the warrior's kit. And now he has a cup of his own. The homosexual relationship and practice between warriors and trainee warriors is commonplace in initiations across the world. At the end, his masculinity achieved, he will never be passive again – just as among the Taifali, a German people described by the fourth-century AD historian Ammianus, this passivity is wiped out by the catching of a boar or a bear (Sergent 1986: 9), and amongst the Keraki of New Guinea, the effects of passivity (amounting even to pregnancy!) are supposedly undone by the drastic remedy of putting quicklime in the mouth (ibid.: 43).

The myth of Ganymede is closely tied to this sort of ritual – it may even be a Cretan myth: in one variant it is Minos not Zeus who is the abductor. Ganymede is abducted in order to bear another's cup. He serves Zeus' pleasure. And Zeus, like a good *eromenos*, gives a generous present of horses to Ganymede's father Tros. Similarly, a story told of the Spartan Lykourgos looks as though it originally belonged here. Stripped of other motifs, it runs thus: the wealthy chase Lykourgos; they hand over a notable youth, Alkandros ('Mighty-man'), to him and escort them both to Lykourgos' home. There he becomes Lykourgos' servant (the other servants are dismissed) and learns good behaviour from

Lykourgos, developing great affection for him (Plutarch, *Lykourgos* 11). Less specifically, we may perhaps wonder whether Herakles' temporary servitude to Eurystheus and Apollo's temporary servitude to Admetus are not ultimately grounded in this type of myth and ritual.

This relationship is described repeatedly in Greek myths. A table in Sergent's book (1986: 262–5) lists 42 examples. Poseidon fell for Pelops and took him off, giving him the present of skill with the chariot. Laios of Thebes fell for Pelops' son Chrysippos and took him off . . . in his chariot, thus inventing homosexuality. Sergent (ibid.: 71–3) has even argued that the oracle to Laios, forbidding him to have children or else his offspring will kill him, is not a punishment for his homosexuality but reflects a ritual requirement for a period of homosexuality before begetting children (adulthood). Furthermore, his son Oedipus' own experience shows the advisability of not rushing into begetting children! The 'Furies of Laios and Oedipus' were worshipped by a rather widespread clan, the Aigeidai, because they supposedly had been unable to have children – both in Sparta and on Thera. They claimed descent from Laios and Oedipus, and were specially associated with the cult of Apollo Karneios, often initiatory in character. His temple on Thera is next to the ephebes' gymnasium, where the gross inscriptions are found (p. 114). It is quite a jigsaw of information, but it certainly casts new light on the failure of Laios and Oedipus to establish successful sexual relations. They were being premature.

If homosexuality had this role in the initiation of warriors, it explains why Herakles, the ultimate hero, is so addicted to pederasty. Plutarch's *Erotikos* (761d) presents him as having had too many such affairs to recount. The fullest story lies behind his constant companion in his labours, Iolaos, who received particular honours in Thebes. Thebes, home of Laios, had a very particular tradition of homosexuality. In 378 BC, homosexual couples in the Theban soldiery were brought together to form a crack squad called the *Hieros Lochos*, the 'Sacred Band'. Such couples, according to Plutarch, customarily visited the Tomb of Iolaos to swear an oath, in virtue of the relationship between Herakles and Iolaos. And next to his tomb, or *heroön* (though Thebans of Pausanias' time 'admitted' he died elsewhere), were the usual (initiatory) sports facilities, the Gymnasium of Iolaos, a stadium and a hippodrome (P 9.23.1) – Iolaos was, after all, according to Pindar (a Theban himself) a champion charioteer (*Isthmian Odes* 1.21–5).

Iolaos also figures at nearby Thespiai (Boiotia). Here he becomes the leader of the Thespiadai, a set of 50 sons of King Thespios. We normally talk about these as the product of Herakles' nocturnal labours (p. 139 below), but they are a group of 50 in their own right, who must go on a long voyage together, in the first instance of colonisation led by a king of a different race from the colonisers: 'The earliest instance was when Iolaos of Thebes, nephew of Herakles, led Athenians and Thespians to Sardinia' (Pausanias 7.2.2). Here it seems to me that Sergent must be right when he views this as a development of an original myth of a local Iolaos leading a voyage of 50 Thespians – diverted to Sardinia because there are Sardinian place- and people-names sounding like Iolaos. In fact, the number 50 is the standard number for members of the initiatory group, the *agele* ('herd'):[3] there were 50 oarsmen (Ap 1.9.16) plus two non-rowers to make up the Argonauts under Jason's leadership.[4] Fifty sons of 'Egypt' chased the 50 daughters of Danaos. Lykaon in Arcadia had 50 sons. And Tarentum was founded by 50 19-year-old Spartan *Partheniai*, whose name is based on the word 'maiden' (*parthenos*) and in some way contrasts them with the concept of marriage. This group size is at home in two further areas: first, it is the size of a dance-group, seen in the chorus for dithyrambs, and this must be related to the dances performed by the age-group (as explicitly attested for the *kleinos* by Strabo); second, and intriguingly, it is the size of the *team* of oarsmen required for a *pentekonteros* (the standard 50-oared galley that preceded the trireme) – a one-way relationship from myth and social structure to the design of the ship, because the group of 50 can be traced back to Indo-European culture long before the use of ships on that scale.

In any case, returning to Thespiai, we can see that Iolaos is the *kleinos* amongst a local group of Argonauts. This is just one of a set of local variants, others including Theseus and his band of 30 who sail in a ship to Crete and the 50 *Partheniai* who sail to Tarentum. In such cases colonisation could be, as Sergent thinks, a late motif in the development of the myth. But I see this differently (1989: 64). Colonisation was not something new in the eighth to sixth centuries BC. It had gone on continuously throughout history (though we tend to obscure this under our wooden term 'migration'). A repeated message of Greek myths is that the age-group and its young leader are associated with the foundation of a new state somewhere else (chapter 9.1). We see it here in the case of the Thespiads and in the case of the Partheniai, though not the Argonauts or Theseus.

Apollodoros (2.7.6) and Diodoros (4.29.4) report that only 40 Thespiads went on the colonising party. This tells us something about how myths are manipulated. Two or three Argonauts have to be retained in Thebes and seven in Thespiai itself: in Thespiai they are honoured as the seven *demouchoi* ('holders of the people'), in Thebes the three had been the ancestors of the major families in the city – i.e. these sets are needed to ground cult and genealogy.

Trickery, transvestism, transexuality

Trickery, though entertaining when you are not involved, is generally regarded as anti-social. Indeed it could be defined as the failure to perform in accordance with the code of behaviour that is thought to be in force. Those, however, who are set outside society may be expected to express their exclusion by rejection of norms. Thus Spartan youths in their limbo phase between boyhood and adulthood were expected to steal and to kill Helots. Responsible married women in Boiotia during a biennial festival of Dionysos would leave the city, wear skins not clothes and behave in carefully defined extravagant ways to invite the amazement and fear of men.

In the myth associated with the Athenian *ephebeia* (the transitional period for Athenian youths), a duel takes place on a border between Melanthos ('Black', with overtones of treacherous)[5] for the Athenians and King Xanthos ('Fair') of the Boiotians. Melanthos shouts out that Xanthos has cheated – there is someone beside him. But he is lying and, having distracted Xanthos' attention, kills him. And becomes king. Pelops, racing Hippodameia's father Oinomaos to win her hand, persuades the latter's charioteer, Myrtilos, to sabotage the chariot (Ap *Ep.* 2.6–8). It works, Oinomaos is killed and presently Pelops kills Myrtilos for good measure (or for attempted rape or so that the House of Pelops may be cursed or so that there may be a 'Myrtoan' Sea). Pelops has made his way to adulthood and power through trickery.

Perhaps this too is why Leukippos, a recurring name of king's sons, wins the land for the colonising party at Metapontion by extracting from the Tarentines an agreement that he and his party may stay there 'day and night', a phrase ambiguous in Greek between one-day-and-one-night and day-and-night in perpetuity.[6]

Another extraordinary feature of Greek myth, surely related to initiation, is the feminisation of heroes before they emerge as adults or warriors. We have seen this in its most literal form in Crete and Thera. But it recurs in other myths: again in Crete, at Phaistos, there is a Leukippos (again this name) who, in answer to his mother's prayer, is at maturity changed from girl to boy – providing a *hieros logos* for the festival of Ekdysia ('Undressing') and becoming a focus for those who are about to marry; or there is the Leukippos who dresses as a girl to associate with Daphne in Arcadia or Elis. Kainis in Gyrton (Thessaly), who lies with Poseidon, is turned into an invincible warrior, Kaineus, by Poseidon. Achilles in a telling moment is revealed amongst the king's daughters on Skyros when he comes forward, responding to Odysseus' strategem, and chooses weapons: now he can participate in the Trojan War.[7] Herakles swapping clothes with Omphale is a variant on this tradition.

This, then, is a taste of initiation ritual and mythology. It will have done its work if we now look more closely at myths to define the site at which the myth is set, the social groups to which their characters are meant to belong and the significance of this moment in their experience.

Part IV

The world of myth

Chapter 8

The world of myth

8.1 LANDSCAPE: THERE'S A STORY ABOUT THIS

Every myth must have come into being *at a particular place*.
(Müller 1825: 226)

We look now at the countryside and at nature. This is not the land of Wordsworthian poems or ecological ideals. This is the wild, only acceptable if subjugated by human activity, if the scene of ritual, if invested with some aura of myth or history.

Pausanias' landscape consists of earth and water: on the one hand, mountains, plains and 'places', on the other hand, springs and rivers. Look at Arcadia. Here is the 'place' *Skope* ('Viewpoint') where the great fourth-century general Epameinondas *looked* dying, unaware that he was passing from history into myth (P 8.11.7). The man who had once inflicted Sparta's most demoralising defeat becomes as he dies (on a rather less successful occasion) an aetiology for their neighbours, the Arcadians. Did Epameinondas in fact look? Or is it in our sense a 'myth'? It does not matter, for its importance is mythical: it is associative and makes a statement about Arcadians and Spartans.

No one will be surprised if the names of two Arcadian rivers (apparently) contain the word 'wash', *lou-*. But myth uses the prosaic meaning as a stepping stone to richer significance: the Lymax is where Rhea cleansed herself after giving birth to Zeus (P 8.41); the Lousios is where Zeus was washed at birth (P 8.28.2). Just so, the people of northern Arcadia liked to think that their god Hermes was washed in the 'triple-spring' *Trikrena* in the territory of Pheneos (P 8.16.1); and Amphion and Zethos were washed in a spring at Eleutherai towards Athens' border with Boiotia (P 1.38.8). In Arcadia, Rhea is a recurring theme: Mt

Alesion above Mantinea is named after her 'wandering' (*ale* –
P 8.10.1)); and when pregnant with Zeus, she came, with only a
few giants to protect her from Kronos, to her cave on the summit
of Mt *Thaumasion* ('Wonderful') – though of course she actually
gave birth on Mt Lykaion (P 8.36.2–3). Rhea, then, invests a
number of features of the landscape with significance. Even at the
level of a story this links the countryside to the cult of Zeus Lykaios
on Mt Lykaion, where Zeus was of course born (P 8.36.3). But the
myth may also imply ritual practices: after all, no one may enter
Rhea's Cave save 'women sacred to the goddess' (P 8.36.3).

Winding rivers are, perhaps, not unlikely to be called 'Snake',
but the Arcadian River Snake has a more special aetiology:
Antinoë, the daughter of Kepheus, son of Aleos (mythic kings of
Arcadia), moved the inhabitants of Mantinea to a new site – using
a snake as a guide, as an oracle instructed. Pausanias, as a good
historian, is concerned that there is no record of what type of
snake it actually was, but deduces from Homer that it must have
been a *drakon* (P 8.8.5). But snakes mean more than this. Having
no feet, they are in direct contact with the land and they live in
holes in the earth. Heroes, who are buried in the earth and watch
over the land, can manifest themselves as snakes. Snakes authenti-
cate the title of these Mantineans to their new site. A snake-given
title is almost as good as autochthony, the condition of having
always been on that land, of having been sprung from it. At Mt
Sepia mythic King Aipytos was killed by a snake, a *seps* presumably; you can see his grave (P 8.16), where, I suppose, he became
one with the land. The landscape reflects mythic history, and
mythic history defines the landscape.

Attica has its similarities. The cape *Zoster* ('Girdle'), so-called I
imagine because of its shape (like the River Snake), contained an
altar to Athene and to Apollo, Artemis and Leto. Leto, the story
goes, undid her *girdle* here to give birth to Apollo and Artemis,
though of course she actually gave birth elsewhere (P 1.31.1) –
Delos according to the approved version. A snake disappearing
into the ground informs Chalkinos and Dais (descendants in the
tenth generation from Kephalos) where in Attica to sacrifice to
Apollo, in accordance with the inevitable oracle; as a result they
find a home in Athens (P 1.37.6–7). Once again a snake expresses
a sense of belonging to the land, an alternative to autochthony. Or
in Salamis there was a stone, presumably fairly eye-catching, not
far from the harbour, on which the mythic hero Telamon sat

looking (like Epameinondas at memorable 'Viewpoint') at the ship carrying his children off to the Trojan War and death (P 1.35.3). And just as 'Viewpoint' served to remind Arcadians of the defeat of their hated neighbours in Sparta, so on the way from Athens to once-independent Eleusis there is a reminder of the murderous faithlessness of the Megarians beyond Eleusis: here is the tomb of Anthemokritos, a herald slain by the Megarians because they did not like his message (P 1.36.3). The past, both historical and mythical (for there is no distinction), continues to live in the landscape of the present.

8.2 HORIZONS

So far we have looked at landscape generally. However, landscape has its own dynamics: mythology has a sense of centre and a sense of distance, a centripetal and a centrifugal nature. Let us proceed gradually from the city.

Outside: cultivation

As we leave the town we come first to the cultivated land, an area perceived as controlled and civilised. This is generally the realm of Demeter who gave us the civilising gift of corn: the land can now be dominated by human activity and the resulting crops undergo a range of processes – grinding, mixing, cooking; consequently, man has less occasion to encroach upon the wild to gain his food by hunting. Agriculture is, however, perhaps more a matter of ritual than of myth: Demeter is a rare participant in Greek Mythology. Her search for Kore predominates, but here the Eleusinian mysteries often stand in the foreground of interpretation, privileging issues of life and death. In cult the same myth partners the Thesmophoria, a widespread festival of the female half of the citizen community, the women and maidens. Perhaps the death of Kore may be interpreted in the light of the changing seasons of the year – the cyclical growth of crops and their death (whether during winter or, in the light of the Greek climate, during the dry season). But the real point is the association of the death and renewal of the crops with the female nature of the participants in Demeter's festival – and that takes us back from the fields to the community.

Otherwise, we hear little of Demeter – except that once she loved Iasion in a thrice-ploughed field: according to Homer he was then blasted by Zeus (*Odyssey* 5.125–8); and according to Hesiod it was in Crete and the result of their union was Ploutos ('Wealth', *Theogony* 969–74). Fields needed their fertility and the myth displays something of the attitude of mind of those not always reputable Athenian women who set up model phalluses in ritual allotments at the Attic festival of the Haloa at Eleusis. Nearby was the Rarian Field, where corn had first been sown.

Corresponding to corn, the gift of Demeter, is Dionysos' gift of wine. That too has its mythology. Wine, as a cultural fact, must be discovered: we have seen such a story in Hekataios (the bitch and the vine-stock, p. 43 above); in another, Oineus, king of Aitolian Kalydon, was the first to receive a vine-plant from Dionysos (Ap 1.8.1). Meanwhile, Anios, the son of Apollo and priest-king on Delos, whom Aeneas meets on his travels (Vergil, *Aeneid* 3.80), has a set of three daughters, the *Oinotrophoi* ('Wine-rearers'). They are called Elaïs, Spermo and Oino (Ap *Ep.* 3.10), thus neatly accounting for 'olive', 'corn' and 'wine' in turn. Another story again probably underlies Polyphemos' 'discovery' of the force of wine in his confrontation with Odysseus (*Odyssey* 9.345–74), in which Polyphemos' handicap is a lack of proper Greek culture and Odysseus' asset is the wine he has received from Maron, priest of (oddly) Apollo (9.197). Wine, however, also reaches out to loss of rational thought, and the god of the rampant vegetation like vine and ivy also propels married women, a symbol of the controlled environment, into the mountain wilds, beyond the pale of civilisation.

Other cultivated plants too had their sacred character. The olive-tree had been Athene's gift to Attica, ensuring her claim to be the land's patron; Poseidon's gift of water did not suffice (Ap 3.14.1). A similar contest had been held at Argos between, this time, Hera and Poseidon (P 2.22.4, 2.15.5). The contrast between the cultivated land and the threatening sea is clearly marked, not least by the subsequent flood which Poseidon's rancour unleashes on both occasions – a force overcome in other stories by heroes (p. 145 below). An extraordinary appendix to this story tells how the Athenians placated Poseidon's wrath by henceforth denying women the vote and denying children the right to be called by their mothers' names.[1] Are women to be associated with the flood that threatens to engulf civilisation? Does this compensate for the selection of a woman rather than a man as patron of the country?

Trees themselves are of more than average significance. The reader should perhaps be aware that trees are part of a seamless continuum of objects of worship which goes back to Mycenaean and Minoan civilisation. Stalagmites in caves, unhewn rocks or stones, pillars, trees, trunks and, finally, the statues made out of those stones or trees have a magnetism as focuses of religious attention. A sacred tree is more than a Christmas tree sent from Norway – it has a power and a real cult. So, in Minoan Crete there were tree sanctuaries, depicted fenced off, an outburst of the sacred into the secular world. This is what lies behind the place trees often assume in Greek myth. The olive-tree of Athene is the sacred tree of the Athenian acropolis. The tree to which Io was tied in the 'grove of the Mycenaeans' is surely the sacred tree of the Argive Heraion. And Peleus' spear, the spear which later only his son Achilles had the strength to wield (*Iliad* 16.140–4), was made from the ash-tree on Mt Pelion.

Some metamorphosis myths are used specially to establish the existence of trees, though admittedly here we are talking not of particular trees but of the first tree of a certain type. As it became part of the prettiness of literature, people thought it worthwhile to tell how the maiden Daphne, pursued by Apollo, escaped by metamorphosis into the laurel-tree, specially important in the cult of Apollo (Ovid, *Metamorphoses* 1.452–567). Pine-trees likewise seemed remarkable enough to identify an island Pityoussa ('Piney') off the coast near Hermione and inspire a myth of how Pitys escaped Pan's attentions in much the same way (Longus, *Daphnis and Chloë* 2.39). Greek culture may not be ecological, but it is sensitive to trees.

Outside: pastoral

Beyond the cultivated land lies a land on which man is more of an intruder and where the forces of nature loom larger. Here goatherds and shepherds tend flocks. From the perspective of the town, these are already marginal people on to whom a myth will ultimately be projected, the pastoral myth so beloved of urban poetry since the third century BC. Their gods are now more pastoral too, though our knowledge of them and their myths will of course always have been mediated through the city. Goatherds don't write – and are depicted about as realistically as Scythians or Egyptians.

From the Hellenistic Age onwards we become aware of Pan and the Nymphs – in literature, landscape-painting and even reality. Pan is a curiosity amongst Greek gods: goat-legged and sometimes goat-headed, not a grand Olympian, but a rather lowly, country god. Maybe he is a spirited god with the sexual drive of a ram, but in cult he only inhabits Arcadia to any extent. He is a Citroën 2CV amongst gods. He haunts the genre-painted countryside, lusty and priapic[2] like those other half-animal gods, the Satyrs and Centaurs, whose plurality he sometimes acquires – so we hear of Pans. Perhaps Pan is pursuing Daphnis the youthful shepherd of the new pastoral mythology – doomed to love and an early death (Theokritos *Idyll* 1, *Epigram* 3). Or perhaps he is pursuing a nymph, Syrinx, who avoids him only by metamorphosis into reed-pipes, the Pan-pipes, another aetiology accomplished (Ovid, *Metamorphoses* 1.687–712). This is a safely twee countryside, immortalised in Longus' second-century AD novel, *Daphnis and Chloë*, where Pan and the Nymphs play a magical role in the preservation of the countryside and those who are attuned to it. Can you hear the pipes (Longus 2.26, 29)? They can on Mt Mainalos in Arcadia, up above the ruins of Mainalos town (P 8.36.8).

Improved communications, increased wealth and the ability of the well-off to own a place in the country underlie this appropriation of the landscape. Yet it could be more awesome. 'Panic' fear is known since the second century BC. Pan appeared to Pheidippides as he ran back to Marathon in 490 BC, running through Arcadia, beyond the limits of human endurance, out there on Mt Parthenion at his sanctuary (P 8.54.6) high above Tegea: why did the Athenians not honour him, he asked (Herodotos 6.105). And now he begins to register on Athenian pottery. But he is not an Arcadian quirk: a reasonable case can be made out for his being a god that goes all the way back to Indo-European, identical with the Sanskrit Pūṣan, a god of cattle and of the (nomadic) margins not so distant in concept from another Arcadian god – Hermes, who tradition claims was Pan's father (Puhvel 1987: 62f.).

Nymphs are an essential part of the generic landscape. They are the apotheosis of marriageable girls at the peak of beauty and desirability, with nice names like Amaryllis and Galatea. They are not yet someone else's, but are there to be courted and pined over by the Daphnises of the pastoral world. But they remain elusive and ungraspable. Even at this late stage in the development of nymphs we perceive the tension in this male mythology between the irresistibility of this class of female and the impossibility (i.e. prohibition) of seduction.

The Nymphs are worshipped in caves – already in Homer, at least in our texts, there is a cave of the Nymphs (*Odyssey* 13.347–8); at Eleusis there was a cave of Pan and the Nymphs where *krateriskoi* (p. 103) were deposited. And, of course, the cave is the prime cult site of Pan and the Nymphs in Longus. But their power spreads further into every aspect of the countryside, lovingly categorised by learned writers: trees have their Dryads (or Hamadryads), groves have Alseids, rivers Naiads (or Hydriads or Ephydriads), mountains Oreads. This does not take account of implausibly tame developments such as Meadow-nymphs (Leimoniads) and Garden-nymphs (Kepids, presumably plastic). It was always an entertaining and pretty challenge to catalogue their names. Thetis heard Achilles' distress at the death of Patroklos:

> . . . and the goddesses gathered around her,
> All of the Nereids who lived in the depths of the sea:
> Glauke was there and Thaleia and Kymodoke
> And Nesaie and Speio and Thoe and Halie ox-faced [!]
> And Kymothoë and Aktaie and Limnoreia
> . . . [20 more names]
> And the other Nereids who lived in the depths of the sea.
> And their gleaming-white cave [NB] was filled with them . . .
>
> (Homer, *Iliad* 18.37–50)

Or perhaps you would like to know about the 'Rainies' (Hyades), who became stars:

> . . . nymphs like unto the Graces,
> Phaisyle and Koronis and Kleeia with her pretty garland,
> And adorable Phaio and Eudoros with her sweeping dress,
> Whom men on the earth call the Hyades.
>
> ('Hesiod', *Astronomia* fr. 291 M–W)

Outside: wild and lush

Nymphe in Greek means not only a 'nymph', but also a girl ready for marriage, a bride or a newly-wed. Indeed, the word itself may be related to the Latin word for 'marry', *nubere*. Their goddess is

Artemis who is frequently attended by them in the wilds, typically hunting. As a result it looks very much as though nymphs originally represent the age-class of girls secluded in preparation for marriage and being true to their liminal condition by being neither maidenly nor matronly. Hence nymphs come to be portrayed as roaming the wilds. It is dangerous to see these forbidden virgins: then you may become *nympholeptos*, 'nymph-seized' – frenzied, possessed. A comparable word is *phoiboleptos*, denoting seizure by Phoibos Apollo. A dreadful warning is given by the case of Aktaion, who stumbles upon Artemis and the Nymphs bathing and, transformed into a deer, is eaten by his own pack of dogs (Ap 3.4.4, Ovid *Metamorphoses* 3.138–252). The hunter Orion, whose tomb is in Tanagra (P 9.20.3), was slain by Artemis too (Ap 1.4.5). But this giant who could stride across the sea is much more complex and deserves a book on his own – which Fontenrose has written.[3]

There is less menacing land in nature's control. The mouth of the River Alpheios is described by Strabo in these terms: 'The whole land is full of shrines of Artemis and Aphrodite and the Nymphs, in groves mostly full of flowers because water is plentiful' (Strabo 8.3.12). This is the sort of landscape where Hades seized Kore (Persephone):

> she was playing with the daughters of Ocean with shapely
> [dresses
> gathering flowers – roses and saffron and pretty violets,
> on the soft meadow, and irises and hyacinth
> and narcissus – grown to trick the bud-faced girl
> by Earth at the behest of Zeus . . .
>
> ('Homer', *Hymn to Demeter* 5–9)

This is a familiar picture in mythology: girls snatched as they pick flowers. Hesiod's *Catalogue* had told of the daughters of Porthaon, a figure of importance for genealogy, who ties the Aitolians to their major centres of Kalydon and Pleuron (cf. Ap 1.7.7). Amongst the papyrus tatters we read an 'Or-like' something like this:

> Or like the daughters who were born to Porthaon
> Three of them, like goddesses, understanding fine crafts . . .
> . . . Eurythemiste and Stratonike and Sterope.
> They . . . as companions of the lovely-haired Nymphs
> . . . through the wooded mountains of the Muses

. . . reached the very peaks of Parnassos
. . . (?rejecting the realm?) of gold-garlanded Aphrodite
. . .
. . . much and . . . reached (mea)dows
. . . dwelling in the tall mountains
leaving the home of their father and their doughty mother.
They then, rejoicing in their beauty (and ign)orance
. . .
flowers to adorn (their hair) . . .
Them . . . Phoibos Apollo
And he went off with . . . Stratonike, undowried,
And gave her to his dear son to be called his buxom wife,
To Melaneus match for a god . . .

('Hesiod', *Catalogue of Women* fr. 26.5–25)

In this myth we see an initiatory type of myth, with an age-group, apparently rejecting sexual maturity, over-confident, secluded from the parental home. Like Europa or Kore the girl is snatched from the correct, sympathetic landscape – well understood by poets throughout antiquity.[4] The fresh, fertile meadow and its flowers ready for picking express the beauty and nubility of the girls that dance there.

In this case incipient femininity harmonises with a positive landscape. But in the case of the wild landscape, its very point is that it contradicts the potential femininity of Artemis and the Nymphs, because in this liminal, limbo condition they are not ready to assume the role that integrates them into society.

Beyond

'Beyond' is always getting further away. Apollo, having killed Python, must flee north to Tempe – a narrow valley, almost a gorge, near the mouth of the River Peneios, at the far end of Thessaly. This is between Mt Olympos and Mt Ossa, the land of gods and of the giants Ephialtes and Otos who had once tried to pile Mt Pelion on Mt Ossa and Ossa on Olympos to reach the gods in heaven (Ap 1.7.4). This end of the earth is where Greeks who count as Greeks (Macedonians don't) stop and is the point Greeks originally intended to hold against Xerxes in 480 BC (Herodotos 7.173) – a conceptual as well as a strategic barrier.

Alternatively, Apollo must flee to the deep south, to the purifier Karmanor in Tarrha in Crete (chapter 6.3). For all its participation in Greek civilisation since the Bronze Age, Crete remains a margin, over the seas and far away. Theseus, as part of a ritual team of seven boys and seven girls, must sail away to meet danger in Crete, and then return. Crete is a 'beyond' for the liminal phase. Its lack of reality is somehow underlined by the role which its most famous king, Minos, must play in the Underworld – judge for dead folk in their daily disputes with each other (*Odyssey* 11.568–71), and later judging them for the lives they have led. He has Rhadamanthys, his brother and legendary Cretan lawgiver, for company too.

A wider world allows Io to wander cow-shaped, not like Proitids across Argive or Arcadian mountains, but round the bounds of the known Greek world. So her itinerary in the *Prometheus Bound* of 'Aeschylus' encompasses the sorts of material that Herodotos included when dealing, as often he does, with far away places. Indeed, she may wander past the very Caucasus where Prometheus is bound (to discuss how Zeus has given them both a hard time). But her ultimate destination is Egypt. Io never returns from this beyond, but her descendants do. Why must the tribal eponym Danaos and his Danaids come to Argos from Egypt? He has a brother by now, Aigyptos of course, and that brother has 50 sons. Like many male representatives of initiatory youth, they are associated with the colour black during the liminal phase. In this case they are themselves black, because they are Egyptians; and Egypt is the marginal land of these liminal people.

Egypt is where the real Helen was whisked away, while the phantom Helen went to Troy – Egypt is off-stage. And in Euripides' imagination (*Helen*), its king is a typical ends-of-the-earth barbarian (like the king of the Tauroi whom Iphigeneia and Orestes must outwit in *Iphigeneia amongst the Tauroi*). Herakles, too, in his duty tour of dangerous places, must deal with the barbarian king of Egypt, Busiris (Ap 2.5.11), who, like Euripides' king of the Tauroi, sacrifices strangers. Human sacrifice is a good sign of a barbarian. Herodotos, for whom Egypt is a very real country, of course specifically denies the truth of this myth: human sacrifice is wholly alien to Egyptian religion (2.45).

Yet Egypt is in the mid-distance, a land where myth and reality merge. It is sufficiently exotic to be surrounded with an impossible aura of learning, tradition, mystery and sacrality, explored in Herodotos' second book. But beyond lie lands cast further adrift from reality. There live the 'Aithiopians'(chapter 5.2). Poseidon has gone to them to receive a sacrifice and that has put him safely out of the way as the *Odyssey* commences (*Odyssey* 1.22–7). This too may be where Andromeda is exposed to Poseidon's sea-monster, for Perseus to rescue (Ap 2.4.3; Ovid, *Metamorphoses* 4.668). And here, in antiquity's greatest novel, Heliodoros' *Aithiopika* (second or fourth century AD), will be found a nation ambivalent between the barbarity of human sacrifice and an ultimate wisdom transcending even that of Egypt, a target for the purest of human souls.

Even beyond Aithiopia there was something more – though only one Iamboulos (perhaps second century BC) seems to have known about it. Deep in the southern sea lay seven blest islands occupied by a fabulous race of amazingly hospitable people. Hairless, with rubbery bones, tongues forked at the base not the tip, they live in meadows (cf. p. 128 above), have hot and cold running springs, study astrology and live to 150. This sort of engaging nonsense was very much to the Hellenistic and post-Hellenistic palate. Antonius Diogenes did a northern version, masquerading also as a thriller (the villain is Paapis, an Egyptian priest), in his *Wonders beyond Thule*. Thule is the utterly remote northern island (*ultima Thule*, as Horace puts it), which you may place somewhere in the Shetlands, Orkneys or – if you prefer – Iceland. According to Pytheas of Marseilles (later third century BC), who set the concept running in an apparently factual account of a voyage round northern Europe, Thule was six days' sail from Britain and one day from the 'frozen sea'. We have to wait until Book 24 of Antonius' book before the narrator, Dinias, finally does travel north beyond Thule: there Dinias (because the earth rises) comes close to the Moon and witnesses various other absurdities too, like nights that last six months. Pytheas had been right about that, but Antonius wasn't to know.

Traditionally horizons up north had been narrower. Greece stopped at Tempe. Certainly Thrace is a marginal land: it is where Dionysos 'came from', a myth powerful enough to delude many modern books (chapter 6.5). The pre-people of Thasos, expelled by Herakles, were Thracians (Ap 2.5.9). And Herakles' cattle, which he has gained from Geryon at a western margin, sometimes have him on the northern margin: they scatter across the foothills of Thrace (Ap 2.5.10) – leaving wild cattle behind. (Or they wandered where Skythians now live – Herodotos 4.8.) Is not the famous Mt Haimos named after the 'blood' that the monster Typhon gushed out (Ap 1.6.3)? Thrace, too, has its barbarian king: Amykos, king of the Bebrykes, who challenged all comers to a boxing match. Only Polydeukes (Latin, Pollux) the Argonaut stopped that (Ap 1.9.20).

Beyond the Thracians at one stage lived the Kimmerioi, who from their name (compare Cymru or Cumberland or Cimbri) should be real, living Celts. But they are Homer's last station before the world of the dead:

> The ship was coming to the limit of Okeanos with its deep
> currents.]
> Here is the people and city of the Kimmerian men,
> Covered in mist and cloud – never on them
> Does the shining Sun look with his rays,
> Neither when he proceeds towards the starry heaven,
> Nor when he turns back again from heaven to earth:
> Deadly night stretches over the miserable humans.
>
> (Homer, *Odyssey* 11.13–19)

The next step beyond these were usually the Skythians, whose land is celebrated in the opening lines of the *Prometheus Bound*:

> We have reached a remote plain of the Earth,
> The Skythian path, an unpopulated desolation.
>
> ('Aeschylus', *Prometheus Bound* 1–2)

The description would doubtless have amused Skythians, but it denotes the limits of popular geography in the mid-fifth century BC. The idea of a map was still new: Anaximander had invented the first one before the mid-sixth century BC, but they remained inaccurate rarities, not a compulsory part of education as today. Real knowledge varied greatly and was accumulated from reports that frequently verged on the mythical. Almost two centuries before the *Prometheus*, Aristeas of Prokonnesos had put together a strange 'faction' of a poem in which he gave some idea of how northern populations, including the Skythians and Kimmerioi, pressed on each other. Indeed he claimed to have travelled, 'seized by Apollo' (so what sort of journey was this?), to the Skythians (Herodotos 4.13). It was beyond Skythia that his creatures of legend lay: one-eyed Arimaspians wresting gold from griffins. And beyond them again lay the blessed Hyperboreans, the happy people of Apollo, encroaching on no one.

Locations in Greek myth have a message relative to the location of the speaker. In this section we have looked at how the distance of a location from the speaker may be set to 'maximum' and therefore divorced from the standard order of things. Where is the 'city of slaves' (Vidal-Naquet 1981: 189)? In Egypt, Libya, Syria, Karia, Arabia or Crete. Geography was – and is – viewed with no more objectivity than history: the one locates us in space, the other in time. When the definition of our view of ourselves takes precedence over accurate reporting of other places and times, we have opened the door to myth.

8.3 OF MONSTERS, GODS AND HEROES

Monsters

Greek Mythology at first sight has plenty of monsters: things from the beginning of time – or at least begotten by the primeval Earth for gods or heroes to defeat; awkward customers like the Hydra of Lerna (always sprouting new heads), the Nemean Lion (with Chobham skin) for Herakles; mistakes with the Lego set, like the Chimaira for Bellerophon, or centaurs or satyrs; and the simply loathsome Gorgon Medousa for Perseus. Add to that the decorative griffins and bogies to scare children – Lamiai and Empousai and so on – and you may think you have a good supply.

Monsters disproportionately attract the attention of *modern* readers, who tend not to notice that in Greek Mythology monsters have a limited circulation, as you may see by counting the proportion of pages given over to them in any complete book of Greek myths. Perhaps the gods themselves sap something of the demand for the non-human and magical in myth – Greek myth is more affected by dungeon-masters than by dragons. But other factors contributed: the exceptional authority of Homer can be viewed as setting a particularly human and realistic tone for later Greek writers to follow; he allows little room for the magical and monstrous. Monsters also lose out in the classical media, in which their distance from reality becomes a liability: they are impracticable for the tragic stage (as any producer of Wagner's *Siegfried* will tell you), and no longer to the taste of vase-painters by the time that red-figure technique takes over (late sixth century BC).

The attraction and importance of monsters is psychological. As they have never existed, their particular construction is likely to reveal more about what is inside man than what is outside. In broad terms we can talk of the fears, loathings and worries they express and perhaps few will disagree. But more specifically, if what psychoanalysts say is valid (cf. chapter 2.2) then this is an area where their work should contribute to our understanding.

Perhaps myths, like dreams, reach into our subconscious where the formative worries of childhood still lurk. Perhaps the baby's deep concern with orality will explain the multiple heads of so many monsters. And is the primal water in which a monster may live 'amniotic'? Is the snake a symbol of the penis? Monsters tend to be snakey and tend to be female: are they then 'phallic' females whom the male child must castrate? And if a female is a serpent from the waist down (as Echidna below), is this a result of the male child's ignorance of the unseen half of his mother? Hypothesis: she must be phallic really.[5] Or the lurking fear later: I know she isn't, but what if she was? A nymph whose lower half is a snake is as penile and threatening as a witch on a broomstick.[6] If, however, the monster is male, then it shall represent the father and his defeat an Oedipal victory (Caldwell 1989: 45). This is a matrix for the convinced reader. Meanwhile, let us return to more pedestrian approaches.

Monsters and gods

Monsters exist in order to be defeated and, preferably, slain. They sprout in the path of those that must prove and establish themselves. Thus at the beginning of his world-order, Zeus must defeat Typhon (Hesiod's 'Typhoeus'). Hesiod describes Typhon's appearance (*Theogony* 823–35): he has 100 snake's heads, eyes blazing fire, voices that could imitate gods' speech or animals' – though artists, under more practical constraints, tended to depict him with one head, a man's, and a snake's body instead.[7] This last child of Earth, the final autochthonous creature, has ambitions to rule the world, which Zeus must suppress in order to rule himself. He is laid low on his mother earth, and cast into Tartaros – thus, I suppose, being un-born (cf. Caldwell 1989: 133–4).

The name of Apollo's opponent at Delphi blends the alleged old name of Delphi, 'Pytho', with 'Typhon' (chapter 6.1). The 'Homeric' *Hymn to Apollo* tells us it was a female of the monster-snake species, a *drakaina*, huge and wild, and that it did much harm to men and flocks (300–4). Routine stuff so far, but it was also the wet-nurse for the super-monster Typhon, who in this version is born by Hera in anger at Zeus (305–7). Thus, by a sort of genealogy, the slaying of a local pest gains wider significance in the world-order. Apollo is thus Slayer of the Foster-Mother of Typhon.

This category of monster is preferably born of Earth, because their slaughter depicts the effective world-order supplanting the raw, autochthonous regime. It is interesting that Typhon is presented as in some way muddling definitions: Typhon is a jack of all voices; or he is ('Homer', *Hymn to Apollo* 351) 'like neither gods nor humans'. His monstrosity reflects the ill-defined nature of his world in contrast with the world we know. As a result of this autochthony, Earth will end up in Greek Mythology as a mother notably of monsters.

The Titans and Giants also present the Olympian gods with a battle to establish themselves, the Titanomachy and the Gigantomachy (chapter 9.2). The Titans are a puzzle. We do not know where their name comes from and individually they are a rag-bag of persons, abstractions and even monsters. Anyone born of Heaven and Earth, rather than from Kronos and Rhea like the Olympian gods, must apparently on that account be a 'Titan'. Titans are the Pelasgians of the gods. But early poets and in particular Hesiod, thinking about the world and how it works, liked to establish quite a range of people or concepts early in their heavenly genealogy ('Theogony'). Thus we find Themis (religious correctness) and Mnemosyne (memory/tradition) in this number. Kronos and Rhea themselves can only be Titans – and similarly Sun and Moon, the 'Hyperion' and 'Phoibe' of Hesiod. Indeed 'Titan' gradually becomes poet-speak for 'Sun' – especially in Roman writers. Tethys, ancestor of sea-divinities, must be a Titan too. Nor can we exclude Briareos and two other 'Hundred-handers' (*Hekatoncheires* – they had 50 heads too): these had, of course, been born of Heaven and Earth, but were released from imprisonment by Zeus and therefore fought on his side, for which Homer, in his wayward inventive way, makes Thetis (Achilles' mother) take credit (*Iliad* 1.104). Also released from imprisonment and also, therefore, primal Titans are the Kyklopes, who forge Zeus' lightning and thunderbolt. Prometheus was also around to help Zeus and so must likewise be a defecting Titan – though by the time of the Aeschylean *Prometheus Bound* (line 332), he has learnt to feel sympathy for Typhon! In the end, Kronos and the Titans are defeated, imprisoned securely in Tartaros 'as far beneath Earth as Heaven is above' (Hesiod, *Theogony* 720). The world is now safely partitioned and formatted: Zeus governs the sky, Poseidon the sea and Hades the Underworld.

Giants and dwarves figure even less in Greek myth than monsters. But 'great Giants [*Gigantes*],[8] shining in their armour, bearing long spears in their hands' are amongst the offspring of Earth in Hesiod's *Theogony* (185–6). A myth of their battle against the gods and the assistance which Herakles gave the gods seems to form around them during the earlier sixth century BC and Apollodoros (1.6) gives an account of which god slew which Giant – very useful when one looks at depictions in sculpture. But in sculpture they are used to make special statements, which we shall look at later (chapter 9.2), all of which draw on a perception of Titans and Giants as *agrioi* ('wild'), thus contrary to the civilised order established by the Olympian gods (Brelich 1958: 329f.).

Herakles

These, then, are the gods' opponents. Heroes face monsters on perhaps a less grand scale, but one more challenging. And it is easier to relate to a hero than a god. There are indeed depictions of Typhon, Python, Giants and (maybe) Titans. But these dwindle into insignificance beside the feats of Herakles ('Hercules' in Latin). There are countless depictions of Herakles and the Nemean lion with its invulnerable hide, and several of Herakles and Kerberos (Latin: 'Cerberus'), the three-headed dog that guards the entrance to the Underworld. Hesiod raises the stakes to 50 heads (*Theogony* 312) and Apollodoros or his source tries a reconciliation: three dog's heads, but umpteen snake's heads on his back (Ap 2.5.12). This just shows how the detail of Greek monsters and, more broadly, myths is not fixed and compulsory, but can be varied to suit an occasion or one's taste. We find about 70 depictions on archaic vases of Geryon, the three-headed (or -bodied) guardian of cattle, often with Orthos his two-headed dog. Even the Hydra was attempted – though that was more of a challenge, as artists find a head-count above three really quite a problem.

Any account of Herakles' supposed life will reveal a multitude of locations in his stories and cause him to wander widely in any composite version. In particular, the myth of Geryon's cattle has been used as an aetiology for a scatter of local sanctuaries, rites and even herds of animals from Spain to Scythia (chapter 8.2). When we look at the various labours, individual local tales of Herakles must have been put together, so forming a series of actions for him. This is the route to the canon of tasks, a set list of tasks, finally settling at 12, though Apollodoros is still struggling to make them 10 (Eurystheus disallowed two – Ap 2.5.11).

The canon of labours invokes a sense of endurance and trials, an extended fiction of an initiatory period. It lasts 10 years (Ap 2.4.12 *fin.*),[9] or the first 10 tasks are complete in eight years and one month (Ap 2.5.11 *init.*). The latter is a recognisable periodicity in Greek festivals, the so-called *enneateris* ('nine-year period', i.e. every eighth year, as Greeks counted inclusively); the former is the Trojan period, the period for which Arcadians were doomed to be Wolves (p. 111 above). This leads to a better understanding of Herakles' *basse couture*. Lion-skin and club are not marks of civilisation, but of the outside: the lion-skin matches the deer-skins of Dionysos' savage Maenads, and the club (and even bow) contrasts with the spear, sword and shield of the Greek hoplite that the *polis* sent into battle – in groups, not as Herculean individuals. Cattle-rustling too is an anti-social activity, practised at borders and associated with initiation by some scholars – like Hermes' rustling of the cattle of Apollo ('Homer', *Hymn to Hermes*), Melampous' rustling of the cattle of Phylakos (Ap 1.9.12) and Nestor's tale of his own cattle-raiding exploits in his youth (*Iliad* 11.671–761).

At the same time, Herakles' combats often share something with myths of gods and with myths of beginnings. A number of Herakles' victims are definitively pigeon-holed by Hesiod as off-spring of Typhon and the viperous Echidna: Orthos, Kerberos and the Hydra (Hesiod, *Theogony* 306–15). Even worse, the Nemean lion is said by Hesiod to be the offspring of Echidna and Orthos, though Apollodoros 'normalises' it as one of Typhon's (Hesiod, *Theogony* 327; Ap 2.5.1). And the serpent that guarded the apples of the Hesperides was said by a source of Apollodoros (2.5.11) to be another offspring of Typhon and Echidna. So snakey, monstrous autochthony is supplanted by a new arrival in Herakles' myth too; and the specific connection with the major enemy of the gods is a sign of the slot which Herakles and his myths are meant to occupy. It is not untrue to the spirit of these myths that Stoic philosophers finally viewed the Labours of

Herakles as the civilising of the world, making it possible for men to live in it. It is a sort of clearance of a primeval jungle. There may also, as Fontenrose (1959: 350–2) thinks, be a hint of primeval creation of order out of the chaos of the primeval waters in Herakles' defeat of the greatest Greek river, Acheloös. It would be a simple matter, too, to patch in the Hydra ('Water'-creature) at this point. Maybe not dissimilar is the fact that Herakles' cattle tend to wander in the marginal territories where Greeks establish colonies and the Greek way of life – as though his slaughter of Geryon had paved the way for them and their stock-rearing (Burkert 1977: 283).

Herakles' labours should fuel psychoanalytical interpetations. Who could resist the massive flushing of the stables of Augeas of accumulated horse-droppings by the diversion of the Rivers Alpheios and Peneios? He has quite enough dealings with snakey monsters. And his winning of the Golden Apples of the Hesperides, as they denote breasts and the maternal, is 'fulfilment of the wish to be reunited with the nurturant mother' – a return to the 'symbiotic paradise' where infant and mother are one and the infant has not become aware of his separate identity (Caldwell 1989: 161).

Tasks in the west have suggested the world of the dead, suitably located where the sun sets. The Garden of the Hesperides is in the remotest west, with its golden apples (we are not told what happens if you eat one, though it seems the obvious question). Geryon, in particular, has been seen as a lord of the dead, with Orthos as his Kerberos, by various scholars since Radermacher in 1903.[10] He lives beyond the River Okeanos on Erytheia ('Red' island, where he keeps his red cattle) and Herakles actually uses the Sun's personal transport, a golden cup, to get there, at least in Stesichoros' *Garyonaïs* (*c.* 550 BC).[11] Geryon is part of a pattern. With monstrous body he is there in the west with cattle which Herakles must win (and gets a helping hand from Menoites, Hades' herdsman, who just happens to be there with his own herd – Ap 2.5.10). Meanwhile, 'Periklymenos', son of Neleus, whose name is a title of the Underworld god, guards cattle which Neleus has stolen from Herakles and which again Herakles must recover, in a cave at Pylos – Pylos, which is known as the scene of a fight between Herakles and Hades and whose name suggests *pyle* ('Gate' . . . to where?). Periklymenos can change the shape of his body (Herakles finally kills him in the shape of a bee), just like the

Indian equivalent of Geryon, Viśvarūpa ('All-shapes'). An Indo-European myth of the winning of cattle from the Underworld looks plausible. Perhaps, too, the Hesperides ('Evening'-maids/ nymphs?) and their apples belong in a twilight world. Even the lake of Lerna, the habitat of the Hydra, may be an entrance to the Underworld and the Hydra its guardian, as Kerényi believed.[12] Thus several of Herakles' labours may be equivalent to, or may originate in myths equivalent to, a defeat of death: the bringing of Kerberos from the Underworld is simply a more overt – or better preserved – version of this type of Herakles myth.

That a hero should overcome death, or attempt to, is no surprise. In Sumerian/Babylonian mythology Gilgameš, accompanied by his friend, his wild (non-urban) counterpart Enkidu, performs a number of feats. But his last is to travel to the edges of the earth to seek – and fail – to acquire immortality. Odysseus too must overcome death and return; and even his period in a *cave* with a one-eyed monster (thought sometimes to be an otherworld characteristic, on no evidence known to me) has been seen as a visit to death – when it is not seen as initiatory, with characteristic loss of name (does he not become 'No one' in order to fool the Kyklops?). The voyage of Argo perhaps itself suggests a visit to another world, beyond the Clashing Rocks – unless they represent the birth trauma. Herakles himself, unusually, will in the end achieve immortality: his mortal flesh burnt away in the pyre on Mt Oite, he will alone of men become a god.

Herakles' character has strange aspects. Naturally he has the strength and ingenuity to defeat interesting and problematic monsters like any folk-tale hero (though they might benefit from more magic and cleverness). The skin of the Nemean lion can only be penetrated by its own claws; the heads of the Hydra must be cauterised by fire – only fire, it seems, can counter the 'Water' beast. The Kerynian hind was sacred and might not be wounded, so he physically caught it. And so on. Yet one cannot help feeling that the brawn of our hero is more apt to be stressed than his brains. He is also a man of superhuman appetites. This was the man who made Thespios' daughters pregnant in one night, all 50 of them (well, 49 – the remaining one becomes his virgin priestess). In another version it was one a night for 50 nights running, though it is not clear that this shows any less stamina.[13] This is the man who, when he feels hungry, unyokes an ox and eats it (Ap 2.7.7 – a similar story is told on Lindos too). However, his strength is extreme and he is exceptional at awful cost. He is always ready to slaughter and seduce. He murders Iphitos, a guest in his own house, and steals his mares or cattle (Ap 2.6.2). And his capture of Oichalia (wherever that was) and the slaughter of its king, Eurytos, can be seen as motivated by his adulterous lust for the king's daughter Iole (Euripides, *Hippolytos* 545; Sophocles, *Women of Trachis* 351–5). Similarly, he captures Ephyre, kills the king and beds the daughter (Diodoros 4.36.1). He is no better with children. He cuffs a boy serving him water and accidentally kills him (accidental killing is characteristic of heroes – Brelich 1958: 69f.). Worse, his strength and energy can spill over into a terrible madness – that is how he comes to kill his own children (Euripides, *The Madness of Herakles*).

However these stories originated, and that too is worth thought, their adoption into a single fiction, with all the systematic views that result, creates an awful and extreme model of heroism which Greeks thought it appropriate to entertain. Greek heroes are not saints, even by Greek standards. The terrible anger of Achilles corresponds to the terrible violence of Herakles. And the impulsive, reckless anger of Oedipus in Sophocles' *Oedipus the King* is at least in part what a Greek audience might expect and even demand of so exceptional a person. Greek supermen are dangerous because they are beyond conforming to the standards which confine ordinary men, and their aberrations are no less typical a feature than their exemplary qualities (Brelich 1958: chapter 4).

The stories of Herakles are not so much diverse (Kirk 1977: 296) as responsive to various views and interpetations: they are *multivalent*. And in that lies the success which they have had in arousing the interest and enthusiasm of ancient and modern audiences. Aetiology, creation, civilisation; heroism and beyond; proof of self and survival of the ultimate trial – death. Yet he also embodies stark contradictions (ibid.: 286). Outlaw, almost savage, to be admired by Greeks in well-tempered cities. A particular case is Herakles' sexuality: the ultimate man, hyperendowed with testosterone, yet subject to King Eurystheus and enslaved to Queen Omphale (though this latter theme is unaccountably missing from archaic and classical art). In some versions (and this is popular in Hellenistic and Roman painting) he even exchanges clothing with her – a motif which reappears when he is reduced to dressing as a woman on Kos to escape the local tribe, the Meropes (so providing a *hieros logos* both for his transvestite priest there and for a marriage custom found also at Argos involving bridegrooms dressing in women's clothing).[14] At some of his shrines women may not even be admitted, yet he spends plenty of time serving women and it was his gallantry to Deianeira, saving her from the attentions of the centaur Nesos, that made her his wife (but led to his death – Loraux 1990: 25, 27).

What we make of these contradictions, particularly the sexual ones, depends very much on our approach to Greek myth as a whole. Loraux (1990: 49) captures current interests when she sees 'the Greeks' as using 'their story of Herakles to pose the problem of their status as sexed creatures endowed with political power'. Personally, I am interested to see how a ritual background leads to the stories and how their paradoxicality motivates their survival: it is precisely because Herakles is generally seen as such a macho hero that a story of him skulking in women's clothing has such force. Or is that just too superficial?

Feats of other heroes

The monsters of heroes other than Herakles are more clearly something to be overcome in order to achieve a target. Viewed from an initiatory perspective, they are an extreme presentation of the dangers encountered and qualities proved in the testing of the liminal period. Viewed from a cosmogonical perspective they represent the dangerous confusion of forms that must be overcome to establish civilisation. Viewed from a psychoanalytic perspective, they hold different meanings, as we shall see.

Bellerophon (Ap 2.3) must overcome the Chimaira, probably a Near Eastern (Burkert 1984: 23) collage of lion, snake and – terrifyingly! – goat. The story is set, rather unusually, not on the mainland but at a margin of the Greek world, in Lykia. Combined with this deed is his defeat of the non-Greek, pre-Greek Solymoi – and those representatives of a disturbed social order, the Amazons. However, King Iobates, who has set him these tasks, does not reward him, but has him ambushed.

> As a result of this Bellerophon stepped into the sea and cursed him, praying to Poseidon that the land might become fruitless and unprofitable. Then he went away after his curse and a wave arose and flooded the land and it was a terrible sight as the sea advanced at a height and hid the plain. The men begged

Bellerophon to relent but failed; so the women drew up their underwear and confronted him. So he went backwards out of shame and the wave is said to have gone back with him.

(Plutarch, *Virtues of Women* 248a–b)

Now the story can proceed and Bellerophon have his reward – the king's daughter and the kingdom.

The extraordinary ending of this story points, I think, to ritual and in particular to those festivals that suspend the normal running of society so that it may be recreated.[15] Floods, whether of Deukalion or as often of Poseidon, belong with prehistory and creation of a definitive order of things, because their function is to blot out the previous order. They go with the time of Kekrops in Athens (Ap 3.14.1) and the time of Nyktimos and his Pelasgians in Arcadia (Ap 3.8.2). Conflict of the sexes and re-creation of the institution of marriage (cf. p. 153 below on matrilinearity) is equally part of the recognition of necessary arrangements for civilisation which are characteristically included in this network of ideas and of rituals.[16] Here the ritual assertion of women's sexuality causes chaos to recede.

The word 'sexuality' immediately lets the psychoanalysts in. Slater (1968: 333–6) underlines the extent to which Bellerophon is involved with women. His initial problems are caused by his rejection of the sexual advances of Proitos' wife (the Potiphar's wife motif);[17] he then slays a female monster, the Chimaira, and defeats the Amazons, only to be defeated by the sexual display of the Xanthian women. 'He does not know how to placate or please the father, and in seeking him is rejected by him.' In Greece the maternal threat is not cushioned, as it is in the biblical family, by 'a strong male role model . . . producing a more brittle, phallic, and narcissistic male, longing for a father but unable to tolerate one' (ibid.: 1968: 335). I am not going to evaluate this interpretation, but I will add two puzzles: (1) what exactly is the story of the Xanthian women trying to tell us through comparison and contrast with the tale of Bellerophon's defeat of the Amazons? (2) is the answer to (1) also applicable to the contrast between Herakles' defeat of Hippolyte, queen of the Amazons, and his demise through the love of Deianeira?

Perseus (Ap 2.4) is very similar. His king, Akrisios, is hostile because of Danaë, who functionally corresponds to Proitos' wife. Her sexuality is an issue, though this time it is Zeus who exploits it to Akrisios' discomfiture. Proitos and Akrisios are of course twins, which forms an interesting link between the two stories. Danaë and Perseus are put in a chest which is washed up on Seriphos. Now enter the secondary king to order the task – Polydektes (the Iobates of this story). The task is to bring back the Gorgon's head (cf. the Chimaira). With magical help (cf. Pegasos) he achieves his objective. Apollodoros mentions no defeat of Amazons, but what is this at Argos . . .

> The tomb nearby is said to be that of a Maenad called 'Dance' [*Choreia*], because they say that she and other women joined Dionysos' campaign against Argos, but that Perseus, when he won the battle, slew most of the women.
>
> (Pausanias 2.20.4)

Finally, Perseus has the task of releasing Andromeda – winning her hand in marriage – which he can only do by overcoming a sea-monster sent against the land by Poseidon. This is set at Joppa in Palestine, even more marginal than Bellerophon's Lykia.

These myths are not just similarly structured, they are versions of the same myth. The association with maenads is especially interesting in the light of our comments on ritual above. It points to the ritual conflict of the sexes in the Argive Dionysos festival, the Agriania, just as we know happened in its Boiotian equivalent, the Agrionia (Dowden 1989: 82–5). This festival is the setting for the whole renewal sequence. Yet this may not exhaust Perseus' ritual connections: Müller (1825: 310) suggested that the cult of Athene on the acropolis of Argos, 'Larisa', was the 'principal factor in the formation of the myth' of Perseus and the Gorgon Medousa. After all, Athene watches over him in this quest and obtains the Gorgon's head for her shield at the end of the day; and Akrisios' tomb was also to be found on Larisa. This Athene is also associated with stories of Diomedes: the Palladion which he and Odysseus were said to have stolen from Troy (Ap, *Ep.* 5.13) was housed in Argos (as well as Athens) and his escapade in *Iliad* 5 where he rides with Athene is reflected in an Argive ritual where the image of Athene is carried off for renewal by bathing – in a chariot accompanied by the Shield of Diomedes (Burkert 1985: 140).

Perseus' myth lends itself to interesting psychoanalytical discussion. However sceptical one is about the whole psychoanalytic method, we have only to look at 'enclosure in a chest with one's mother in sea' to understand what words will follow this colon:

ante-natal, intrauterine state, amniotic fluid. The Gorgon will generally end up as female, even maternal, genitalia: 'there are several representations of castrating "phallic" females in the monsters of Greek myth: for example the Gorgons, who had snakes for hair and rendered a man impotent by their look' (Caldwell 1989: 153); 'a symbol of the mother's sexual demands on the child' (Slater 1968: 32).

Perseus indeed, in Slater's view, reflects what the world was like for Greek children (at least, upper-class Athenian ones in the Classical Age): closeted with the womenfolk, the father absent doing what a man has to do. Perseus is 'in effect fatherless' (Slater 1968: 313); he is his unmarried mother's champion (ibid.: 32); his mother is, however, so close that her intense interest in him causes anxiety. It is mothers who have ambitions for their sons (ibid.: 31): Danaë is close to Perseus, Thetis to Achilles – and Olympias, we might add, to Alexander the Great. The bogies that terrify children – Lamia, Gorgo, Empusa, Mormo – are all (ibid.: 64) connected with fears of the mother's sexuality. Here perhaps we see the method's over-indulgence in sex. It is simpler to view these monsters as, yes, reflecting the role of mothers in Greek society (as in other societies – cf. Dvořák's *Noonday Witch*), but in a different way: do they not rather project the mother's power to frighten children by means of the hurtful characteristics that she denies herself?

It is difficult to know quite how far to follow the sometimes tempting reconstructions of the psychoanalysts. Personally, the point at which I lose confidence is when Caldwell (1989: 43) asks why the (of course) Oedipal son Bellerophon rejects his 'mother's' advances. True, the orthodox psychoanalytic explanation might be that he fears punishment by his father. But Caldwell prefers 'performance anxiety' as an explanation. Only subsequently does he gain Pegasos, doubly phallic because he flies and because riding him has the virility of riding a powerful motor bike (Caldwell 1989: 42, 191). Then he defeats the snakey female. And after that he is 'equipped' to take Andromeda – whose name, AndroMEDa uncannily reflects the same word for 'mastery' that gives us MEDousa (Slater 1968: 332). It is best to keep the 'sea monster' away from her (ibid.).

The prominence of **Theseus** is usually said to go with the rise of democratic Athens at the end of the sixth century BC, though that is not the whole story. He compares with Bellerophon and

Perseus in his defeat of Amazons and in his slaughter of a monster resulting from Poseidon's anger. The Minotaur results from the coupling of Minos' wife with a bull which Minos had fraudulently retained after Poseidon had sent it to him in response to a prayer. This theme connects with Minos' desire (successful, it appears) to rule the sea. This is the creature he slays, and as a result he wins Ariadne, though she then passes to Dionysos (Ap *Ep.* 1.9), lord of the Agrionia. So there may be something of the Bellerophon–Perseus type here. If we now add in the death of Theseus' father Aigeus, it becomes fairly clear that renewal is the purpose: Theseus returns to replace Aigeus.[18] Other details connect with a more detailed form of renewal, initiation: two of his party of seven youths dress in girls' clothing (cf. p. 118 above) and the black sails with which he returns to Athens are the *aition* for the black cloaks of Athenian ephebes. More specifically, the expedition to Crete and back is closely associated with the Oschophoria at Athens which involved a procession led by two boys in girls' clothes towards the marginal, boundary village of Skiron (Vidal-Naquet 1981: 156–8). So in this case we appear to have a myth to go with a passage rite.

Slater (1968: 390) finds Theseus interesting because, unlike Bellerophon or Perseus, he has a supportive father, Aigeus. But the Labyrinth in which the Minotaur lives is constructed in psychoanalytic mode as 'reversal of the birth journey . . . encountering a phallic paternal object and destroying it' (ibid.: 391).[19] Thus an Oedipal conclusion is reached. Others have thought more of his reaching adulthood by penetration with the assistance of a virgin. Meanwhile, his defeat of Amazons 'seems quite in keeping with the misogyny of Athenian thought' (ibid.: 393) and the Potiphar's – or Proitos' – wife motif displaying 'the danger of mature feminine passion' is transferred to his stepson Hippolytos.

Personally, I am more intrigued by the shifting figure of Poseidon. He occurs in contexts of male initiation – it is he who lies with 'female' Kainis (like a Cretan?, cf. chapter 7.2) and then grants her a sex-change and invincibility as Kaineus (Ap *Ep.* 1.22). In these myths he supplies monsters, just as he will beget monstrous and formidable sons, Busiris for Herakles and Polyphemos for Odysseus. The sea over which he rules threatens to overwhelm the land in primordial times. And yet he has some special connection with the heroes who succeed: the wave recedes with Bellerophon son of Glaukos ('grey', name of a sea hero) son of

Poseidon; one candidate for father of Theseus is Poseidon – and Müller (1825: 271f.) argued temptingly that Aigeus was another Poseidon. Perseus himself comes out of the ocean. So it is that these heroes have power in the very element that is the antithesis of civilisation.

The typical hero-story

Another approach to the mythology of heroes is to observe the similarities between their sequences of stories. To what extent is there a common formula that holds them together?

This type of approach emerges from the study of folk-tales, where more specific social approaches are excluded by the lack of local data in the tales themselves. Hence, though a psychoanalytic approach is possible (Bettelheim 1976), much rests on the identification of the basic building-blocks or motifs out of which the stories are constructed (which have been indexed in the remarkable volume of Aarne-Thompson 1964) and of the typical patterning of those motifs into recognisable sequences. Even the study of the diffusion of tales from one culture to another rests ultimately on this sort of analysis, because one has to be able to identify the stories which one alleges are spreading from culture to culture. The relationship of Greek myths to folk-tale is a thorny one, but inasmuch as both are sets of traditional tales composed from recurring motifs the same analysis of structure should be applicable. Indeed, folk-tale motifs often appear in Greek myth, though they may be more visible in some myths than in others, for instance in the Perseus and Andromeda sequence.

The hero, with his feats and trials, suggests it may be possible to draw up a typical classification of motifs. Such a classification was suggested by Lord Raglan and applied to a sequence of heroes from classical, biblical, medieval and other cultures:

1 The hero's mother is a royal virgin;
2 His father is a king, and
3 Often a near relative of his mother, but
4 The circumstances of his conception are unusual, and
5 He is also reputed to be the son of a god.
6 At birth an attempt is made, usually by his father or his maternal grandfather, to kill him, but
7 He is spirited away, and
8 Reared by foster-parents in a far country.

9 We are told nothing of his childhood, but

10 On reaching manhood he returns or goes to his future kingdom.

11 After a victory over the king and/or a giant, dragon, or wild beast,

12 He marries a princess, often the daughter of his predecessor, and

13 Becomes king.

14 For a time he reigns uneventfully, and

15 Prescribes laws, but

16 Later he loses favour with the gods and/or his subjects, and

17 Is driven from the throne and city, after which

18 He meets with a mysterious death,

19 Often at the top of a hill.

20 His children, if any, do not succeed him.

21 His body is not buried, but nevertheless

22 He has one or more holy sepulchres.

(Raglan 1936: 179f.)

The reader will, I am sure, find this a most interesting attempt at defining a common structure of hero-tales, though it is not clear what conclusions could be drawn from its application, even if it could be successfully applied – and Brelich (1958: 66) viewed Raglan's scheme as 'an undoubtedly mistaken attempt'. This is a problem altogether with motivic analysis, that it requires some further theoretical explanation or context – perhaps structuralist or psychoanalytic?

A more abstract and sophisticated sequence was developed by Vladimir Propp, who in 1928 published a Russian book classifying Russian folk-tales (*byliny*), though since his ideas became more widely known (English translation, 1958) his method has been seen as having wider applicability. Like Raglan, he viewed a story as a sequence of slots ('functions') which might be realised by various particular motifs. The order of these 'functions' was constant, but stories did not generally include all functions. I hope it will be helpful to the reader to see these laid out, even though it will be necessary to turn to Propp's book (1968) for any adequate understanding of what is implied:

1   One of the members of a family absents himself from home.
2   An interdiction is addressed to the hero.
3   The interdiction is violated.

4   The villain makes an attempt at reconnaissance.

5   The villain receives information about his victim.

6   The villain attempts to deceive his victim in order to take possession of him or of his belongings.

7   The victim submits to deception and thereby unwittingly helps his enemy.

8   The villain causes harm or injury to a member of a family.

8a   One member of a family either lacks something or desires to have something.

9   Misfortune or lack is made known: the hero is approached with a request or command; he is allowed to go or he is dispatched.

10   The seeker agrees to or decides upon counteraction.

11   The hero leaves home.

12   The hero is tested, interrogated, attacked, etc., which prepares the way for his receiving either a magical agent or helper.

13   The hero reacts to the actions of the future donor.

14   The hero acquires the use of a magical agent.

15   The hero is transferred, delivered, or led to the whereabouts of an object of search.

16   The hero and the villain join in direct combat.

17   The hero is branded.

18   The villain is defeated.

19   The initial misfortune or lack is liquidated.

20   The hero returns.

21   The hero is pursued.

22   Rescue of the hero from pursuit.

23   The hero, unrecognised, arrives home or in another country.

24   A false hero presents unfounded claims.

25   A difficult task is proposed to the hero.

26   The task is resolved.

27   The hero is recognised.

28   The false hero or villain is exposed.

29   The hero is given a new appearance.

30   The villain is punished.

31   The hero is married and ascends the throne.

Propp's method, whose application his enthusiasts have extended, perhaps has a tendency to empty narratives of their contents rather than to uncover a structure which makes sense of the narrative, as a Lévi-Strauss or a Detienne might. This indeed was Lévi-Strauss' criticism of Propp.[20] Much more educative a method, if not yet attuned to the contradictions and ambivalences perceived by structuralists, was the thoroughgoing examination of the characteristics and associations of Greek heroes in Brelich's 1958 study. The richness of his account does not lend itself to summary, but broadly his approach is as follows. The ancient elements of individual myths cannot be securely identified (1958: 45) and in any case what is most characteristic of hero-myths is recurring themes and concerns (ibid.: 67). As a result it is best to take hero-myths as a whole and identify theme by theme their place in Greek culture and values. Thus Brelich discusses in order: death, combat, competitions, prophecy, healing, mysteries, the transition into adulthood, the city, kinship groups, human activities and later in the book the relationship of heroes to other beings, in particular the gods. This is more plainly a route to the understanding of Greek mythology than schematic lists.

Chapter 9

Mythic society

9.1 POLITICAL POWER IN MYTH

Kings

Myth's distance from real political life is specially marked by the convention that mythic states are ruled by kings. There are no oligarchies or democracies. In this light, it is a *tour de force* that Theseus is portrayed (e.g. by Aristotle, *Constitution of the Athenians* fr. 4) as having encouraged democracy and rolled back the frontiers of autocracy, the Gorbachev of myth.

How do men of myth become kings? Nestor reminds Achilles in *Iliad* 1.279 of the special position of 'the sceptre-holding king to whom Zeus has granted *kydos* [glory]'. They are *diogeneis* (Zeus-born). And naturally, as Zeus is the Olympian model of their sovereignty. Every ninth year Minos communes with Zeus at Knossos (*Odyssey* 19.178f.). And the festival of Zeus Lykaios comes round every ninth year – where Zeus reviewed Lykaon's kingship and found it wanting. Some kings of myth are simply there from the beginning. Some inherit from their father, like Agamemnon from Atreus. Yet it is not always the oldest who inherits – there are hints of *ultimogeniture*, inheritance by the youngest. Thus Nestor, king of Pylos, is the youngest son of Neleus; in Arcadia it is Lykaon's youngest son, Nyktimos, that succeeds him (Ap 3.8.1–2); and, of course, Zeus is Kronos and Rhea's youngest. Is it that renewal demands a reversal of the laws of succession?

There is some recognition of the spread of power from one centre to another: thus Orestes becomes king of Sparta as well as Mycenae. And Menelaos, Agamemnon's (younger?) brother, becomes king of Sparta. Yet here there are conflicting signals: Sparta is acquired by the Mycenaean family twice in two generations. This story is sending a message linking these two centres and asserting, maybe, the authority of old Mycenae over a Sparta now out of its control. Further, the Mycenaean duo Agamemnon and Menelaos, rescuers of Helen, replay the role of the twin Dioskouroi, equally rescuers of Helen. Authority should have passed from Tyndareus to the Dioskouroi, but their fate takes them elsewhere, Tyndareus steps aside and we are left with Agamemnon and Menelaos in their slot – a slot which historically is filled by the strange Spartan institution of the dual kingship. In mythic terms Agamemnon and Menelaos look like Sanskrit **avatars**, human realisations of gods (just as in the *Mahābhārata*, the twin Nāsatyas are avatars of the Dioskouroi equivalent, the Aśvins).

Marriage matters too: Orestes acquires his entitlement to the throne of Sparta by marriage with Menelaos' daughter, Hermione. Menelaos came to the throne through his marriage with Tyndareus' daughter, Helen. Odysseus' winning of Ikarios' daughter, Penelope, has a high profile in the mythology – a myth which Homer, in his characteristic way, replays through the perverted attempt of the suitors to win Penelope's hand in Ithaka. Is she also implicitly the key to the throne? In these cases the succession to the throne passes via a woman. This is not matriarchy (see the next section), for women are not queens in their own rite, nor is it matrilinearity, for power passes via daughters and wives, not mothers. Indeed the marriage is called into existence precisely because the daughter cannot wield power herself. This belongs in the broader Greek cultural picture of the restrictions upon women inheriting property. Property can only pass to a household, an *oikos*, of which a man must be in control, and a man who dreams of wealth and power should look to marry an heiress. The marriage of Oedipus and Jocasta (apart from its incestuous difficulties) is based on this type too: as the old king is dead and there is no suitable relative to marry Jocasta and take the *oikos* (Kreon is her brother), an outsider is needed.

More unusual is the story of the prophet Melampous, who cures the Women of Argos (and/or the Daughters of Proitos) and thereby gains a third of the kingdom for himself, and another third for his brother Bias – whilst the remaining third goes to the son of the present king (Ap 2.2.2). Bias does well out of Melampous in an earlier story too, when Melampous by his skill obtains cattle that will persuade Neleus to give his daughter Pero to Bias

(Ap 1.9.12). But in that case the throne is not on offer: it is, presumably, Nestor's.

A final way to become king is of course by ousting. This happens in various ways. Zeus overthrows his father Kronos. Pelops, seeking to win a throne by marriage to Hippodameia, in fact causes the death of her father Oinomaos in a motoring accident. Theseus' return causes the death of his father Aigeus. Perseus turns Polydektes of Seriphos to stone – does he gain the throne? Should not Herakles' labours lead to the replacement of Eurystheus? These sorts of examples, considered together with Minos' renewal of power after a fixed period and with Frazer's notions of a dying king, led to the mirage of actual kings ritually being slaughtered by their successors at the beginning of the twentieth century (see, for example, Harrison 1912: 223). The mistake, however, is only a slight one: the theme of renewal of kingship is certainly present and fits in well enough with other aspects of renewal (p. 145 above); the old scholars simply took it too literally, a perpetual danger with myth.

Matriarchy, matrilinearity

> Greek myths of matriarchy, like the South American, are didactic rather than historical.
>
> (Lefkowitz 1986: 22)

Homer recounts an oddity of the Lykians, a non-Greek people who support the Trojans. Their Bellerophon had two sons and one daughter, but Zeus lay with the daughter, Laodameia, and power apparently passed (thus legitimised) through her to Sarpedon (*Iliad* 6.196–9). It is a real question, which a Byzantine scholar asked, why Bellerophon's sons did not rather inherit the kingdom.[1]

Is this perhaps one of those topsy-turvy foreign practices, like Egyptian women urinating standing up (Herodotos 2.35)? This model of what it is to be a foreigner leads to Herodotos' view (1.173) that the Lykians named their children after their mothers, not their fathers, and reckoned their descent (and legitimacy) by the female line – by **matrilinearity**. But is it historically true? Herodotos' statement follows on from a mention of this Homeric case of Sarpedon, scarcely itself founded on genuine ethnographic observation of how power was inherited amongst the Lykians. We should think rather of a clever predecessor of

Herodotos (Hekataios?) reading his Homer and deducing Lykian matrilinearity, perhaps with a little support from the rather less surprising system of primogeniture – inheritance by the eldest whether male *or female* (Pembroke 1967: 21f.). After Herodotos, Greek authors have their usual lack of scruples in elaborating on flimsy evidence and on each other: Nikolaos of Damascus tells us how amongst the Lykians only daughters could inherit property – and Herakleides Pontikos (a pupil and associate of Plato and Aristotle) even asserts that the Lykians had been ruled by women since time immemorial (tell that to Sarpedon!). In the real world, Lykian inscriptions may not quite reach back to Herodotos' time, but they give no hint that what he says is true. A myth has been conjured up around these Lykians, pigeon-holing them as pre-civilised, as Pembroke saw (ibid.: 34), because matrilinearity belongs with the state of lawless promiscuity which (of course) prevailed before the invention of marriage.

Homer's myth and Greek historians' myths about their neighbouring peoples are an even worse basis for Bachofen's (1815–87) romantic idea that once long ago, before classical culture, **matriarchy** (*Mutterrecht* or 'Mother-Right') – had prevailed in these primal Aegean cultures and indeed in all societies during the course of their evolution. Homer's Lykian myth is not, however, wholly exceptional: Argive myth told how King Temenos precipitated a crisis by transferring his authority not to his sons but to his son-in-law Deiphontes who married his daughter Hyrnetho (P 2.19; Ap 2.8.5). And Spartan myth can be viewed as diverting power past Kastor and Polydeukes to Helen and son-in-law Menelaos. Here it may be appropriate to note that the Helen and Hyrnetho who share this format of story are both recipients of cult.[2]

Matriarchy, according to Greeks, belongs at the ends of the earth: Amazons lived beyond the Black Sea, or, when that was no longer far enough (as Lefkowitz wryly observes, 1986: ch.1), in Skythia, or maybe in Aithiopia. Or perhaps they had once existed but were defeated by a male emblem, a Herakles, Theseus, Perseus or Achilles. Amazons are there to tell us how the world isn't. It is not so different from the disenfranchisement of women under Kekrops in the wake of Athene's victory over Poseidon (chapter 5.6). In other societies, too, the myth of matriarchy belongs to 'a prior and chaotic era before the present social order was established' (Bamberger 1974: 276). In our own day, however, the myth of matriarchy has gained new power in relation to a feminist present and is perceived not as a period in prior times ripe for termination, but as a model which recalcitrantly refuses to exemplify itself in history. We make myths serve our times, just as Bachofen did for the upright Victorian matron.

King's power in colonies

A different way of becoming king is to be sent out to lead a new colony. So, for instance, Leukippos son of King Makareus ('Blest') of Lesbos founds a colony on Rhodes, and another Leukippos is sent out by King Admetos of Pherai (Thessaly) to become the founder of Magnesia on the (River) Maeander (Dowden 1989: 63f.). Colonisation is a frequent occurrence in Greek history and prehistory and has one key difference from migration, namely that some stay in the original centre while others depart. As a result a new source of authority must be created for those that depart and this is presented sometimes in the mythologem of the colony being founded by the king's son. Looking back across Greek history colonies were founded (1) in the Mycenaean period (e.g. Lesbos, Rhodes), (2) in the early Dark Ages by Aeolian Greeks (in the Troad for instance, but also as far south as Smyrna) and (3) in succession to the Aeolians by the Ionian Greeks (hence what we call Ionia). There had been kings in some and maybe all of these colonies (we hear of kings at Miletos, for instance) and it would indeed be likely that a monarchy would found a monarchical colony (by ultimogeniture so as to preserve the succession at home?). So myth in this case may not be inaccurate in depicting the leadership of the colonising party. As forms of government changed, this monarch whose key role it is to found the new colony (like the legendary founder of cities) becomes more narrowly viewed: less a king or king's son now, more an *oikistes* ('founder') to receive cult after his death. Even in classical times colonies had an official *oikist*, not a committee of management, and in some ways this is the only significant survival of monarchy into the Classical Age.

Priests and prophets

Priests are quite rare in Homer and perhaps only become a necessity when the habit of building temples is developed. These temples belong very much to *polis* culture and have been seen as substituting divine authority for the authority that had once been the king's, as in the cases where temples are built on the site of the old palace.[3] We therefore do not expect priests in myth. On the other hand, prophets must once have been part of the regular apparatus of society. Kalchas in Homer, though he has a wider history than Homer implies, at least occupies a recognisable augur's place beside the *wanax*. And the skills such as understanding bird-song (even woodworm-language!) enjoyed by Melampous reflect those professed regularly in other societies. Teiresias may be best consulted dead, as by Odysseus in Book 11 of the *Odyssey* and by real Greeks at Orchomenos, but again he shows the status of 'approved prophet'. Similarly, Amphiaraos may be consulted dead in Boiotia, but in the campaign of the Seven against Thebes he has a clear role and also a status which matches that of the overlord, Adrastos, himself.

So in mythic times, archetypal prophets were valued consultants. There is likely to be some justification for this in facts about pre-historic society, but we must not forget either that prophets of historical times, whose ability was more open to question, needed myth's justification of their predecessors to enhance trust in their own powers. The Klytiads of Elis traced their descent back to Klytios, grandson of Amphiaraos, and one of them, Teisamenos, appears in a traditional role as prophet to the Greek army at Plataia (Herodotos 9.33). Iamos, mythic ancestor of the Iamids, was a child of Apollo who lived by the River Alpheios in Elis, where Melampous also gained his skills from Apollo. Iamos' descendants supplied the prophets of the oracle of Zeus at Olympia.

Warriors or heroes

Beyond the king and prophets stand the warriors. In Greek parlance these warriors, like the king, are 'heroes'. And this is the use from which all our senses of the word 'hero' in the end derive: to be 'heroic' is to behave like one of these heroes (on a good day); and the modern 'hero' of a play is so named because the leading figures of Greek plays had been these heroes. In Greece, we should be aware also that heroes are a class of being between man and god, receiving honours at their special cult-place, their grave. Thus heroes in myth have a nasty habit of living hard and dying young. In Dumézil's system (chapter 2.2) one expects a warrior-class separate from the kingly class and it is true that the kingly function is sometimes separated from the warrior: Eurystheus is the king, Herakles the warrior; Adrastos may lead the Seven against Thebes and even participate, but the focus may be more on the (other) warriors; Agamemnon may do some fighting at Troy, but not on Achilles' scale, as Achilles is made to complain (*Iliad* 1.226–31). Yet the message of Greek myth is not that warriors are a class apart from kings: some (Diomedes) already are kings, others will be or could have been kings. Herakles has a right to Eurystheus' position and Achilles and Hektor would in due course have become kings if only they had lived – and not died young in order to have their identity fixed for ever as warriors. Being a warrior is thus depicted as a transitional stage for a particular class, whereas being a king will involve greater age, marriage, offspring and genealogy. It is therefore to be expected that kings see their sons fight: Priam rules, Hektor fights; Nestor fights his best, but his son Antilochos occupies the Hektor slot; Peleus is left elderly and pitiable at home, but Achilles fights.

It is at this point that it becomes evident that Greek myths are fixated on the upper class, like the mythology of medieval knights. A single man – or Seven – can cause terror to a city because the rest of humanity is filtered out of the picture. Rarely in Homer do we catch sight of the others: 'and the people [*laos*] were falling'. The importance of the heroes has some partial historical justification in that they alone would have been able to afford armour, horses and chariots in the Bronze Age; they are therefore bound to become the formidable *promachoi* ('fore-fighters', usually translated 'champions'). But the justification is only partial: 20 peasants with clubs would make short shrift of Achilles. Slaves, on the other hand, are invisible in Greek myths. They existed in the Mycenaean Age as in classical times, but belong to the mechanics of society in which myth itself takes no interest. Only when a myth must be realised on the fuller canvas of epic or tragedy do serving-women, nurses, *paidagogoi* (tutors) and herdsmen appear. On the other hand, we find the servitude of Herakles to Eurystheus and to Omphale, and of Apollo as a herdsman to Admetos. But this is to reduce the great hero to the otherwise invisible servile condition for a limited period.

Heroes sometimes have one particular close friend, a *hetairos* ('companion'). It is not clear what this represents. Is it an economical image distilled from the relationship between a whole group of warriors? Is it the homosexual relationship found in initiation or the next stage, when the younger man has become a full warrior in his own right? Or is it just an exemplar for friendship, which is after all frequent enough in real life? Herakles and Iolaos belong, as we have seen, with initiatory apprenticeship – Iolaos is a 'squire' in medieval parlance. In the case of Patroklos and Achilles, we (and most Greeks) think of Achilles as the dominant partner, but Homer (perhaps wilfully) depicts Patroklos as the elder who is to guide Achilles (*Iliad* 11.786–9), surely evoking the trainee-model. Others – Theseus and Peirithoös, Orestes and Pylades – simply become bywords for friendship. There is of course no truth to uncover about these fictional friends, only questions of original context and subsequent use. The Greeks themselves differed on the extent to which the Achilles–Patroklos relationship might have been sexual (the middle road is represented in a fragment of Aeschylus' *Myrmidons*: 'our association, respectful of your thighs'!) and the mythic tradition provides no definitive answer.

Changing times

Occasionally, in the grey area between myth and history, one finds material outside the picture we have sketched and closer to later reality.

Lawgivers are a particular concern of the Archaic Age but have no niche in myth, which depicts an illiterate world and would talk about founders in any case. Lykourgos at Sparta, as we have seen, is probably entirely mythical, but his depiction as the guardian of an under-age king is more detailed than we expect of myth. The effect, whether in myth or reality, is to distance him from the system he revises, as one might expect of a lawgiver or arbitrator (compare ombudsmen). Solon, as arbitrator and lawgiver for the Athenians, added to this distance by going into exile to give his reforms a chance to work (a motif shared by the Lykourgos story). The laws of the archaic lawgivers Zaleukos (seventh century BC?)

and Charondas (sixth century BC?), figures surrounded by 'legend', were adopted by many towns in Italy and Sicily other than their own, obviously appreciating a system brought in from elsewhere. Pythagoras was welcomed from outside to Croton as an authority on moral life and law (Iamblichos, *The Pythagorean Life* 9). Perhaps we are out of myth into history by now, but the same ways of thought persist. Aristotle, in identifying lawgivers, produces what will become a new mode of genealogy for defining the authority of persons relative to each other: '[some claim that] Lykourgos and Zaleukos heard [i.e. learnt from] Thales and Charondas heard Zaleukos' (*Politics* 1274a). A few centuries earlier, Charondas would have been Zaleukos' son.

Something new is also represented by Thersites ('Rash-man'). In the epic *Aithiopis* he insults Achilles by claiming that Achilles, who has just slain the Amazon queen Penthesileia, had been in love with her. The result is that he himself is killed by Achilles. Dissension then results from this death. Back in the *Iliad* (2.212–77), Thersites is depicted as a trouble-maker for the kings, maybe in anticipation of this incident in the *Aithiopis*. Homer is clear about Thersites: he is uneducated and ugly and of a lower class than the kings. This is usually, and I think correctly, treated as an intrusion from social conditions in Homer's own time and associated with the rise of a larger armed fighting class, the hoplites. His is a lone voice, denigrated by his creators, railing against the privilege of myth.

9.2 REPELLING THE FOREIGNER AND -*MACHIES*

Art may use myth for decoration, just as narration may use it for entertainment. In neither case, however, should we lose sight of its potential for making a statement about the world and our place in it. Repelling a foreign enemy is a case in point. When the Persians were driven back in 490 and 480–479 BC, Greek culture had been saved and reasserted. This is why Herodotos' history takes the form it does: an analysis of what it is to be a foreigner and what it is to be a Greek, leading up to the successful preservation of Greek culture from the 'barbarian'. This was especially important at Athens, as Athens had undergone a major form of accreditation through her part in the defeat of Persia.

The battle of the Lapiths and the Centaurs, the **Centauromachy**, is depicted three times on the Athenian acropolis in the decades that followed the Persian Wars: on metopes on the Parthenon, on the shield of the statue of Athene Promachos on the Acropolis and even on the sandal of Athene Parthenos (Carpenter 1991: 166). It is also depicted on the west pediment of the Temple of Zeus at Olympia. How far can this be associated with the defeat of the Persians?

The role of centaurs is to be disorderly and immoral. They are half-animal; they drink too much; they cannot control their lusts; and, worst of all, they show this behaviour at a dinner party to celebrate a wedding, that of Peirithoös and Hippodameia (Ap, *Ep.* 1.21). They thus violate the laws binding guests and hosts and dissolve the social bonds which eating together creates. They represent everything which society must restrain in order to survive and it is therefore no surprise that they live in mountains. Who ever heard of a city of centaurs? How could it possibly work? To celebrate the victory of the Lapiths over the Centaurs is to celebrate the victory of the civilised *polis*. The threat from the Persians appears to have stimulated this celebration in art, though it cannot of course be guaranteed that the Persians continued to be the principal reason for the use of this socially relevant and colourful theme on public works.

The reception of such work by visitors and passers-by must have varied in its depth of resonance in any case. This, for instance, is what Pausanias, an intelligent man of the mid-second century AD, made of the Centauromachy at Olympia: 'In my opinion Alkamenes chose this topic because he learnt from Homer [*Iliad* 14.318] that Peirithoös was a son of Zeus and he knew that Theseus was the great-grandson of Pelops' (P 5.10.8). So the scene is chosen because it features Peirithoös and Theseus, who can be related to Zeus, whose temple it is, and Pelops, the local hero. Once again we are confronted by the surprising literalism of the Greeks – on whom we are trying to impose rich, subtle ideas. But of course Pausanias even mistakes the Apollo in this scene for Peirithoös.

What associations, I wonder, would occur to a viewer of Mikon's painting (*c.* 450 BC) of Theseus helping the Lapiths in their fight with the Centaurs in the Theseus shrine at Athens (P 1.17.2)? One might say that Theseus represents the Athenian role in the defeat of the Persians and their continuing naval deterrent. Equally, the scene is appropriate on the simpler grounds that it is part of the mythology of Theseus and it makes good art – as

Mikon would have known if, as is possible, he had worked on the pediment at Olympia.[4] Conversely, the statue of Athene Promachos on the Acropolis is actually a tithe from the defeated Persians (P 1.28.2), which would seem to clinch the connection. And it must be remembered that there are no literal depictions of defeated Persians in classical Athens: art like tragedy (Aeschylus' *Persai* aside) preferred to talk through myth. It is not until the time of Pergamon that we find literal Persians, even in Athens[5] – and of course by then they are to all intents and purposes mythic.

But the Centauromachy is only one of a series of mythic battles depicted on the Acropolis. The **Gigantomachy**, the battle of the Olympian gods with the Giants, has deeper roots. Obviously it is an appropriate theme to celebrate on any sacred building, confirming as it does the order imposed by the gods as a team. It is perhaps specially appropriate to Delphi, which came as close as anywhere in Greece could to general responsibility for religion: there the theme can be found on the north frieze of the Siphnian Treasury, the pediment of the Megarian Treasury and on the west pediment of the Temple of Apollo (Carpenter 1991: 75). All these depictions belong to the later sixth century BC.

At Athens, likewise, the theme erupts in the sixth century – on large, very public vases dedicated on the Acropolis around 560–550, and is traditionally woven into the *peplos* presented to Athene's statue at the Panathenaia (it is depicted there on the pediment of an archaic temple around 520 BC). Why? It is not just a question of a poem, the *Gigantomachia*, suddenly arriving on the scene and exciting artists (it doesn't seem to have excited anyone else). The mid-sixth century at Athens is the time of the tyranny of Peisistratos (except 555–546 BC) and the creation of Athens as a major power. In some way this myth, which underpins the totality of the divine order, has been made part of the image of the newly-amplified Panathenaia, which under Peisistratos became penteteric (= held every four years) like the major Panhellenic festival at Olympia. From now on, the myth is part of the grand apparatus of the Athene cult: it will be found on the east metopes of the Parthenon and on the interior of the shield of Athene Parthenos. This shield seems to have depicted the Giants in a new way and brought about a change in their iconography, to judge by contemporary vases. Giants now have skins not armour and rocks not weapons (Carpenter 1991: 75). They have been relegated to the wild and uncivilised and, in effect, reduced to the condition of

Centaurs. A new layer of meaning has been superimposed. Perhaps some may even have thought of the Persians.

The Persians are certainly at issue in our third battle, the **Amazonomachy**. Amazons, typically depicted with caps, bows, Persian trousers, axes, reflect a Greek view of barbarian gear in general (because non-Greek) and Persian gear in particular. Maybe too the servile Persians, in contrast to the freedom-loving Greeks, were classed as 'women' (Tyrrell 1984: 50–2). This battle provided the theme for the west metopes of the Parthenon and was the principal subject of Pheidias' shield of Athene Parthenos. Thus Athene's shield showed the battle with the Amazons (front) and Giants (back) and her sandal showed the battle with the Centaurs; together they encapsulated the victories of Athens and declared her image to the world.

This message was not lost on the artists of the Hellenistic Age in Pergamon, which based its claim to superpower status on its defeat of the Gauls in Asia Minor in the 230s BC. The cultural language of this remarkable art echoes that of Peisistratean Athens and deliberately evokes that of Athens after the Persian Wars. Dead Giants and dead Amazons pick up the themes of world order (this is after all an altar of Zeus) and defeat of the barbarian. Dead Persians drive home the Athenian intertext: what Athens was in the Classical Age, Pergamenes are now (much as the north metopes of the Parthenon had depicted the defeat of those earlier Asians in Troy). Dead Gauls, visibly assimilated to Giants, maybe introduce a new literalism, but transmute present achievement into myth.[6] What, no Centaurs? Look again at the agonised expressions of Pergamene Giants: do they not uncannily recall the deaths of Athenian Centaurs?[7]

9.3 MYTH AND SEXUALITY

It emerges then from an examination of Greek myth that male attitudes to women, and to themselves in relation to women, are marked by tension, anxiety and fear.

(Gould 1980: 57)

Greek mythology is by and large a man's mythology, describing a world from a man's point of view. Women are seldom considered in isolation from men, though we will consider important exceptions below, and they seldom have scope for action on their own initiative. Mostly, females are either (a) children, (b) nubile maidens or (c) married. What is absent from this female career structure is any stage between initiation and marriage – the stage which allows the male to become a warrior, prove himself and discover himself: men marry later than women. Widows are mostly ignored and single women cannot be allowed to exist, except for goddesses like Circe and Kalypso.

The tribulation of the Greek virgin

One myth plainly for women is that of Demeter and Kore (Persephone). Even this presents a grim portrait of marriage as abduction from the mother with the connivance of the father (Zeus). Yet the myth is grounded in a festival for citizen women and their daughters, the Thesmophoria, and celebrates their relationship with each other and their affinity with the productiveness of nature.

Other myths, concerning nubile maidens, can often be viewed (as in chapter 7.1) as going back to stories which must have had currency amongst females concerned with the initiation of girls. But once we set aside that antiquarian background, most often inaccessible to classical Greeks, the mythical environment becomes very hostile to these maidens. Io is the victim of the lust of Zeus and the jealousy of Hera (Ap 2.1.3); her situation is tragically explored in 'Aeschylus', *Prometheus Bound* and can only be resolved by the family line to which she gives rise: Herakles, who will incidentally release Prometheus, and ultimately Danaos and the Argives. Her consolation, then, for being exploited lies in the *oikos* to which she will give rise, as in a sense it does with every Athenian maiden. The Danaids do not murder their Egyptian husbands on their own initiative, but on their father's, because he has been forced into arranging these matches. Herakles wants the maiden Iole, but he does not woo her: he must seek the consent of the family. When they refuse he kills them all and has her anyway, though he then bequeaths her to his son Hyllos, whose influential offspring she will doubtless bear. Kreousa in Euripides' *Ion* foolishly thinks Apollo did wrong by raping her, but her offspring is Ion, eponym of the Ionians. And Kallisto, raped by Zeus, may have a rough time, what with being transformed into a bear and maybe even shot by Artemis, but never mind: her son Arkas will be the ancestor of the Arcadians.

However, the gods' lusts, though in themselves something which would get them life imprisonment in a modern society, are not trivially exercised but exist in order to beget significant offspring who will have a god at the head of their genealogy. It is doubtful therefore whether this mythology is best viewed as implementing irresponsible male fantasy, though the case of heroes, who can step beyond normal constraints (p. 140), may be different. Seduction of free-born girls was after all a crime and myth considers no others.

Some girls in Greek myth are presented as inviting their fate. The Proitids at Tiryns mocked the statue of Hera (or refused the rites of Dionysos); a girl in the *hieros logos* of Brauron sets a chain of calamities under weigh by poking fun at a tame bear (that scratches her, is killed by her brothers, and the result is plague and expiation). Two of the daughters of Kekrops, Agraulos and Herse, pry into a forbidden chest, and, seeing a snake wrapped round the infant Erichthonios, are driven mad and hurl themselves from the Acropolis (Ap 3.14.6). These strains of hazardous impulsiveness amongst girls may be reflected in a tendency of mythology to produce *hippos* ('horse') names for maidens (*Melanippe, Hippolyte, Hippodameia*), inviting Calame's suggestion (1977: 411–20) that marriage and female education both are designed to 'tame' these dangerous maidens. Of course male names also contain this element, suggesting that pride in horses went back to the Greeks' Indo-European forebears whose most momentous technological advance was horsemanship. But that does not exclude the possibility that hippic names indeed registered in the way Calame observes.

Faithless wife, passionate woman

It perhaps matches the double standards of Greek males that though men and male gods do a lot of begetting in myth, the issue of faithlessness arises only with women (the only male issue is adultery – see Thyestes, Aigisthos, Paris – where the consistent message is that adultery fails). Astonishingly, a chorus of Euripides' *Medea* puts this stress on female faithlessness down to the absence of women authors who might redress the balance ('since it would have sounded a counter-hymn to the race of males' (*Medea* 426–7)). That would imply that there was a competing women's value-system centred on securing the devotion of Greek males to their marriages, which indeed there must have been. Medea in Euripides' play, for all her excesses, plainly wins sympathy based on Jason's behaviour; Deianeira in Sophocles' *Women of Trachis* acts, with adequate approval, to restore Herakles' interest in their marriage; Clytaemestra in Aeschylus' *Agamemnon*, though a clear monster who has subverted and perverted the restraints required of women, nevertheless has an intelligible pretext for her hostility to Agamemnon in his introduction of Cassandra to the house. But for all this the real force of moral opprobrium in male–female relationships falls upon the woman: Clytaemestra (who murders her husband), Medea (who destroys her family twice, at least in the prevalent, Euripidean, version),[8] Phaidra (who attempts to seduce Hippolytos), Stheneboia (who attempts to seduce Bellerophon), Eriphyle (who makes her husband Amphiaraos join the Seven against Thebes and go to his death – selling him for a necklace – Ap 3.6.2).

The predominant message is that women are disproportionately subject to their passions. One reflection of this is Euripides' interest in the dramatic psychological colour resulting from the tragic situations so produced (nicely satirised by Aristophanes, *Frogs* 1043–54). Another, cruder, reflection is the myth of Teiresias, who alone of all human beings had been both man and woman: asked the obvious question, he replied that women enjoyed it more (as of course on a Greek male view they would) and was promptly blinded for his pains by Hera (Ap 3.6.7). It is difficult to know what stress one may appropriately put on the point, but plainly the arrangements for the Greek *oikos* and near-purdah of respectable Athenian women in the Classical Age rest on a supposed need to contain women's sexuality and the heroines of the classical stage (the most direct form of communciation through myth) often show the dangers when that sexuality is insufficiently controlled. Even locking Danaë in a chamber of bronze does not work. Zeus simply descends in a shower of golden rain (Ap 2.4.1) – later allegorised as a bribe to the servants, something which might be thought to work if your Danaë was locked (as women sometimes were) in the women's quarters:

> There is no wall, nor possession,
> Nor anything else so hard to watch over as a woman.
>
> (Euripides *Danaë* fr. 320 Nauck[2])

Tragedy extracts from mythology the themes it wishes and the versions of myths which survive, for instance in Apollodoros, are often drawn from the tragedians. It is perhaps a fine line between the dramatist's interpretation of existing values in selected myths and the creation of a new value-system by more radical re-interpretation of myth. There is no need to view the Hippolytos myth (Ap *Ep.* 1.18–19, from Euripides) as necessarily involving a harsh view of the gods, though we come away from Euripides' play with that view. In perceiving a system of values in myths as a whole, we must, I suppose, be careful to describe values which are inbuilt or consistently perceived rather than those which are peculiar to particular works of literature. So it is worth observing that this picture of the dangers of women's passion does not begin with tragedy. The story of Stheneboia (another Phaidra) is already in Homer's *Iliad*. And the *Odyssey* contrasts the intelligent and responsible mistress of the *oikos*, Penelope, with the brute sexual passions of Kalypso that restrain our Greek man from achievement of his purpose. Odysseus is also advised by Hermes, in a most curious passage, to refuse Circe's bed until he has imposed an oath on her and thereby avoided the loss of his manhood (*Odyssey* 10.301): it is not clear what exactly is envisaged, but in any case our Greek male needs some reserve and assertion before an offer of sexual relations in order to maintain his male-ness. More broadly, the whole distrust of women ('misogyny', hatred of women, seems an exaggeration) has a special place in Greek poetry from Hesiod onwards. His is, of course, the image of Pandora, the nearest thing the Greek tradition has to the biblical Eve, though like much of Hesiod's writing, this story may be new to Greek mythology.

Male sexuality: satyrs

The unacceptable extremes of male sexuality are exported from men to satyrs. These licentious creatures are part animal, like centaurs, and therefore define behaviour which is beyond the human pale. Their penises, like those of animals such as donkeys, are enormous, usually erect and not so much shown in pictures as displayed and brandished – balancing wine-cups on them is the least of their sins. Greek men, as Lissarrague has observed in this context, may not have been required to hide their genitals but equally they were expected to be discreet about them.[9] The satyrs' endless masturbation, bestiality, mutual orgies and frustrated assaults on maenads denote an excess, even if the excess is to be found amusing. These forces are, of course, part of the apparatus of the Dionysos procession and display at once the suspension of normal society implicit in much Dionysos religion and the control which the religion is none the less able to exercise over these wild instincts. It is really no different with the maenads themselves, who are at once released from their subservience as matrons to roam with menacing violence out of the city with phallic-looking poles tipped with pine-cones (*thyrsoi*) but at the same time contained within a religious organisation controlled by a male god. Perhaps Dionysos is perceived as effeminate but his most frequent processional symbol is the phallos.

Satyrs and maenads are both good material for art: they can be captured in a characteristic moment. But their strength is their weakness: they have no time-depth, no story, no names. Their iconography, their context and their behaviour define them. They are 'mythical' creatures because they belong to the common Greek imaginative inventory, their *imaginaire*.

Behaviour detrimental to the *oikos*

Mythology offers, in the end, a dialogue on the *oikos*. All heroes must in some way be legitimate, even if their parenthood involves gods and nymphs – a privilege and a convenience not open to babies of historical times. Thus Euripides in his *Bacchae* (28–9) casts Semele's sisters as wicked doubters who take a historical not a mythic view and suppose Semele's child Dionysos in fact to have been illegitimate. Adulterous liaisons cannot have offspring: Aigisthos and Clytaemestra may have consorted for 10 years, but their contraceptive practice was, it seems, immaculate. This is not of course the same as a hero born out of wedlock – that does happen, for example, Hippolytos, son of Theseus and the Amazon (Ap, *Ep.* 1.16), and all the liaisons with immortals, who with the exception of Thetis are never actually married to mortals.

Adulterous liaisons, as they cannot produce offspring, cannot succeed either. Aigisthos rules temporarily before being slaughtered by Orestes. Thyestes adultery with Atreus' wife results in his banqueting on his own children – a mushrooming disruption of the *oikos*: though Thyestes continues to exist, to the embarrassment of mythographers who shuffle him to and fro, he can only continue his influence by (unwittingly) begetting Aigisthos by his own daughter (Ap, *Ep.* 2.14), leading to a most unpleasant recognition scene in Sophocles' lost play the *Thyestes*. Thus the saga of an *oikos*, as may be expected, has something to say about the relationships that are necessary for more successful *oikoi*. Adultery is only one disruption in a house which can run to Agamemnon's sacrifice of his daughter Iphigeneia, and Orestes' slaughter of his mother Clytaemestra. A similar story results from the saga of the House of Laios at Thebes. Laios' interest in Chrysippos, however it originated (chapter 7.2), becomes the invention of a perversion of sex and is associated by an oracle with his begetting of a son, Oedipus, who will kill his father and marry his mother. In the next generation Oedipus' sons fight and kill each other – and Antigone might just be seen as over-attached to the dead Polyneikes. This is what Lévi-Strauss referred to in his treatment of the Oedipus myth (chapter 2.2) as the 'underrating' and 'overrating of blood relations'.

Conflict between the sexes

In the course of the story of Dionysos at Thebes our attention becomes fixed on King Pentheus ('Mourning'-man). He is torn apart alive, as animals are in cult, after being pursued by the maddened women. Perhaps something similar befell King Megapenthes ('Much-mourning') in the lost myth of the Agriania at Argos.

Conflict between men and women is integral to this mythology and the associated Dionysos cult, depicting the termination of the normal condition of society and the need to begin it again. At Chios and Tenedos the women are found pursuing or (in myth at any rate) killing a man; at Chaironeia they even pursue Dionysos; and conversely at Chios, Orchomenos and maybe Sikyon a group of men or an individual pursue a group of women (Dowden 1989: 84). This too is where Lykourgos, son of Dryas, fits: supposedly he is a king of the Thracian Edones (Antimachos thought he was better as an Arabian – Diodoros 3.65.7), but he has a clearly Greek name and his father Dryas rather reminds one of Dryops. In any event, according to Homer (*Iliad* 6.130–40) this Lykourgos on a fabulous (Mount) Nyseion pursued the 'nurses' of Dionysos and suffered as a result.

Conflict between the sexes occurs elsewhere too. The women of Lemnos murder their husbands, interpreted by Burkert (1970) as relating to another renewal festival, and the Danaids at Argos kill their first set of husbands, the Egyptians – though that may be more a matter of their progress to the acceptance of marriage, as befits a myth possibly once associated with a passage rite of girls (Dowden 1989: ch. 5). Likewise Amazons exist in order to fight men and to be defeated by the likes of Herakles, Theseus and Perseus (chapter 8.3).

Thus in ritual, myth and imagination, the separation and distinctive roles of the sexes are explored and presented as a hostility which is periodically in ritual, and once for all in myth, resolved in favour of the men and the taming institution of marriage. There is no lesson that the sexes are necessarily in conflict. Exceptional disruptions serve only to underline the harmony and undisputed male supremacy on which Greek mythology and ritual believe successful societies are built.

Conclusion: what Greek myth is

The picture which now emerges of Greek myth is hard to sum-
marise. Plainly it is not enough to allege that myth does some one
thing or another. Greek myth is a complicated organism, with a
history of its own, in both ancient and modern times. At one
extreme, Greek myth reaches back to an Indo-European past
which we can scarcely conceive; at the opposite extreme stand
modern ideas and interpretations of myth, which, irrespective of
any value they may have for a correct understanding of Greek
myth (and is there such a thing?), are part of the intellectual fabric
of our times. In between lies the entire culture and history of the
Greeks, with which myth is continually in dialogue and in which it
is continually redeployed. I hope that this book, with its shifting
standpoints and its little heap of samples, has captured something
of what Greek myth is and given some initial guidance on the
limits within which it can be used, safely or precariously, to tell us
about Greek history, society and values.

What we think matters about Greek myth will naturally vary
according to our tastes, preferences and the framework of ideas
within which we think. I do not think there is any possibility of an
objective account of Greek myth and I think it would be the
poorer if there was. As a mere example, let me state the conclusions that I myself would draw at this point:

1 Myth is a local heritage. Each local city has its local mythology as
   it has its local system of gods and festivals. Sometimes that
   mythology carries a visible message, as in genealogies. Sometimes it explains. Sometimes it expresses a feeling for how their
   culture feels and thinks. Sometimes it is a good story and their
   good story.

2 Myth is a national heritage. The system of Greek Mythology is a means of communication between all who subscribe to it. To recognise it is to be Greek, just as to speak the Greek language is a sign of being Greek. A community which sets up a myth in sculpture on its temple talks not just to itself, but to all who come to visit it. If we today can enjoy recognising a Labour of Herakles on a metope, how much more thrilling must it have been to see the original, gloriously painted, at the forefront of art and technology, and showing a powerful Greek traditional story? Local pride grows greater too if it can show that a great national story actually happened here.

3 Myth is the story of a lost and powerful past that created the present. It tells of the age of gods, heroes, beginnings and explanations. It tells too of the human sequence which led to our societies now: then Pelasgians and Karians, now us Megarians. Carbon-14 dating does not have the same ring.

4 Myth expressed in its own way the key factors that rituals also expressed, and sometimes worked, or had worked, in partnership with them. The moment of initiation, in particular, had been prolific in spawning rituals and myths. Even when those rituals had faded (as they mostly had by the Classical Age), the myths continued, carrying with them much of the original force of these moments. It is no coincidence that stories of departure, difficult experience and return to a new sense of identity have their own vitality – that is why initiation mattered in the first place. The cycle of Labours of Herakles, though put together at a relatively late date (12 was a good number for metopes), displays the power of this pattern – quite as much in its hold over modern audiences as in its hold over ancient. The *Odyssey* is a return, but a return of a man reshaped by his experiences and endurance. The *Iliad* is not a tale of the Trojan War, though that too could, and presumably did in hands other than Homer's, deliver this result by including preliminaries, nine-year period of endurance and segregation, and return. The *Iliad* is the tale of Achilles, who is excluded from the warrior society to which he belongs, who suffers and reflects and who returns, not just physically to slaughter Hektor, but through a supreme moral and emotional reincorporation by confrontation with Priam in the last book.

5 Greek myths often avoid happy endings. This explains why they are ideally suited to tragedy and is reinforced by the collection

of myths from tragedy. It would however be shallow and inaccurate to suppose on this account that it is a prime function of myths to serve as warnings (Bettelheim 1976: 38). What after all are we warned against by the Oedipus myth? Not to be fated to marry our mothers? Or by Agamemnon? Not to have accursed ancestors? Or to learn through suffering (between axe-strokes)? Especially in the hands of the tragedians, the myths give a more stationary sense of how things are: problems of the divine order, of man's place, of society even and of character are raised, exacerbated, displayed, but not resolved except in the sense that there is an ending. Neither tragedians nor Greeks as a whole drew up divine and social charters through the language of myth.

Here the ideas of Lévi-Strauss and the structuralists have helped us to focus on the different logic of myth-language (if indeed it is a language): myth expresses opposites and conflicts, it balances them out or reaches for other issues that can act as intermediaries. It clearly would be very satisfactory and very tidy for us writers and students of myth to be able to say that myth solved problems. But we must beware of imposing our own problem-solving intellectual culture on a medium conceived in a different world.

I have no intention of imposing this list as a definitive conclusion. Readers must compose their own. Perhaps this book will help.

Notes

1 Myth and mythology

1 On folk-tale and initiation rites see Versnel 1990: 50 and his bibliography at 81 n.109.
2 Problems with defining myth in terms of religion: Kirk 1970: 11.
3 Raglan 1955: 129, citing work of W.J. Gruffydd on the *Mabinogion*; cf. Dowden 1989: 3–5.
4 Edmunds (1990: 16) attempts to define oral literature as 'scripts' and to include all myth within this category.
5 Apart from a couple of probably false identifications, he figures only as one of the E metopes in the Gigantomachy sequence.
6 For an example of this problem see Dowden 1989: 185–7.
7 Frazer 1921: vol. i, xlv–lviii, following earlier work by R. Wagner (*Mythographi Graeci*, vol. i, Leipzig, 1894).
8 The concept of *in illo tempore* is Eliade's, for example M. Eliade, *Le mythe de l'éternel retour*, new edn, Paris, 1969: 20, 33–41.
9 *Odyssey* 4.423 (Eidotheë to Menelaos), 7.302 (Odysseus to Alkinoös), 10.516 (Circe to Odysseus); *Iliad* 20.104 (Apollo to Aeneas). Compare *Iliad* 23.645, where Nestor speaks of excelling amongst the heroes.

2 How myths work: the theories

1 Examples of historicism in prehistorians: F. Stubbings, 'The rise of Mycenaean civilization', IV 'Danaans and the Hyksos', *CAH3* 2.1 (1973): 635–8; Hammond 1976: ch. VI. See the Topic bibliography, p. 179.
2 P. Faure, 'Aux sources de la légende des Danaïdes', résumé in *REG* 82 (1969) xxvi–xxviii, rightly criticised by Detienne 1979: 13f. D.W. Roller, 'The enigma of the tribe of Dan', *LCM* 16 (1991): 38.
3 E. Rohde, *Psyche: The Cult of Souls and Belief in Immortality among the Greeks*, Eng. translation, W.B. Hillis, London, 1920: 287; contrast Dowden 1989: 97, 106.
4 G. Pilot, *Le code secret de l' Odysée: les grecs dans l'atlantique*, Paris, 1969; V. Bérard, *Les navigations d'Ulysse*, 4 vols, Paris, 1928–35.

5 Puhvel 1987: 153; G. Dumézil, *Camillus: a study of Indo-European religion as Roman history*, Berkeley, 1980: e.g. ch. 1 and table on pp. 101f.
6 Graf 1987a: 44f. E. Durkheim, *Elementary Forms of the Religious Life*, Eng. translation, London, 1915 (French: Paris, 1912).
7 This originates with Dumézil 1953: 26-8; cf. Littleton 1982: 212.
8 Cf. Ap 2.6.1 (Iole), 2.7.7 (Ormenion, a place, not a father of Astydameia), 2.7.8 (Astydameia and Ktesippos): the version in Diodoros looks secondary to me, despite its convenience for Dumézil.
9 The term comes from Jean Starobinski, *Trois fureurs*, Paris, 1974: 26 – a reference I owe to Loraux 1990: 23.
10 Caldwell 1989: 15. Caldwell is in fact particularly didactic, though this of course helps the exemplary clarity of his book.
11 Lloyd-Jones 1990: 282, citing E. Gellner, *The Psychoanalytic Movement, or the Coming of Unreason*, London, 1985.
12 W.M. Calder III in *LCM* 16 (1991): 67.
13 The sources for this version are given by Brelich 1958: 75: Cicero, *Aratea* 424 ('In his frenzy with insane heart he was killing animals'), 431 ('hunting enthusiastically'); scholiast on the Latin Aratea, p. 196 M ('killing practically all the beasts'); Ovid, *Fasti* 5.451 (' "there is no wild animal", he said, "that I do not wish to defeat" ').
14 R.S. Caldwell, 'The psychoanalytic interpretation of Greek myth', in Edmunds 1990: ch. 7.

3 Greeks on myth

1 Fragments of Greek prose writers who can, however doubtfully, be classed as historians are collected in the many volumes of F. Jacoby, *Die Fragmente der griechischen Historiker*, Berlin, 1926–30, Leiden, 1954–8. In, for example, 2F23, 2 indicates that Akousilaos is author number 2 in the collection, F that the reference is to a fragment (not a T for testimonium, i.e. information more broadly about the author) and 23 is the number of the fragment. A fragment is a passage from a lost work of an author, usually recovered as a result of being quoted by other authors who survive in full. In Jacoby's volumes, some volumes contain the (usually) Greek text of the authors; others contain commentary on those texts (German in earlier volumes, English in later), others again contain the footnotes for the commentary.
2 The text is found in *FGH* 239.

4 Myth and prehistory

1 See Topic bibliography, p. 181.
2 Another example is surely the comparability of Herakles with Indra as slayers of three-headed figures, see Burkert 1979: 85; Puhvel 1987: 51–3. For Dumézil's fuller comparison of Herakles with Indra, more controversial in its detail, see pp. 29f. below.

3   Müller (1844: 49) claimed this as evidence for an Achaian phratry at Sparta to which kings belonged. I think this was to take a genealogical claim too literally; after all, one would not hypothesise an Egyptian phratry on the basis of Herodotos 6.53.
4   The name actually looks more like the *Tagos* ('commander-in-chief') of the *lawos* ('armed forces').
5   R. Hope Simpson and J.F. Lazenby, *The Catalogue of Ships in Homer's Iliad*, Oxford, 1970.
6   Eur. *Archelaos*, fr. 228 N² (Dowden 1989: 148).
7   Other interesting examples include the Abas and the Abantes, inhabitants only of Euboia in classical times, yet Abas is the father of Akrisios and Proitos (see further Dowden 1989: 156, 162); and, of course, the Achaioi – a major name in Homer, but only the inhabitants of the northern coast of the Peloponnese in classical times (myth deals with them through the figure of Teisamenos, P 7.1.7).
8   Cf. R.M. Cook, *CAH3* II.2: 778f.
9   O. Gurney, *The Hittites*, 2nd edn, Harmondsworth, 1954: pp. 56–8; M. Wood, *In Search of the Trojan War*, London, 1985: 186–206.
10 Burkert 1984: 99–106; F.H. Stubbings in *CAH3* II.2: 167–9.
11 J. Chadwick, in *Parola del Passato* 31 (1976): 116f.
12 This goes all the way back to Müller 1844: 47. Argive invention according to Tigerstedt 1965: 35.
13 Tigerstedt (1965: 36) observes that the myth in effect certifies the existence of a Dorian invasion against modern doubters.

5 Myth and identity

1   The Heraion may once have belonged not to Argos, but to Mycenae, cf. Dowden 1989: 127f.
2   On *ethnos* and federation see Larsen 1968: xivf., 8f.
3   One would, of course, expect the odd lame eponym, like Hoples (Ap 3.15.6). Dumézil once thought that these subdivisions represented his three Indo-European functions (see Dumézil 1953) and Jeanmaire (1939: ch.2) likewise tries this type of approach.
4   G. Neumann in *KlP*, s.v. 'Leleger', attributes this view to Shevoroshkin, *Issledovaniya po deshifrovke kariiskich nadpisej*, Moscow, 1965: p. 28 ('Investigation into the decipherment of Karian inscriptions').
5   Perhaps Indo-European *$Pl_{H_2}sgoi$ (cf. Greek *pelas*, 'near'). There are obvious phonological difficulties, but perhaps not beyond resolution: the voiced g might be caused by the laryngeal in a contraction at the Indo-European level of a word for 'neighbours', *$pel_{H_2}s$-wikoi*; the Germanic w- rather than the expected f- may be explained by the l in the environment. What is clear is that the sequence of consonants is labial, lateral, dental spirant (the s does not have to be written out of the proto-Germanic form), velar plosive. This formula would embrace also the Volsci and maybe the Falisci (*Falesci, cf. Falerii?) in Italy.
6   Hes. fr. 234 M–W (Str. 7.7.2 [322]). Deukalion's stones, for example, Ap 1.7.2.

7   Another example: the autochthon Anax ('Lord') ruled over Kares (Karians – of which Leleges are a subdivision – P 7.2.8) in Anactoria, until Miletos sailed in with an army of Cretans, the populations mixed and the place was called Miletos (P 7.2.5).
8   Scholiast on Eur. *Orestes* 932; Sakellariou 1977: 108.
9   Baton *FGH* 268F5 (Ath. 14.45 639d–40a), Sakellariou 1977: 108f.
10   De Polignac 1984: 134, summarising *AC* 49 (1980): 5–22.
11   Genealogical authors and Athens, cf. Parker 1987: 200.
12   Klearchos in Ath. *Deipn.* 13.2 [555d]; Harrison 1912: 262; primal promiscuity, Pembroke 1967: 30f.
13   On the Aigeidai see Vian, 1963: 216–25; and C. Robert, *Oidipous: Geschichte eines poetischen Stoffs im griechischen Altertum*, 2 vols, Berlin, 1915: vol. i, 2f., 565–74.
14   But the Spartans felt as justified as the Argives in their claim to hegemony through Pelops and Agamemnon (Herodotos 7.159). Huxley (1983: 7f.) comments, 'Pelops is mentioned by Syagros because Sparta claimed to rule his island, the Peloponnese; Agamemnon, because he led the Achaeans against Troy, as Sparta must lead the Hellenes in the defence of Greece.'
15   Orestes was said to have moved from Mycenae to Arcadia as the result of an oracle (P 8.5.4). But Teisamenos' bones (equally as a result of an oracle from Delphi) were moved from Achaia too, where tradition said the inhabitants were those dispossessed of Sparta and Argos by the Dorians (P 7.1.5, 7.1.8). Bones were always powerful: compare the bones of eponymous Arkas, that were brought from Mainalos to Mantinea (P 8.9.3).

6 Arrival at the cult-site

1   This inhibits the position of Demeter: as an Olympian she cannot be autochthonous, but as Earth-Mother she cannot be anything else. Hence her sense of not quite belonging with the Olympian family.

7 Myth and initiation ritual

1   P.M.C. Forbes Irving, *Metamorphosis in Greek Myth*, Oxford, 1990: 50–7.
2   J.N. Bremmer and N.M. Horsfall, *Roman Myth and Mythography*, [BICS Suppl 52], London, 1987: 38–43.
3   Sergent 1986: 145f., building on R. Roux, *Le problème des Argonautes: recherches sur les aspects religieux de la légende*, Paris, 1949: 129, 134f. On the number 50 see also, for example, J. Bremmer, 'The suodales of Poplios Valesios', *ZPE* 47 (1982): 138; Dowden 1989: 157f.
4   Another crew of 50 + 2: Odysseus' ship has 46 on Circe's island (*Od.* 10.203–8) after losing six to the Kikones.
5   On this point and the whole myth: Vidal-Naquet 1981.
6   Str. 6.1.15 [265]; Dionys. *Ant.Rom.* 19.3 [17.4]. Cf. Dowden 1989: 64.
7   These examples are in Dowden 1989: 65f.

8 The world of myth

1 Varro in Augustine, *City of God* 18.9; Vidal-Naquet in Gordon 1981: 198; less revealing version at Ap 3.14.1.
2 Pan, Priapus, and shepherd-boy: Boardman 1975: ill. 335.1 (Athenian, early 460s, p. 181); Theok. *Epigram* 3.
3 J. Fontenrose, *Orion: the myth of the hunter and the huntress*, Berkeley, Calif., 1981.
4 Examples are collected by Richardson 1974: 6ff. Compare too Ov. *Met.* 2.861, 864 (Europa), 5.385–94 (Persephone at Henna in Sicily); Claudian, *de Raptu Proserpinae*, 2.71–150.
5 For these views see Caldwell 1989: 42 and 191 n.10, 153, Campbell 1959: 64 (amniotic fluid).
6 Caldwell 1989: 33 – but for the penile stick compare the thyrsos of the Maenad.
7 Carpenter 1991: ills. 96, 99 (550–540 BC), 97 (late fourth century BC).
8 The reader may not be aware that *Gigantes* sounds rather like a tribal name such as *Abantes*.
9 If 10 tasks not 12, following the usual amendment of the text, then surely 10 years not 12.
10 L. Radermacher, *Mythos der Hellenen: Untersuchungen über antiker Jenseitsglauben*, Bonn, 1903: 42.
11 Stesichoros fr. 185 Page; full story in Ath. *Deipn.* 11 (470c).
12 C. Kerényi, *The Heroes of the Greeks*, Eng. translation, H.J. Rose, London, 1959: 143.
13 Herodoros, a practical man, reckoned it took seven nights (*FGH* 31F20).
14 Plutarch, *Greek Questions*, 58 [304c–e]. Loraux 1990: 35 – I do not however understand her general argument on the feminisation of Herakles.
15 Dowden 1989: Subject index s.v. 'renewal of society', for example, 183, 191.
16 Dowden 1989: Subject index s.v. 'chase'.
17 Writers assume this biblical myth to be familiar: it is found in *Genesis* 39. There are five examples in Greek myth: Slater 1968: 335.
18 This point is made, if in outmoded terminology, by Harrison 1912: 323.
19 Labyrinth as womb, for example, Campbell 1959: 69.
20 C. Lévi-Strauss, 'Structure and form: reflections on a work by Vladimir Propp', in *Structural Anthropology 2*, Eng. translation, M. Layton, London, 1977: ch. viii.

9 Mythic society

1 Eustathios *ad loc.*; J.J. Bachofen, *Myth, Religion, and Mother Right: selected writings of J.J. Bachofen*, Eng. translation, R. Manheim, Princeton, NJ, 1967: 73.
2 Hyrnethion, P 2.28.6–7. Both also are removed from a would-be husband by two brothers in a chariot: Helen from Theseus (for

example) by the Dioskouroi, Hyrnetho from Deiphontes by Kerynes and Phalkes, P 2.28.5.

3   For example, F. de Polignac, *La naissance de la cité grecque*, Paris, 1984: 16.

4   P. Levi, *Pausanias: Guide to Greece*, vol. 1, Harmondsworth, 1971: 48 n.92.

5   J. Onians, *Art and Thought in the Hellenistic Age: The Greek World View 350–50 BC*, London, 1979, ill. 83 (at Pergamum); P 1.24.2 (at Athens, dedicated by Attalos, together with, NB, Gauls defeated in Mysia).

6   Onians 1979: 81–5.

7   Onians 1977: 85–7.

8   In fact in the original Corinthian myth the Corinthians themselves slaughter Medea's children – and ever since must expiate this by a ritual involving children dressed in black.

9   F. Lissarrague, 'The sexual life of Satyrs', in D.M. Halperin, J. J. Winkler and F. I. Zeitlin (eds), *Before Sexuality: The Construction of Erotic Experience in the Ancient Greek World*, Princeton, 1990: 53–81, esp. 55–6.

Topic bibliography

This is a guide to further reading, both on the whole subject and, chapter by chapter, on its various topics.

The best **introduction** to Greek mythology is (in German) Graf 1987a. In English, Kirk 1974 is well written, learned and deservedly popular, though I am not satisfied that progess in the study of myth is sufficiently helped by his choice of categories. The best **bibliography**, though now old, is Peradotto 1973. Examples of **older approaches** are conveniently collected in B. Feldman and R.D. Richardson, *The Rise of Modern Mythology 1680–1860*, Bloomington, Indiana, 1972. For collections of works by various scholars exemplifying **modern approaches**, see Bremmer 1987, Edmunds 1990.

COLLECTIONS OF GREEK MYTHS

Ancient (see also under chapter 1.2): The only conveniently available compendium is that of **Apollodoros**: Greek text and translation in J.G. Frazer, *Apollodorus: The Library*, 2 vols, Cambridge, Mass. and London, 1921 (Loeb Classical Library).

Modern: R. Graves, *The Greek Myths*, 2 vols, Harmondsworth, 1955, despite extensive worthless comments, gives a good basic account of the full range of Greek mythology, with sources for each myth. P. Grimal, *The Penguin Dictionary of Classical Mythology*, London, 1991 (French, 1951), excels in range and detail, but does not cite sources; R. Stoneman, *Greek Mythology: an encyclopedia of myth and legend*, London, 1991, again in dictionary format, also offers some intriguing medieval and modern material, gives skeletal indications of important sources and, occasionally, discussions, and adds a helpful bibliography. M. Grant, *Myths of the Greeks and Romans*, London, 1962, though readable and alert, is unduly limited in range and focuses excessively on high literature. Rose 1928 overemphasises gods and, though a solid, methodical book, is badly dated in style and content.

CHAPTER 1.1

Veyne 1988 is a reliable and sensitive guide to where myth really fitted in Greek culture. Nestle 1941 propounds the old-fashioned romantic view of the Greeks as a whole advancing from *mythos* to *logos*. *Mythos/ logos* and the relationship to the spread of writing: Vernant 1982: 186– 90; Edmunds 1990: 2–15.

Kirk 1970 (ch.1, section 3) discusses differences between **myth** and **folk-tale**, taking the issue more seriously than I recommend. Graf (1987a: introduction, esp. p. 12) is more discriminating. Bremmer (1987: ch. 1) is brief and clear on tradition, collective significance and the relationship to folk-tale, legend, etc.

CHAPTER 1.2

Ancient authors where myths or traditional narratives are in plentiful supply: **Homer**, **Hesiod**; **Aeschylus**, **Sophocles**, **Euripides**; **Ovid**, *Metamorphoses*; **Pausanias** – all available in the Penguin Classics series or in the Loeb Classical Library (Harvard University Press). For the **Epic Cycle**, turn to M. Davies, *The Epic Cycle*, Bristol, 1989. For **Antoninus Liberalis**, see Francis Celoria, *The Metamorphoses of Antoninus Liberalis*, London and New York, 1992.

Mythology in art: *Lexicon Iconographicum Mythologiae Classicae*, Zurich, 1981-date lists alphabetically all known ancient artistic representations of mythological subjects; part one of each volume is the catalogue, part two the illustrations. Especially good value is Carpenter 1991 – profusely illustrated, if more interested in data than in interpretations; NB his topic bibliography at pp. 247–9. The handbooks by John Boardman in the same series (see General bibliography below) each have a section on myth.

CHAPTER 2.1

Theories of myth: Graf 1987a: chs 1–2. Puhvel 1987: ch.1 is fresh though he omits Modern Myth-Ritual. Vernant 1982: 207–40 gives a thoughtful review of theories and possibilities from a post-structuralist viewpoint. A swift review of theories by an anthropologist, with some useful comment on Lévi-Strauss: P.S. Cohen, 'Theories of myth', *Man* 4 (1969): 337–53.

Historicism: Amongst prehistorians the worst offender is J. Zafiropoulo, *Histoire de la Grèce à l'âge de bronze*, Paris, 1964. Good overall discussion of myth and prehistory (if not quite sceptical enough): R.B. Edwards, *Kadmos the Phoenician: a study in Greek legends and the Mycenaean Age*, Amsterdam, 1979, pp. 192–207. Tigerstedt (1965: 26f.) touches on modern credulity in myth as history and cites in particular (322 n. 94) J.L. Myres, *Who Were the Greeks?*, Berkeley, Calif. 1930: 297ff.

Allegory: **Ancient**: J. Pépin, *Mythe et allégorie: les origines grecques et les contestations judéo-chrétiennes*, Paris, 1958; F. Cumont, *Recherches sur le symbolisme funéraire des romains*, Paris, 1942. **Renaissance**: E. Wind,

Pagan Mysteries in the Renaissance, 2nd edn., Harmondsworth, 1967.
Romantic: K. Raine and G.M. Harper, *Thomas Taylor the Platonist: Selected Writings*, Princeton, NJ and London, 1969; F. Creuzer, *Symbolik und Mythologie der alten Völker, besonders der Griechen*, 3rd impr., 4 vols, Leipzig, 1836–43. (Useful, brief account of Creuzer in Rose 1928: 3f.).
Natural allegory: Manifesto: Max Müller 1898. On Max Müller himself see N.C. Chaudhuri, *Scholar Extraordinary: the life of Professor the Rt. Hon. Friedrich Max Müller, P.C.*, London, 1974.
Cambridge myth-ritual: Versnel 1990, esp. 30–44, is the major modern discussion. Edmunds 1990: 23f. Principal text: Harrison 1912. A later, enthusiastic association of myth with ritual was found in Raglan 1936, taking in (for example) Robin Hood, King Arthur, Irish and Norse saga, Troy and the hero, ritual drama. For a lucid account of his position, see Raglan 1955.

CHAPTER 2.2

New comparative mythology: Littleton 1982. Dumézil's views have now been closely examined and found unverifiable by W.W. Belier, *Decayed Gods: Origins and Development of Georges Dumézil's 'Idéologie Tripartite'*, Leiden, 1991. Attempts to explore Greek mythology according to this method: Dumézil 1953 (in French); Dumézil 1970: ch. 5 (Herakles); Puhvel 1987: ch. 8.
Psychoanalysis: Bibliographies of psychoanalytic treatment of Greek myth: R.S. Caldwell, 'Selected bibliography on psychoanalysis and classical studies', *Arethusa* 7 (1974), 119–23 on 'Greek mythology' – a brief survey by an enthusiast. J. Glenn, 'Psychoanalytic Writings on Classical Mythology and Religion: 1909–1960', *Classical World* 70 (1976) 225–47 – a thorough and critical survey. Withering review of the whole approach: Lloyd-Jones 1985. Interesting modern examples of this type of method: Slater 1968; Caldwell 1989.
Jung: Jung and Kerényi 1949. There is a whole sequence of volumes by C. Kerényi on 'Archetypal images in Greek religion', for example *Dionysos: Archetypal Image of Indestructible Life*, Eng. translation, R. Manheim, Princeton, NJ and London, 1976.
Structuralism: C. Lévi-Strauss, *Structural Anthropology*, Eng. translation, C. Jacobson and B.G. Schoepf, Harmondsworth, 1972: ch. xi; with E. Leach, *Lévi-Strauss*, London, 1970, rev. 1974.

CHAPTER 2.3

Modern myth-ritual: H. Jeanmaire, 'La cryptie lacédémonienne', *REG* 26 (1913): 121–50; Jeanmaire 1939. L.J. Alderink, 'Greek ritual and mythology: the work of Walter Burkert', *Religious Studies Review* 6 (1980) 1–14; and Versnel 1990: 44–90. Brelich 1969; Burkert 1983; Brulé 1987; Dowden 1989.
'Rome school': Brelich 1977, on the Rome school, is a useful preliminary to the study of mythology altogether. Brelich 1958: 23-78 usefully reviews the problems posed by Greek myth. His 1958 and 1969 studies

are the major works of the school. G. Piccaluga, *Lykaon: un temo mitico*, Roma, 1968.

'**Paris school**': Detienne sites himself relative to structuralism in Detienne 1979: ch.1 (originally in French as 'Mythes grecs et analyse structurale: controverses et problèmes' in Gentili and Paioni 1977: 69–89). On J.-P. Vernant: 'A bibliography of the works of Jean-Pierre Vernant', *Arethusa* 15 (1982) 11–18; C. Segal, 'Afterword: Jean-Pierre Vernant and the study of ancient Greece', *Arethusa* 15 (1982): 221–34. Froma I. Zeitlin has now edited a particularly useful collection of Vernant's writings, in English translation: J.-P. Vernant, *Mortals and Immortals: Collected Essays*, Princeton, NJ, 1991.

CHAPTER 3

Greek **Attitudes** to myth: far-reaching survey, Veyne 1988; see also Vernant 1982: 200-4. **Myth and history**: C. Brillante, 'History and the historical interpretation of myth', in Edmunds 1990: ch. 2. A deeper study, showing something of why history, even when available, must on occasion be turned to myth: M. Eliade, *Le mythe de l'éternel retour*, new edn., Paris, 1969, 48–64.

CHAPTER 3.4

Homer the **Theologian**: R. Lamberton, *Homer the Theologian: neoplatonist allegorical reading and the growth of the epic tradition*, Berkeley, Calif. 1986.

CHAPTER 4.1

Borrowing from the **Near East**: R. Mondi, 'Greek mythic thought in the light of the Near East', in Edmunds 1990: ch. 3 (bibliography: 194–8), seeks to refine the notion of diffusion. Burkert, 'Oriental and Greek mythology: the meeting of parallels', in Bremmer 1987: ch.2, is a useful, but brief, set of samples and reflections. Burkert's 1984 monograph cast the net wider (extensive bibliography: 121–31). P. Walcot, *Hesiod and the Near East*, Cardiff, 1966; M.L. West, *Hesiod, Theogony*, Oxford, 1966: esp. 18–31 (bibliography at 106f.); Centre d'Etudes Supérieures Spécialisées d'Histoire des Religions de Strasbourg, *Colloque, 1958, Strasbourg: Eléments Orientaux dans la religion grecque ancienne*, Paris, 1960. Interesting material also, if intermittently, in Burkert 1979.

CHAPTER 4.3

Trojan war: M.L. Finley, J.L. Caskey, G.S. Kirk and D.L. Page, 'The Trojan War', *JHS* 84 (1964): 1–20; J.T. Hooker, *Mycenaean Greece*, London, 1977, 165–8, 214–16; L. Foxhall and J.K. Davies, *The Trojan War: Its Historicity and Context: papers of the first Greenbank Colloquium, 1981*, Bristol, 1984. Popularising: M. Wood, *In Search of the Trojan War*, London, 1985. Look too at Bremmer 1987.

CHAPTER 4.4

Dorian migration: the historicity is challenged by, for example: R.M. Cook, 'The Dorian invasion', *Proceedings of the Cambridge Philological Society* 188 (1962): 16–22; John Chadwick, 'Who were the Dorians?', *Parola del Passato* 31 (1976): 103–17; J.T. Hooker, *Mycenaean Greece*, London, 1977, 168–80. The traditional view is defended by P. Cartledge, *Sparta and Lakonia: a regional history*, London, 1979: 77–88 (bibliography at 100 f.).

CHAPTER 5.2

Genealogy, Aetiology: Veyne 1988: 24–6. Attempt to restrict the significance of aetiology for the explanation of Greek myth: Kirk 1974: 53–9. Vansina 1965, index s.v. 'genealogies' for genealogy in traditional societies.6

CHAPTER 5.5

Pelasgians: Düller 1937: 36–39 on Pelasgians and myth; Sakellariou 1977: 81–230, with excellent documentation of other views. The monograph on the Pelasgians is F. Lochner-Hüttenbach, *Die Pelasger*, Vienna, 1960, which I regret I have not seen.
Modern treatments of **Orpheus**: Graf 1987b; J.F. Nagy, 'Hierarchy, heroes and heads: Indo-European structures in Greek myth', in Edmunds 1990: ch. 4.
Sparta: Tigerstedt 1965: ch.1; Calame 1987; G.L. Huxley, 'Herodotus on myth and politics in early Sparta', *Proceedings. Royal Irish Academy*, 83 Section C (1983): 1–16.

CHAPTER 5.6

Athens: Parker 1987.

CHAPTER 6.1

Delphi: C. Sourvinou-Inwood, 'Myth as history: the previous owners of the Delphic Oracle', in Bremmer 1987: ch. 10; Fontenrose 1959.

CHAPTER 6.3

Sikyon: Brelich 1969: 377–87.

CHAPTER 6.5

Dionysos: E. Rohde, *Psyche: the cult of souls and belief in immortality among the Greeks*, 8th edn, Eng. translation, W.B. Hillis, London, 1920 (in German, 1st edn, Freiburg, 1890); W.F. Otto, *Dionysus: myth and cult*,

Eng. translation, R.B. Palmer, Bloomington, Indiana, 1965; Burkert 1985: 161–7.

CHAPTER 7.1

On the profile and features of **Initiation** that are relevant to an understanding of myth, see Versnel 1990: 44–59. **Girls' initiations** in general: Brelich 1969; Calame 1977; Brulé 1987; Dowden 1989. **Bears** in particular: Brulé 1987: Ch. 2; Dowden 1989: Ch. 1; P.H.J. Lloyd-Jones, 'Artemis and Iphigeneia', *JHS* 103 (1983) 87–102; C. Sourvinou-Inwood, *Studies in Girls' Transitions: Aspects of the arkteia and age representation in Attic iconography*, Athens, 1988.

CHAPTER 7.2

Wolves: in Arcadia, Burkert 1983: 84–93; in Greek myth and history, Kunstler 1991. **Troy** and initiation: Bremmer 1978. **Homosexuality** and myth: first-rate treatment in Sergent 1986.

CHAPTER 8.2

Iamboulos: Diodorus Siculus, 2.55–60, for example, in C.H. Oldfather, *Diodorus Siculus*, vol. 2, Cambridge, Mass. and London, 1935 (Loeb Classical Library, vol. ii).
Antonius Diogenes: summary preserved in the Byzantine bishop Photios, *Library* 166, translated by G. Sandy, in B.P. Reardon (ed.), *Collected Ancient Greek Novels*, Berkeley, Calif. 1989: 775–82.

CHAPTER 8.3

Greek **monsters** in general: Kirk 1970: 191. **Titans** and Titanomachy: Ap 1.1–2; Hesiod *Theogony*: 133–53 (list, apparently, of Titans), 501–6 (Kyklopes), 617–28 (100-handers), 664–745 (battle and imprisonment).
Cattle-raiding and initiation: B. Lincoln, 'The Indo-European cattle-raiding myth', *HR* 16 (1976): 42–65; P. Walcot, 'Cattle-raiding, heroic tradition and ritual: the Greek evidence', *HR* 18 (1979): 326–51.
Geryon, cattle and the dead: J.J. Croon, *The Herdsman of the Dead*, diss., Amsterdam, 1952; Fontenrose 1959: 334–46; Burkert 1979: 85–8, based on Burkert 1977.
On **Theseus**, now see the extensive work of C. Calame, *Thésée et l'imaginaire athénien: légende et culte en Grèce antique*, Lausanne, 1990.
Folk-tale and typical story-structures: Burkert 1979: 5–10, 83 f.; A. Aarne, *The Types of the Folktale: a classification and bibliography*, Eng. translation and amplification, S. Thompson, Helsinki, 1964; V.J. Propp *Morphology of the Folktale*, Eng. translation, L. Scott, 2nd edn, L.A. Wagner, Bloomington, 1968.

Psychoanalysis and Heroes from Oedipus to Lohengrin via Jesus: O. Rank, *The Myth of the Birth of the Hero: a psychological interpretation of mythology*, Eng. translation, New York, 1914.

CHAPTER 9.1

Matriarchy: J.J. Bachofen, *Das Mutterrecht: eine Untersuchung über die Gynaikokratie der alten Welt nach ihrer religiösen und rechtlichen Natur* ('Matriarchy: an investigation into rule by women in the ancient world with respect to its religious and legal character'), Basel, 1861, repr. in K. Meuli (ed.), *J.J. Bachofen: Gesammelte Werke*, vols 2–3, Basel, 1948. Criticism of Bachofen: Pembroke 1967; S. Pembroke, 'Last of the matriarchs', *Journal of the Economic and Social History of the Orient*, 8 (1965): 219–47; Bamberger 1974; G.G. Thomas, 'Matriarchy in early Greece: the Bronze and Dark Ages', *Arethusa* 6 (1973): 173–95; P. Vidal-Naquet, 'Slavery and the rule of women in tradition, myth and utopia' in Gordon 1981: 187–200. Some bibliography on Feminism and ancient matriarchy/matrilinearity issues: S.B. Pomeroy, 'Selected bibliography on women in antiquity', *Arethusa* 6 (1973): 125–57, esp. 132–5.

CHAPTER 9.2

Amazons: Tyrrell 1984 is the standard book; more provocative is P. duBois, *Centaurs and Amazons: Women in the Pre-History of the Great Chain of Being*, Ann Arbor, Michigan, 1982. For briefer perspectives see P. duBois, 'On horse/men, Amazons, and endogamy', *Arethusa* 12 (1979): 35–49; and A.W. Kleinbaum, 'Amazon legends and misogynists: the women and civilization question', in F.R. Keller (ed.), *Views of Women's Lives in Western Traditions: frontiers of the past and the future*, Lewiston, NY, Queenston, Ontario and Lampeter, Wales, 1990; and, judiciously, Lefkowitz 1986: ch. 1.

CHAPTER 9.3

Misogyny/women in Greek myth and literature: N. Loraux, 'Sur la race des femmes et quelques-unes de ses tribus', *Arethusa* 11 (1978): 43–87; Lefkowitz 1986: ch. 7; and, particularly forceful on sexual polarisation in myth, F.I. Zeitlin, 'The dynamics of misogyny: myth and myth-making in the Oresteia', *Arethusa* 11 (1978): 149–84, esp. 150–60. But one of the major needs in literature on myth is for a book comprehensively reviewing mythology from a woman's standpoint. In the meantime, some understanding may be gained, for instance, from: A. Cameron and A. Kuhrt (eds), *Images of Women in Antiquity*, London, 1983; M.Z. Rosaldo and L. Lamphere (eds), *Women, Culture, and Society*, Stanford, Calif., 1974.

General bibliography

This part of the bibliography serves as a key to (a) the text references and notes; and (b) the Topic bibliography on pp. 178–84. For 'further reading', please refer to the Topic bibliography.

Bamberger, J. (1974) 'The Myth of matriarchy: why men rule in primitive society', in M.Z. Rosaldo and L. Lamphere (eds), *Women, Culture and Society*, Stanford, Calif.: 263–80.

Bettelheim, B. (1976) *The Uses of Enchantment: The meaning and importance of fairy tales*, London.

Boardman, J. (1974) *Athenian Black Figure Vases*, London.

— (1975) *Athenian Red Figure Vases: The Archaic Period*, London.

— (1978) *Greek Sculpture: The Archaic Period*, London.

— (1985) *Greek Sculpture: The Archaic Period*, London.

— (1989) *Athenian Red Figure Vases: The Classical Period*, London.

Brelich, A. (1958) *Gli eroi greci: un problema storico-religioso*, Roma.

— (1969) *Paides e parthenoi*, Roma.

— (1977) 'La metodologia della scuola di Roma', in B. Gentili and G.Paioni (eds), *Il Mito Greco: Atti del convegno internazionale (Urbino 7–12 maggio 1973)*, Roma: 3–29.

Bremmer, J. (1978) 'Heroes, rituals and the Trojan War', *SSR* 2: 5–38.

— (ed.) (1987) *Interpretations of Greek Mythology*, London.

Brulé, P. (1987) *La fille d'Athènes*, Paris.

Burkert, W. (1970) 'Jason, Hypsipyle and new fire at Lemnos', *CQ* n.s. 20: 1–16.

— (1977) 'Le mythe de Géryon: perspectives préhistoriques et tradition rituelle', in B. Gentili and G. Paioni (eds), *Il Mito Greco: Atti del convegno internazionale (Urbino 7–12 maggio 1973)*, Roma: 273–84.

— (1979) *Structure and History in Greek Mythology and Ritual*, Berkeley and Los Angeles, Calif.

— (1983) *Homo Necans: The Anthropology of Ancient Greek Sacrificial Ritual and Myth*, Eng. translation, P. Bing, Berkeley and Los Angeles, Calif.

— (1984) *Die orientalisierende Epoche in der griechischen Religion und Literatur*, Heidelberg.

— (1985) *Greek Religion: Archaic and Classical*, Eng. translation, J. Raffan, Oxford.

Calame, C. (1977) *Les choeurs de jeunes filles en Grèce archaique*, vol. I, 'Morphologie, fonction religieuse et sociale', Roma.

— (1987) 'Spartan genealogies', in J. Bremmer (ed.), *Interpretations of Greek Mythology*, London: Ch. 8.

Caldwell, R. (1989) *The Origin of the Gods: a psychoanalytic study of Greek theogonic myth*, New York, NY and Oxford.

Campbell, J. (1959) *The Masks of God: Primitive Mythology*, New York, NY.

Carpenter, T.H. (1991) *Art and Myth in Ancient Greece*, London.

Cave Brown, A. (1976) *Bodyguard of Lies*, London.

Detienne, M. (1979) *Dionysos Slain*, Eng. translation, M. and L. Muellner, Baltimore, Maryland and London.

— (1986) *The Creation of Mythology*, Eng. translation, M. Cook, Chicago, Ill.

Diller, A. (1937) *Race Mixture among the Greeks before Alexander*, Urbana, Ill. (repr. Westport, Conn., 1971).

Dowden, K. (1989) *Death and the Maiden: Girls' initiation rites in Greek mythology*, London and New York, NY.

Dumézil, G. (1953) 'Les trois fonctions dans quelques traditions grecques', in *Hommage à Lucien Febvre: Eventail de l'histoire vivante*, vol. 2, Paris: 25–32.

— (1970) *The Destiny of the Warrior*, Eng. translation, A. Hiltebeitel, Chicago, Ill.

Edmunds, L. (ed.) (1990) *Approaches to Greek Myth*, Baltimore, Maryland and London.

Fontenrose, J. (1959) *Python: A Study of Delphic Myth and its Origins*, Berkeley, Calif.

Frazer, J.G. (1921) *Apollodorus: The Library* (Loeb Classical Library), 2 vols, London.

Freud, S. (1913) *Totem and Taboo*, Leipzig and Vienna (Eng. translation, ed. J. Strachey, London, 1955).

Gentili, B. and Paioni, G. (eds.) (1977) *Il Mito Greco: Atti del convegno internazionale (Urbino 7–12 maggio 1973)*, Roma.

Gordon, R.L. (ed.) (1981) *Myth, Religion and Society*, Cambridge.

Gould, J. (1980) 'Law, custom and myth: aspects of the social position of women in Classical Athens', *JHS* 100: 38–59.

Graf, F. (1987a) *Griechische Mythologie: Eine Einführung*, 2nd rev. impr., München and Zürich.

— (1987b) 'Orpheus: a poet among men', in J. Bremmer (ed.), *Interpretations of Greek Mythology*, London: ch. 5.

Hammond, N.G.L. (1976) *Migrations and Invasions in Greece and Adjacent Areas*, Park Ridge, NJ.

Harrison, J.E. (1912) *Themis: A Study of the Social Origins of Greek Religion*, Cambridge.

Jeanmaire, H. (1939) *Couroi et Courètes: essai sur l'education spartiate et sur les rites d'adolescence dans l'antiquité Hellénique*, Lille.

Jung, C.C. and Kerényi, C. (1949) *Science of Mythology: Essays on the myth of the divine child and the Mysteries of Eleusis*, Eng. translation, London.

Kirk, G.S. (1970) *Myth: Its meaning and functions in ancient and other cultures*, Cambridge.

— (1974) *The Nature of Greek Myths*, Harmondsworth.
— (1977) 'Methodological reflexions on the myths of Heracles', in B. Gentili and G. Paioni (eds), *Il Mito Greco: Atti del convegno internazionale (Urbino 7–12 maggio 1973)*, Roma: 285–97.
Kunstler, B. (1991) 'The werewolf figure and its adoption into the Greek political vocabulary', *CW* 84: 189–205.
Larsen, J.A.O. (1968) *Greek Federal States: their institutions and history*, Oxford.
Leach, E. (1974) *Lévi-Strauss*, London (1st edn 1970).
Lefkowitz, M.R. (1986) *Women in Greek Myth*, London.
Littleton, C. Scott (1982) *The New Comparative Mythology: an anthropological assessment of the theories of Georges Dumézil*, 3rd edn, Berkeley and Los Angeles, Calif.
Lloyd-Jones, P.H.J. (1985) 'Psychoanalysis and the study of the Ancient World', in P. Horden (ed.), *Freud and the Humanities*, London and New York, NY: 152–80 (reprinted in P.H.J. Lloyd-Jones, *Greek Comedy, Hellenistic Literature, Greek Religion, and Miscellanea: The Academic Papers of Sir Hugh Lloyd-Jones*, Oxford, 1990: 281–305).
Loraux, N. (1990) 'Herakles: the super-male and the feminine', in D.M. Halperin, J.J. Winkler, and F.I. Zeitlin (eds), *Before Sexuality: The Construction of Erotic Experience in the Ancient Greek World*, Princeton, N.J.: 21–52.
Max Müller, F. (1873) *Introduction to the Science of Religion*, London (repr. 1899).
— (1898) 'Comparative Mythology' (1856), in F. Max Müller, *Chips from a German Workshop*, reissue, vol. IV, London: 1–154.
Müller, K.O. (1825) *Prolegomena zu einer wissenschaftlichen Mythologie*, Göttingen.
— (1844) *Die Dorier*, part 1, 2nd edn., Breslau.
Nestle, W. (1941) *Vom Mythos zum Logos: Die Selbstentfaltung des griechischen Denkens von Homer bis auf die Sophistik und Sokrates*, 2nd impr., Stuttgart.
Nietzsche, F. (1872) *Die Geburt der Tragödie aus dem Geiste der Musik*, Leipzig.
Nilsson, M.P. (1932) *The Mycenaean Origin of Greek Mythology*, Berkeley, Los Angeles, Calif. and London.
Parker, R. (1987) 'Myths of early Athens' in J. Bremmer (ed.), *Interpretations of Greek Mythology*, London: ch. 9.
Pembroke, S. (1967) 'Women in charge: the functions of alternatives in early Greek tradition and the ancient idea of matriarchy', *Journal of the Warburg and Courtauld Institutes* 30: 1–35.
Peradotto, J. (1973) *Classical Mythology: An Annotated Bibliographical Survey*, American Philological Association, Urbana, Ill.
Polignac, F. de (1984) *La naissance de la cité grecque: cultes, espace et société, VIIIe–VIe siècles avant J.-C.*, Paris.
Puhvel, J. (1987) *Comparative Mythology*, Baltimore, Maryland and London.
Raglan, Lord (1936) *The Hero: A study in tradition, myth, and drama*, London.
— (1955) 'Myth and Ritual' in T.A. Sebeok (ed.), *Myth: a symposium*, Philadelphia (repr. Bloomington, Indiana, 1958): 122–35.

Richardson, N.J. (1974) *The Homeric Hymn to Demeter*, Oxford.

Rose, H.J. (1928) *A Handbook of Greek Mythology*, London.

Sakellariou, M.V. (1977) *Peuples préhelléniques d'origine indo-européenne*, Athens.

Sergent, B. (1986) *Homosexuality in Greek Myth*, Eng. translation, A. Goldhammer, London.

Slater, P.E. (1968) *The Glory of Hera: Greek Mythology and the Greek Family*, Boston, Mass.

Tigerstedt, E.N. (1965) *The Legend of Sparta in Classical Antiquity*, vol. 1, Stockholm, Göteborg and Uppsala.

Tyrrell, W.B. (1984) *Amazons: A Study in Athenian Mythmaking*, Baltimore, Maryland and London.

Van Gennep, A. (1960) *The Rites of Passage*, Eng. translation, M.B. Vizedom and V.L. Caffee, London.

Vansina, J. (1965) *Oral Tradition: a study in historical methodology*, Eng. translation, H.M. Wright, London.

Vernant, J.-P. (1982) *Myth and Society in Ancient Greece*, Eng. translation, J. Lloyd, London.

Versnel, H.S. (1990) 'What's sauce for the goose is sauce for the gander: myth and ritual, old and new', in L. Edmunds (ed.), *Approaches to Greek Myth*, Baltimore, Maryland and London.

Veyne, P. (1988) *Did the Greeks Believe in their Myths?: An essay on the constitutive imagination*, Eng. translation, P. Wissing, Chicago, Ill.

Vian, F. (1963) *Les origines de Thèbes: Cadmos et les Spartes*, Paris.

Vidal-Naquet, P. (1981) 'The black hunter and the origin of the Athenian *ephebeia*', in R.L. Gordon (ed.), *Myth, Religion and Society*, Cambridge (an earlier version appeared in *PCPhS* 194 (1968): 49–64).

Ward, D.J. (1968) *The Divine Twins: an Indo-European myth in Germanic tradition*, Berkeley and Los Angeles, Calif.

West, M.L. (1985) *The Hesiodic Catalogue of Women: its nature, structure, and origins*, Oxford.

Index of ancient authors

Index of modern authors

Index of peoples, characters and places

Spelling of Greek names: I have kept Greek names as close as possible to the Greek alphabet, which for instance has no letter C. So look under K rather than C and expect AI and OI not AE and OE, except in the commonest words – e.g. Aigeus (not Aegeus), Akrisios (not Acrisius), Kaineus (not Caeneus), Kouretes (not Curetes). The exceptions are such words as Circe, Oedipus, Corinth – where Kirke, Oidipous and Korinthos seemed in varying degrees excessive.

d. = *daughter of* k. = *king of* r. = *river*

Index of topics and themes